N

AL CAPP

AL CAPP

A LIFE TO THE CONTRARY

MICHAEL SCHUMACHER AND
DENIS KITCHEN

BLOOMSBURY

NEW YORK · LONDON · NEW DELHI · SYDNEY

Published by Bloomsbury USA, New York

All papers used by Bloomsbury USA are natural, recyclable products made from wood grown in well-managed forests. The manufacturing processes conform to the environmental regulations of the country of origin.

LIBRARY OF CONGRESS CATALOGING-IN-PUBLICATION DATA

Schumacher, Michael, 1950–
  Al Capp : a life to the contrary / Michael Schumacher and Denis Kitchen. —1st U.S. ed.
    p. cm.
  Includes bibliographical references and index.
  ISBN 978-1-60819-623-4 (alk. paper)
  1. Capp, Al, 1909-1979. 2. Cartoonists—United States—Biography. I. Kitchen, Denis, 1946–
II. Title.
  NC1429.C295S38 2013
  741.5'6973—dc23
  [B]

                                  2012027508

First U.S. Edition 2013

1 3 5 7 9 10 8 6 4 2

Typeset by Westchester Book Group

Printed in the U.S.A.

CONTENTS

PREFACE

Once upon a time, long before Garry Trudeau entertained newspaper comic strip readers with his astute political commentary in "Doonesbury," before readers visited the Okefenokee Swamp and followed the social satire in Walt Kelly's "Pogo," before comic strips were aimed at the hearts and minds of adult readers, Al Capp introduced his followers to a hilarious mythical Kentucky hillbilly hamlet known as Dogpatch. The strip, "Li'l Abner," created and drawn by Capp from the very beginning, ran for forty-three years and, at the height of its popularity, reached a worldwide readership of more than ninety million.

Although it had its charm, Dogpatch was populated by folks just a few steps behind modern big-city ways. Turnips provided the town with its only known source of income, pigs were raised as both pets and a primary food source, single women literally chased eligible bachelors in the annual Sadie Hawkins race (with the captured men forced into wedlock), and creatures with such unlikely names as shmoo, kigmy, and bald iggle dropped by as figures in Capp's humorous observations on the human race. Politicians and businessmen did their best to bilk Dogpatchers out of the puny bit they did possess. The typical story ran for weeks on end, until even Capp himself seemed occasionally befuddled over where his winding plots would end up.

Abner Yokum, the strip's title character, lived with his parents, Mammy and Pappy Yokum, and by all appearances had everything a perennial nineteen-year-old could possibly want. He was tall, handsome, muscular, and constantly being pursued all over the hills by Daisy Mae Scragg, the most beautiful single girl in Dogpatch, who, for reasons escaping any other male in the vicinity, wanted only a man totally uninterested in her. Abner was naïve on his best day, dumb as a fencepost on his worst, and always caught up in an adventure more complicated than his native intelligence

vii

could handle. Al Capp delighted in working him in and out of trouble, using his predicaments as stagings for satire, parody, and a brand of comedy that won the praise of Charlie Chaplin, John Steinbeck, Hugh Hefner, John Updike, and a host of others.

Capp's rise to prominence was swift and unprecedented. As far back as the turn of the twentieth century, comic strips had bolstered newspaper circulations and earned their creators fame and fortune. "Hogan's Alley," an early comic dynamo featuring a kid wearing what appeared to be a yellow nightshirt, touched off newspaper wars, while a beautiful surrealistic strip called "Little Nemo in Slumberland" guided its readers through previously unexplored regions of the subconscious. Other strips and one-panel cartoons aspired to do little more than deliver daily punch lines. Action and adventure strips, boasting of long-running plots that held readers' attention for weeks and even months, were capturing the country's fancy right about the time "Li'l Abner" made its debut.

Capp had no idea where his strip would take him; he only knew that he wanted to succeed as a cartoonist. He knew, from an early age, that he could draw, and he'd kicked around art schools and worked on a few short-lived jobs before landing a breakthrough job as an assistant to Ham Fisher, the creator of the enormously popular boxing strip "Joe Palooka." It was only a matter of time before Capp struck out on his own.

The world was ready for "Li'l Abner," which started out as an adventure strip but quickly developed into a humorous feature with long-running stories usually associated with such comics-page favorites as "Flash Gordon," "Dick Tracy," or "Little Orphan Annie." Readers, still bruised from the Depression and fearing the events in Europe leading to World War II, connected with Capp's adult humor, outrageous adventures, buxom female characters, and snide but spot-on commentary. "Li'l Abner" shot to the top in very little time and would become one of the most widely read strips in comics history. Capp was a wealthy man before he celebrated his thirtieth birthday.

But this was only the beginning. Restless and hypercreative by nature, Capp trained his sights on how to broaden his artistic and financial horizons. His marketing genius led the way. Besides developing ideas for new comic strip titles, he pushed to find ways to nudge his "Li'l Abner" characters off the comic strip pages and into previously unexplored or barely explored territories. There were product endorsements and, more lucrative yet, merchandising blitzes tied into the strip. In one year alone, the shmoo, a cuddly little critter capable of providing humanity with everything it ever needed, grossed $25 million in merchandising—and this was mid-twentieth-century dollars.

Capp created a new template for the successful comic strip artist as he went along. "Li'l Abner" blazed the trail for such future marketing phenoms as "Peanuts" and "Garfield." Then, when Dogpatch USA opened its gates in 1968, Capp became the only cartoon creator other than Walt Disney to have his own theme park. By that point, Capp's face had appeared on the covers of *Time* and *Newsweek*, he was a regular contributor to *Life*, his mug had been seen on countless newspaper and magazine ads, and he was a regular guest on television, most notably *The Tonight Show*. Comics artists had almost always been solitary figures spending hours alone at the drawing table, collecting good salaries but remaining relatively unknown to the public. Al Capp changed all that, through the force of sheer ambition, talent, marketing know-how, and a winning personality.

Capp created his own success, but he might have been destroyed by it as well. A contrary individual by nature, he was more apt to argue than agree with you. If someone or something was popular, chances were Capp would find a way to skewer it in "Li'l Abner." The high and mighty would be cut down to size, sometimes playfully, as in Capp's parodies of Frank Sinatra and John Steinbeck, sometimes savagely, as in the case of his commentaries on Joan Baez and the antiwar activists of the 1960s. Anyone or any idea could be a target. Even when he was at his silliest, as in "Fearless Fosdick," his long-running send-up of Chester Gould's "Dick Tracy," something dark seemed to be bubbling just beneath the surface.

This contrary attitude, once so amusing to his readers, lost its charm when his political views took a sharp turn to conservatism and he crisscrossed the United States in a lucrative but dizzying series of appearances on college campuses, where he aggressively confronted his student audiences. When he was implicated in a couple of sex scandals while touring the universities, even his close friends Richard Nixon and Spiro Agnew couldn't save him. His career's downward spiral rivaled its ascent in sudden and dramatic fashion.

Capp's fall from grace, the retirement of "Li'l Abner" from the daily papers, and Capp's death in 1979 did little to lessen the comic strip's legacy. "Li'l Abner" has been available in reprint editions (nearly forty volumes, in total) for all but a few years since Capp's death, and it has been the subject of numerous scholarly studies and theses. *Li'l Abner,* the play, at one time a smash hit on Broadway, continues to be performed by professional, student, and local theater groups. Sadie Hawkins Day, an annual feature in the "Li'l Abner" strips, is still celebrated in dances and events across the country. Expressions originating in the strip—"double whammy," "hogwash," and "going bananas," to name a few—are still part of the everyday vernacular.

For Capp, it all began with a traumatizing yet defining moment early in his life, a fateful meeting with a trolley car.

1 FLASHPOINT

No one will ever know the precise, unvarnished details surrounding Al Capp's losing his left leg at the age of nine. He'd claim that it was the turning point of his life, and there is no reason to doubt it, any more than there is good reason to question his assertion that he never enjoyed a pain-free day over the next six decades.

Capp, a first-rate storyteller, comic strip artist, humorist, inventor of tall tales, occasional liar, entertainer supreme, and hair-trigger wit, offered many versions of the accident that cost him a leg, each account slightly different from the others—each, one suspects, tailored for a specific audience or readership.

"Al Capp may have been his own greatest creation," Dave Schreiner, a comics historian and editor, once wrote. "He built around himself out of his personal history a pyramid of truth, near-truth, and myth which helped transform the already colorful and interesting Alfred Gerald Caplin into the controversial and legendary Al Capp, world's best-known newspaper cartoonist."

Schreiner, whose significant work in comics included editing all but two of comics giant Will Eisner's graphic novels, believed that Capp had the ability to make any story believable, including his account of losing his leg.

"Capp was one of the very best storytellers," Schreiner observed, "and he did not confine his enormous talent to the funny pages. He mixed plausibility and outrageousness in his work, and when he related anecdotes and incidents from his life, the same rules applied."

What is known about the accident that claimed Capp's leg is that Capp, then answering to his given name of Alfred Caplin, was in need of a haircut. The eldest son of Otto and Matilda "Tillie" Caplin, of New Haven, Connecticut, Alfred was five weeks shy of his tenth birthday and had a full head of thick black hair that, more often than not, looked as if it had been groomed with a mixing spoon. Alfred's parents would let it go until it had grown too long for the day's standards, at which point one or the other would hand him enough money for a haircut.

On this day—Friday, August 21, 1919—father and son were on their own. Tillie was upstate with the other children: younger sons Bence and Elliott and daughter Madeline, all afflicted with the mumps. She had rented rooms in a farmhouse, hoping the clean country air would do them good. That afternoon, Otto Caplin pressed a fifty-cent piece into the palm of Alfred's hand: thirty-five cents for the haircut, with five cents as a tip and ten cents to cover trolley fare.

But Alfred had other ideas. He knew something about money, even at that young age, and after some quick calculations, he figured that he could get more bang for his half-buck if he made a few adjustments to the plan. He knew of a Prof. Amoroso's Barber Academy, where, he later remembered, "you could get a haircut for fifteen cents and they'd bind your wounds," a place of wonder where tips were rejected—the perfect transaction.

There was one hitch to the plan. The academy was across town, a fair distance from the Caplins' Stevens Street house. Rather than catch a trolley and cut into his potential savings, Alfred decided to hitch a ride on the back of an ice wagon. The free ride, not to mention a sliver of ice on a hot day, seemed to be the ideal solution. "I hopped on that wagon, in a state of bliss," he'd write many years later.

Somewhere, somehow, Alfred tumbled off the wagon. It might have occurred as he was dismounting near the academy, as Alfred would claim in his accounts, or he might have simply walked in front of the trolley without looking, as Otto Caplin later suggested. Whatever happened, the result was horrific: Alfred wound up sprawled out on the tracks, directly in the path of an oncoming trolley. Unable to stop, it rolled over Alfred's left leg, crushing his thigh well above the knee. Mercifully, the boy blacked out.

When he regained consciousness, he was in a hospital emergency room, surrounded by people in white, all trying to bring him around long enough to determine his identity. Alfred stole a peek at the damage. The sickening mess reminded him of scrambled eggs. "There was just nothing that you could call a 'leg' left of it," he'd remember later.

In 1946, Al Capp created a booklet distributed to amputee veterans by the Red Cross. In these autobiographical panels, he depicts himself as slightly older than the nine-year-old he was at the time of his life-changing accident.

Indecision was the rule of the hour. Hospital personnel didn't want to take action until they had talked to the boy's father. Otto Caplin didn't want to make a decision until he'd talked to his wife. Tillie Caplin, stuck in the middle of nowhere with three kids under the age of nine, didn't know what to think.

Elliott Caplin would never forget the call from home. His mother, in the kitchen of the farmhouse, was handed the phone, and she struggled to get details while a group of people stood around the kitchen, listening to Tillie and trying to piece together what had happened. Something was wrong, and it had to be bad. No one called long distance in those days unless it was serious.

"Her expression never altered," Elliott recalled. "Her face had lost all color, but her hand remained steady throughout what must have been a nightmare."

Otto told her someone would be picking them up as soon as he could arrange the ride. Then he rushed to the hospital and joined Alfred, who lay on a table near the emergency room. Alfred, sweating profusely, stared ahead in a daze.

"How are you doing?" Otto asked.

"All right," his son answered. He looked like he was about to nod off, but suddenly opened his eyes. "Don't you tell Ma," he implored.

Doctors didn't immediately remove Alfred's damaged leg. Instead, he was given painkillers but very little hope. When the hospital emergency physician insisted that Alfred's leg would have to be amputated, Otto Caplin demanded a second opinion. Two other doctors confirmed the original finding, but rather than allow the hospital staff to work on the leg, Otto insisted that another specialist handle it. Hours passed. The doctor couldn't be located. Finally, the following morning, the doctor arrived and Alfred's left leg was amputated well above the knee.

In writing about the procedure in his unpublished autobiography many years later, Al Capp played down the trauma. "There is no more drama about the amputation of a leg than about a pedicure," he wrote. "The offending mess is lopped off, and the remains sewn up. It makes no difference whether it's down near the ankle or six inches from the hip, as mine was."

At the time, however, the boy was in agony. Alfred was not immediately told that his leg had been removed, and for days on end he lay in a daze, heavily medicated, in and out of consciousness. Tillie refused to leave his bedside. When Alfred finally discovered that he'd lost his leg, he was angry and accusatory.

"They took my leg off!" he shouted at his mother.

"We had to, to save your life," she assured him. She attempted to explain how they had consulted the best doctors, how they had prayed for him to survive, how he was now like the brave soldiers who came home from wars without arms or legs.

Alfred wasn't interested in explanations.

"But they have lived," he said of the soldiers. "I'm only a kid. I've just started to live!"

Alfred healed quickly, and three weeks after the accident he returned home. His childhood, at least the one he knew, had ended.

Alfred hated being a one-legged curiosity. Classmates who once had no interest in him at all were suddenly overflowing with concern and pity.

"With two legs I had been a nobody," he observed bitterly. "With one leg I was somebody."

Nor did he care for the smothering he received from his mother, who fretted over his condition and cooked him heaps of steaks and lamb chops, protein-laden foods that doctors recommended for the healing process. He was relieved when the money ran low, as it always did, and she was forced to serve the usual meals.

Alfred could be a terror around the apartment. He'd always been temperamental, but following the loss of his leg, he became even more stubborn and surly, prone to explosive fits of rage, usually directed at his mother. He did not attend school for a prolonged period following the accident, and his sense of isolation and immobility fueled his dark moods.

"Alfred fidgeted," his father later wrote in his own account of his son's life. "He hated dark days; he hated monotony. He had an insatiable urge to keep moving."

He was tormented by phantom pains and itches in his missing leg and toes. He'd experience these sensations—not uncommon for amputees—for the rest of his life.

Getting around on one leg at home was relatively easy. Alfred could hop from room to room in the apartment. When he had to leave home, he'd use crutches, his left pantleg pinned up and out of his way. But traveling any kind of distance, like to his school on Davenport Avenue, was problematic. Otto Caplin would take Alfred on those occasions when he was at home; otherwise, the job fell to Alfred's Uncle Ellie, whose difficulties meeting car payments made the week-to-week arrangement precarious.

Alfred's parents plotted to rearrange their finances in a way that would permit them to buy him an artificial limb. The nearest supplier, a man with the unfortunate name of Butcher, worked out of Hartford, and his services weren't cheap. Otto managed to come up with a twenty-five-dollar deposit, and Butcher began custom-designing a prosthetic leg that would fit Alfred.

Alfred hoped the artificial limb would allow him to walk around with little effort—and look normal while he was doing it. Those hopes were dashed as soon as Butcher showed up in New Haven with the leg. The older man led Alfred into a bedroom and, while the Caplin family waited anxiously in the living room, instructed him on how to use the leg. Alfred strapped it on.

There was nothing natural about moving with the leg, and after a few tentative, stumbling, uncomfortable steps, he grew frightened. He could barely maintain his balance, let alone move around smoothly and naturally.

In his memoir, *Al Capp Remembered,* Elliott Caplin recalled his older brother attempting to demonstrate the device. Alfred slipped and cursed; he was held on his feet by Butcher. He shook off Butcher's support and promptly fell to the floor. Tillie Caplin screamed. "Shut up, Momma," Alfred said.

"My brother never mastered the art of walking with a wooden leg," Elliott Caplin wrote. "He would sway precariously with every step like a damaged airplane making an emergency landing."

Later in his life, when he was a wealthy comic strip artist with a face instantly recognizable from magazine covers and television appearances, Al Capp would speak of a recurring nightmare in which he fathered a son born with one leg. One might escape the immediate effects of an accident such as his, but its residual effects were never distant.

In the first years following the accident, Alfred grew intimately acquainted with just how much he'd lost. He could make light of the fact that, as a marginally gifted athlete, he would no longer embarrass himself on the playing field. But there was no joking about what the loss of a leg meant to his choices in career or even his relationships with others. His limitations were spelled out every time he took a step or tried to negotiate stairs.

Bitter realities and lessons hit him in unexpected ways. For instance, he was always aware that his parents had very little money. It was a reality he accepted without much thought—until, that is, he lost his leg. When something went wrong with his prosthesis, and it often did, he couldn't simply consult with the company that sold him the leg. That would have eaten more money than the Caplins could afford. Of course, the fact that Otto Caplin hadn't been making timely payments on the leg didn't help, either. So, instead of having the leg repaired by a specialist, Alfred would take it to a garage where an automotive mechanic would put it back together properly.

Then there was the issue of growth. Alfred's right leg was growing at the normal rate; his left leg, fashioned out of wood, was going nowhere. By the time Alfred was reaching his teen years, one leg was substantially shorter than the other. His walking, awkward to begin with, became almost grotesque.

There was also the problem of shoes. Alfred wore out the sole and heel of his right shoe at a very quick pace, due to the exertion placed on his "good" leg, whereas the left shoe wasn't nearly as worn. As an adult, he'd buy three pairs of shoes at a time, storing or tossing out a couple of the left shoes while wearing out the right ones, but this wasn't an option when Alfred was a boy.

The physical problems compounded the psychological suffering that Alfred did his damnedest to deny. He would be able to shrug off a lot of it in later years, but he felt isolated at the time, removed from his friends and schoolmates, with no hope of ever really belonging. He addressed this feeling in a brief autobiographical fragment, written in 1922 and 1923, and published posthumously in the collection *My Well-Balanced Life on a Wooden Leg*. In the fragment, "The Autobiography of a Freshman," Alfred wrote about living an Eden-like existence for his first ten years, when he had companions and an uncluttered life in the garden. That changed dramatically when he lost his leg and suddenly found himself outside the garden gate:

> To this day, I sit at the gate, vainly waiting for the day when I may enter. Sometimes the children come to the edge of the gate and speak a few words of pity to me—but not for long. They hear the call of health and, hastening back, resume their play.

* * *

By the time he began attending Central High School in Bridgewater, Connecticut, Alfred was aware that he would never be regarded the same as his male classmates, especially when it came to dating. He was as rowdy and obsessed with girls as the next guy, but as he later complained, "My rooster toughness and rowdiness was forgiven with sweet understanding [by the girls] when all I wanted was the same thrilled contempt that was accorded two-legged rowdies for the same behavior."

To be successful, he decided, he would have to trick girls into seeing him as normal. But since he gave himself away as soon as he took a step or two, he had to come up with a way to be noticed while he was standing stock-still.

He began staking out street corners. A favorite was on the corner of the city's busiest intersection, at D. M. Read's Main Street storefront. He'd lean against the building, looking as cavalier as any other smart-ass high schooler, and call out to girls in passing cars or to those going by him on the sidewalk. Alfred considered it a victory if someone turned back and gave him a withering look. It would be a great day if he received several of these.

It was a technique that, by its very nature, was bound for failure. A time would come when he'd have to move, and later in life, Capp would recount one of these failures in a story whose tragic irony is almost too perfect to believe. The question of accuracy doesn't lessen its impact, though.

One day, while he was holding down his preferred spot, the boy's ritual took a new and intriguing turn. Three teenage girls pulled up in a car nearby and, waiting in traffic, presented Alfred with an opportunity. Alfred shot them a look—a leer, as he would describe it. Two of the girls would have nothing to do with him, but one, to Alfred's delight, smiled back. Then she did the unthinkable: she dropped her school pad out of the car window and into the street. It was a ruse; the girl wanted him to retrieve the pad and hand it back to her. Alfred froze, unwilling to hobble out to the street. The car moved on. The pad stayed in the street.

When it was safe to move, Alfred limped away from the building and picked up the pad. The girl's name and address were written inside, which, under other circumstances, would have been nothing less than a triumph. For Alfred, there were logistics to consider. The young woman hailed from the wealthy section of town, where all the houses had porches or verandas, with steps leading up to them. On flat ground, Alfred could at least make a noble effort to walk like the average Joe; steps required his reaching back and physically pulling his left leg to the next step. If she were to witness this . . . well, it wouldn't be good. But could he really pass up this rare opportunity?

Alfred, in the end, concluded that the rewards might be worth the risks, especially if he could minimize the chances of her seeing him negotiate the steps. The plan he hatched was simply to call the girl, arrange the meeting, show up before the agreed-upon time, and try to make it up the stairs and onto the porch before he was noticed. He'd wait until the appointed time, they'd meet, and, if all went well, they'd spent the evening on the veranda.

The early portion of the arrangement went without a hitch. Alfred called and explained that he wanted to return her pad, preferably tonight, and she invited him to drop by at seven o'clock for a glass of lemonade. Alfred arrived at the girl's house fifteen minutes early. He made it up the stairs without attracting any attention, and shortly before seven he was sitting on the veranda, waiting for her to come out.

His perfect plan blew up on him when she opened the door a few minutes before their scheduled meeting time, started outside, saw him, and stopped abruptly. She said nothing for a few moments. She finally told him that she couldn't see him that evening; she had somewhere else she had to be. She thanked him for his trouble and asked him to leave the pad on the chair. That said, she turned and walked back into the house.

Alfred didn't try to call her back.

"It would have been too much for both of us to bear," he wrote in his account of the incident,

> for we both had been playing the same game. I had arrived early so she
> would not see me walk. She had planned to be waiting on the porch so
> I would not see her walk. For in the instant of her turning away at the
> door, I had seen the stiffening of her shoulder, the outthrust movement
> of her hip—the sure signs that she, too, of all sad, shy girls on earth, had
> an artificial limb.

* * *

Alfred tried to compensate for the loss of his leg in a variety of ways, in his youth and throughout his life. To build upper-body strength, Alfred, too poor to own barbells or dumbbells, developed a workout program that involved hoisting a piano bench high above his head, over and over, until, in time, his arms, shoulders, and upper back developed enough muscle tone to help with his self-image.

Not that he would ever be considered small or frail. He had a thick but not especially overweight physique, with broad shoulders, a barrel chest, and meaty arms; his waist, though far from tapered or undersized, seemed to fit the rest of his frame. It was his head that you noticed: it appeared to be a size too large for the rest of him—leonine, as writers would describe it on more than one occasion later in his life—and it was made to look even larger by his coarse black hair. Alfred took special pride in his hair, even if its grooming seemed to be a challenge a bit out of his range. Years later, in a magazine interview, he'd tell an interviewer that he had nightmares about losing his hair, that he'd actually drawn self-portraits of what he might look like if he went bald. Toward the end of his life, when his health was fleeing and he found it difficult to take a normal breath, he would mutter impatiently about how his hair was thinning.

Ultimately, though, it was the strength of his intellect and formidable wit that would carry him through. He could lurch down the street, his artificial limb squeaking and, at the worst of times, locking up or falling apart, but he could rely on his wits to bail him out of awkward situations.

It all came down to attitude. There was no point in pretending that he wasn't different. What he needed to do, he decided, was to have a sense of humor about it.

In time, he would use his situation to help others. As an adult, he worked as a volunteer for organizations devoted to people with similar challenges. He acted as the honorary national chairman of the Sister Elizabeth Kenny Foundation, an organization dedicated to assisting people with disabled or missing limbs. He created an autobiographical comic book and poster addressing the way he lost his leg and how he moved on from it, for the Red Cross, both distributed to World War II amputees. He tirelessly visited army and navy hospitals, giving pep talks and personalized drawings to GIs.

Over the years, whenever he learned that a young person had lost a limb, Capp would send a letter, typically in care of the patient's hospital, working in conjunction with the Sister Elizabeth Kenny Foundation. Receiving a personal letter from such a luminary, especially one with a similar handicap, was no doubt a significant morale booster to distressed young patients and their distraught parents. In a typical example, from 1964, Capp wrote, in part:

> Dear Chip,
>
> I understand you have lost a leg and of course you are not exactly happy about it. I was about your age when I lost mine, and I have learned a few things since then which you probably have not yet had time to find out for yourself.
>
> The main trick is not to keep remembering what you've lost, but all the rest you have left. When you can do that, other people will too, not just because they are afraid of hurting you, but because it just won't be important . . . I will not tell you that your artificial leg will do the job of a real one, any more than glasses are better than eyes, but it does a pretty darn good job . . . Of all the major misfortunes that can happen to the human body, the loss of a leg is perhaps the least. I don't expect you to know that now, but you will know it.

One of his favorite anecdotes, repeated many times over the years and preserved in a cartoon in the *Saturday Evening Post*, as well as an entry in *My Well-Balanced Life on a Wooden Leg*, involved a stay at the posh Savoy Hotel in London. A room-service waiter had visited his room to take his breakfast order, and as Capp gave it from his bed, the waiter looked down and saw Capp's artificial leg, wearing a shoe and sock, sticking out from under the bed. When he realized that Capp had caught him staring, he made as good a recovery as anyone could have expected.

"Very good, sir," he said to Capp when he had completed his order. "And what will the other gentleman have?"

2 YOUNG DREAMS AND SCHEMES

The marriage of Al Capp's parents, Otto Caplin and Tillie Davidson, was arranged in the Lithuanian shtetl of Yanishok, a tiny hamlet a stone's throw from the Latvian border.

For thirty years, Capp tried to learn something about "Yaneshek," as he spelled it, which had disappeared from the map. Whenever he was in New York and had a Russian-sounding cabdriver, he'd ask the cabbie if he knew of the town. His persistence eventually paid off. A driver knew of the village, which he described in a single line: "If you walked to the center of the town and bought a lemonade, that was a big day in Yanishok."

Yanishok, Capp decided, was probably like the hamlet depicted in *Fiddler on the Roof*—groupings of huts and a synagogue. The Jews there lived meager existences based largely on survival. In a village such as this, the only hope was to escape to America.

Capp envisioned the day that his grandfather Sam Cowper, a young peddler of some education, heard from three cousins living in New Haven, Connecticut. The cousins had moved to the United States, established themselves, and, over time, pooled together more than enough money to bring Sam, his wife, and their two-year-old son, Otto, to New Haven. The money he needed—and more—was enclosed in the letter.

Overjoyed, Sam repaired to the local tavern, where he hoped to share the news of his good fortune with friends. No one was around. The only people in the bar were a half-deaf bartender and a customer so ancient that some villagers already figured him to be dead. Sam ordered a drink and waited. After a while, Rabbi Fivel (Philip) Davidson entered, aiming to enjoy his customary beer, compliments of the house. Sam asked the bartender to pour him a vodka.

The rabbi sipped on his drink and listened as Sam told his story. He, too, had relatives in the United States, in New Jersey, but they didn't have the money to bring him over.

The conversation turned to their children. Sam spoke of his little boy, Otto, while the rabbi talked glowingly of his daughter, Matilda, who was the same age.

"Any Jewish father would be proud to have his son marry your daughter," Sam told Rabbi Davidson. "That father would never have to worry about his boy growing up in such a strange place as America, knowing that, at 21, that boy would marry the daughter of Rabbi Fivel."

The ritual played out to its desired conclusion. Sam offered to lend the rabbi the money he needed to move his daughter to America. It was only right and proper: after all, his family had sent him more money than he needed. The rabbi was a man of God.

After a token rejection of Sam's offer, the rabbi tearfully accepted it, but only under two conditions. First, he would repay the loan, with 6 percent interest, within five years. Second, Sam's son and his daughter would marry on Matilda's eighteenth birthday.

The two shook hands, completing the transaction. Sam gave the rabbi the addresses of his cousins in New Haven.

The two men's lives took very different paths after they moved to their new country. Rabbi Davidson settled in New Jersey, and over the years he worked his way to the highly respected position of chief rabbi of Newark. As Al Capp would remember, his maternal grandfather's word was law. No one of the faith in that community was married, got divorced, or began a business partnership without his prior approval.

Sam Cowper changed his name to "Caplan" (which would later be changed again to "Caplin"). He, too, continued the career he'd had in the old country. He pushed a cart through the streets of New Haven, selling dry goods, working every day from dawn to dusk until he had saved enough to buy his own store. As Capp would remember, his paternal grandfather's early years in the store were characterized by success and expansion—until, that is, he discovered the works of Alexandre Dumas. To that point, he'd read virtually nothing but the Talmud, but he quickly determined that the swashbuckling adventures described in *The Count of Monte Cristo, The Three Musketeers,* and other Dumas novels were much more exciting. He was hooked. Capp recalled seeing a photograph of his grandfather, cutting quite the figure with his long, Russian-style hair and beard, seated outside his store, reading Dumas rather than waiting on customers. He went out of business, his store purchased by creditors. Even then, he had the chance for a new beginning. He had enough left from the sale of his store to open a small apron-manufacturing plant, but he took little interest in it. He stayed home more and more, and his wife, who knew nothing of aprons, took over. This place, too, was taken over by creditors. With the money left over from the sale of the plant, Sam bought a two-family house in a middle-class neighborhood in New Haven.

Al Capp revered his paternal grandmother—"my favorite creature," he'd call her—and the way she endured the foibles of her husband reminded him of the way his own mother dealt with the shortcomings of his father. Like Capp's own parents', his grandparents' marriage had been arranged when both were children. The relationships of both couples would later be essentially reflected in their "Li'l Abner" counterparts, Mammy and Pappy Yokum. If his grandmother was unhappy, Capp didn't notice. She might not have been a good enough cook to tempt a starving man, and she might not have known the first thing about how to balance a ledger or run a business, but she showered her grandchildren with unconditional love.

And that, to little Alfred Caplin, was more than sufficient.

Otto was his parents' great hope: bright, witty, good-looking, and seemingly ambitious. When he enrolled at Yale to study law, they were certain they had the family's first American success story on their hands. By the time he began attending Yale in the fall of 1908, Otto was courting Matilda Davidson. As far as Al Capp knew, neither of his parents ever dated anyone else. Otto and Tillie Caplin married before the end of Otto's freshman year, and Tillie soon became pregnant.

Alfred Gerald Caplin arrived on September 28, 1909, just a few weeks after fall classes at Yale began for Otto's second year. Otto hadn't registered. Instead, saying that he needed more money to support his family, he took a

This is the sole surviving photo of Alfred Caplin prior to the amputation of his leg, taken in 1913.

job as a traveling salesman, hawking industrial oils. His son would never believe his father's version of that story. Instead, he preferred to think that his father took the job as a means of escaping a new family, a wife who was becoming increasingly addled with every new addition, and responsibilities that weighed heavily on his carefree nature.

Alfred's brother Jerome, nicknamed Bence, was born a year after Alfred; Elliott was four years younger. Madeline, the only girl in the family, arrived a year later. Alfred was very close to Bence, whereas, by his own admission, he had virtually no use for the two youngest while still living at home.

By all indications, the Caplin household was loud but far from joyful. Otto was away more than he was home, leaving Tillie with the difficult job of raising the children and managing very meager finances, which normally amounted to holding creditors at bay. Alfred was surly and vile tempered, and his three siblings lived in fear of upsetting him—and it didn't take much. Bence ate alone in the kitchen on nights when Tillie served soup, because he slurped the hot liquid and that was enough to send Alfred into a rage.

Tillie hung on, hoping for a change for the better. She would anxiously await the day's mail delivery, praying for the check her husband promised to send, and as the days went by and the checks seldom found their way to the mailbox, Tillie would look for ways to talk the landlord into allowing her a little more time to make rent, or convince the grocer to extend her a little more credit. She hoarded everything she bought when she did have money, and when there was no money and things got really bad, she would take the children out after dark, when they could go unobserved while they scrounged through trash cans for discarded clothing or even bits of coal.

Perhaps more humiliating were the loans and handouts she and Otto received from family members, particularly Otto's brother-in-law Harry, who married Otto's sister Rose and always seemed to slip Otto urgently needed money for bills or, on occasion, when Otto was feeling really motivated, a new business. Harry had troubles of his own, including his own string of failed businesses, but when times were good he found ways to help Otto and his family.

The constant lack of money, the moves to squalid apartments after the family was evicted by landlords, the difficulties of raising four children with very little help, the loneliness she felt when Otto was away for long stretches of time—all exacted a steep price, physically and mentally, from Tillie Caplin. On nights when she was alone and the kids were off to bed, she would sit in a rocking chair in the kitchen, sipping tea and talking to herself about the days of her youth, which seemed happier, despite the fact that she had lost her mother at fourteen and, as the oldest of her parents' eight children, wound up raising her younger brother and sisters.

On those rare occasions when he did talk about the matter, Al Capp would characterize his mother with a tinge of sadness.

"Her hair turned white before she was thirty-five," he recalled. "She was cheerful enough but she had sort of a haunted look—she never had any pretty clothes or good times." Her voice, once melodic and sweet, became "anxious and scolding and shrill."

A life of disappointment reached its lowest point when Alfred lost his leg. Alfred would never quite understand her feelings. While he wrestled with the harsh realities of going from room to room on a clumsy artificial leg, or dealing with the feelings of isolation he experienced when he watched his classmates running and jumping and carrying on the way kids do, his mother concerned herself with his future—whatever that might be. What kind of jobs could he possibly hold? What would women think of this man? Would he ever have a wife and children? Could he even live in a way that was close to normal? She wept when she considered it.

Albert had little patience for this. In his mind, his mother's worries were manifestations of weakness. He wasn't interested in merely surviving. He would learn to thrive on one leg, no matter what it took.

Al Capp would claim that he could not remember his life with two legs. He would talk of his childhood in only the most general terms. It had been a happy childhood, he'd declare, even though the evidence—and the memories of his younger brothers and sister—said otherwise. He could be surly and difficult; he had little sympathy for others. He'd fought his mother when she tried to get him to learn to play the piano; he tolerated school, achieving average grades, even though it was clear that he had an above-average mind.

He loved to read and draw and go to the movies, all of which fed into a prodigious imagination. When his father returned from a sales trip, he'd bring home piles of hotel stationery. Alfred would fill the sheets with drawings and his own little comic strips, which were mostly imitations of what he saw in the newspapers or on the screen in the movie houses.

His father encouraged him at every turn. Otto Caplin was himself an amateur comics artist, and he drew his own strips on grocery bags or butcher paper. Most of his comics were about a married couple, not unlike him and his wife, and their daily travails. "He always triumphed over her in those strips," Alfred would say, many years later. "But only in them. Never in real life."

Comic strips enjoyed widespread followings at that time. Comics had been around since before the turn of the century, when the immense popularity of R. F. Outcault's Yellow Kid ignited newspaper wars, inspired weak imitations, and, ultimately, began a newspaper tradition that continues to this day. The funnies, as they were called, sold newspapers—lots of them. The competition to get the best artists and comic strips was fierce. Some of Alfred's favorite artists, like Rudolph Dirks ("Katzenjammer Kids"), Bud Fisher ("Mutt and Jeff"), George Herriman ("Krazy Kat"), Cliff Sterrett ("Polly and Her Pals"), and Billy DeBeck ("Barney Google"), were not only extraordinarily creative and influential; they earned lucrative incomes. When he heard that Bud Fisher was pulling in two thousand dollars a week for "Mutt and Jeff," and "constantly marrying 'Follies' girls," Alfred reasoned that this might be a career for him.

His earliest work received much more modest compensation. Alfred had a businessman's sensibilities, and he recognized that the basic single-joke comic strip was not going to guarantee him a continuing readership. The kids in his neighborhood liked his strips, enough so that Alfred would create his own publication featuring his comics and have Bence and Elliott sell them on the street for a penny or two each. He'd try to pump out an issue a week; to keep interest up, Alfred ended each adventure strip with a "cliffhanger" that assured him a readership the following week.

But Alfred lost the readership he'd been building when Otto moved his family from New Haven to the Brownsville section of Brooklyn, a neighborhood Capp later described as a "block-gang warfare jungle." Otto had just watched another of his businesses go under and was back with his old stand-by employer, the Atlantic Paint Company, and his new territory included New York City and Long Island. Alfred's new school, P.S. 62, was, he would later claim, experimenting with a new classroom organization: rather than follow the accepted practice of separating the students according to their scholastic abilities, the school decided to mix the high achievers with the underachievers, the theory being the more intelligent kids would help elevate the others.

Alfred was terrified. Not only was he the new kid in school, and a one-legged one at that; he found himself surrounded by some of the most frightening classmates he could imagine—kids destined, he was convinced, for one of the state's finer penal facilities.

"The experiment went on for a couple of months, and it made thieves and monsters out of us nice kids," he said of the experience. "It was horrible, like a leper colony."

His art became his salvation—and again, a source of income. When his classmates learned that he could draw just about anything, they paid him—first pennies, then nickels, and eventually dimes—to sketch their fantasies on paper. No moral imperatives were involved: Alfred drew whatever they asked him to draw. The typical request found Alfred sketching one of his classmates in action, often as a cowboy. One kid asked him to portray him as a cowboy shooting his older brother. Before long, Alfred had more work than he could manage. He considered enlisting the help of an assistant.

Then the heat was really turned up. The class's art instructor was a young, attractive teacher named Miss Mandelbaum. When Alfred proved that he could sketch a reasonably convincing likeness of her, all of his commissions changed. The typical sketch now pictured a pubescent student's leering at a nude or scantily clad Miss Mandelbaum. The price for such a drawing: twenty-five cents.

"I was just a kid from the country, but soon I became an expert in pornography," he'd recall. "My price was a quarter a drawing, and with twenty-five steady customers, I was doing fine until I got so many commissions that I starting taking extra work home and my father found out about it."

It would have been a short-lived gig in any event. Otto Caplin, always restless, had resigned his sales position and was moving the family yet again, this time to start up a toy store. Alfred would have to rebuild the audience for his art once again.

The family's constant movement, necessitated by Otto Caplin's failed business enterprises, combined with the evictions from landlords when the rent was late, was hard on Alfred. Otto Caplin didn't fail for lack of effort. His list of business enterprises included a wholesale silk stocking store, a boot store, a wholesale toy distributorship, and still another silk place. He'd manage to scrounge up some backing money from a sympathetic relative, open the business with the highest of hopes, and shut down after a relatively short and sad run, when he could no longer get credit from suppliers and he was overwhelmed by waves of debt. He'd return to a traveling sales position until the next big idea hit him.

For Alfred, movies were the ultimate escape. He had felt that way since he was very young. His life at home could be difficult, but a nickel could buy him a way out for at least a couple of hours. He had little use for the main attraction, which tended to be a romance. Alfred and his friends would hang around for about ten minutes of the film, catching just enough to supply them with a week's worth of contempt and fodder for discussion; they'd be long gone before the serious kissing and loving hit the screen.

The comedies and adventures were an entirely different matter. Alfred never tired of watching the pratfalls, the triumphs of the little (but more clever) guy over much bigger foes, the absurdist heroism, or the acts of bravery that defied all logic. A couple of hours at the White Way or DeWitt theater—or, if he was really doing it up, the Bijou in downtown New Haven—would transport Alfred to worlds that even his own imagination couldn't invent. A new film by Charlie Chaplin, Alfred's favorite, was the manifestation of genius.

The serials influenced the young comic artist in him. He loved the way each installment ended with a damsel in distress, facing her demise in seemingly impossible and inescapable circumstances that were somehow resolved within the first ninety seconds of the following week's segment. Of course, that installment would end with a similarly inescapable brush with death—or so it would seem until the following week, when the resolution was so simple and obvious that Alfred couldn't believe he hadn't thought of it. Alfred studied these carefully. He learned how to create characters in an abbreviated period of time, how to build and pace a story, and how to mount suspense. The little comics magazines that he created and sold around the neighborhood became indications of a quick learner at work.

Books educated him further. As a boy, he loved visiting his grandparents' home and reading the adventure novels that Zayde Caplin favored. By the time he reached his teen years, he was moving on, devouring Dickens,

George Bernard Shaw, and others. He haunted Whitlocks, the local bookstore, whenever he could put together any money. As his brother Elliott remembered, he especially favored the thick, bound volumes of *Harper's Monthly*, which could be purchased used for two bits. These volumes contained some of the most memorable writing and illustrations produced in America in fifty years. According to Elliott, Alfred also looked through newspapers and the backs of magazines for ads offering bound editions of the complete works of such authors as Joseph Conrad, Anthony Trollope, and William Makepeace Thackery. He sent away for these volumes and read them cover to cover until threatening letters to "Alfred Caplin, Esquire" began arriving in the mail, stating that there would be hell to pay—or at least police action—if he didn't pay for or return the books. Alfred's library shrank substantially when his mother intercepted one of these letters.

"Momma hastily packed whatever volumes she could find and mailed them, parcel post, back to the irate publisher," Elliott Caplin explained. "Alfred didn't seem to mind very much. He was a reader, not a collector."

As acerbic as he could be when contending with his mother and siblings, Alfred cared deeply for his father. He looked forward to Otto's return from sales trips, he enjoyed discussing his art with him, and while he was well aware of his father's shortcomings as a father and provider, Alfred sympathized with the difficulties of his life. He couldn't imagine how it would be to struggle with earning a living, facing failure after failure, and dealing with a wife constantly carping at him and children always whining and demanding attention. This wasn't the life he would have chosen. He thought his father, "a gifted artist and brilliant man," should have pursued cartooning, where he might have managed the world he created. "He was a dreamer," Alfred told Elliott, when both had grown older and discussed their father. "He did his best and never deserted us. Poppa was O.K."

If Otto Caplin taught his son anything, it was how to think quickly on his feet. Otto Caplin might have been a dreamer, but he was realist enough to know that, for all his grandiose plans, he would never own the mansion on the hill; if everything fell into place, he just might be able to hold on to an apartment in a good Jewish neighborhood, with furniture for everyone in the family, and enough food in the icebox to offer a few choices. To accomplish this, he had to plan beyond the next minute, even if living in the present seemed impossible.

Alfred understood this, and it served him well throughout his life. He was always on the lookout for something that gave him a little edge, boosted his income, or set him up for success somewhere up the road.

One of his earliest lessons in this occurred when he was fifteen. He had befriended a classmate named Stanley, a kid he liked to describe as "solid." Stanley played on the football team, pulled C+ grades, and dressed very fashionably. Alfred admired his self-confidence, a characteristic you didn't always see in kids that age. Stanley worked at a gas station, and Alfred dropped by one afternoon to see if he wanted to sneak into the movie theater with him. Stanley replied that he was paid a dollar a night for his work pumping gas, so he could afford to pay his way into the theater.

Alfred liked the response, which impressed him as being honest rather than highfalutin', but it also nudged him into doing some on-the-spot math. Stanley had only been working at the station for a couple of weeks, yet here he was, buying clothes that he could never afford on his modest salary. Something didn't add up. Alfred kept an eye on him, and soon enough he had an answer: Stanley was running a game on the gas station's customers. A car would drive in and, without getting out of the car, the driver would order his gas. Stanley would pump the gas, but he always stopped a gallon short of the customer's order. If the customer ordered ten gallons of gas at twenty-five cents a gallon, Stanley would put nine gallons in the tank but charge the customer for ten. He'd pocket a quarter and drop the rest in the gas station's cash register. It worked perfectly. Sam Moscow, Stanley's boss, was receiving full payment for the gas leaving the pump, while Stanley was getting a quarter for every customer stopping by the station. On those occasions when a customer did leave the car, Stanley played it straight and pumped what the driver ordered.

This was a scam that Alfred could stand back and admire. It was beautifully conceived, and the quarters added up to a nice sum by the end of Stanley's shift. By Alfred's calculations, Stanley was probably padding his dollar salary by four to five dollars every time he worked.

Alfred congratulated Stanley on his little enterprise. Stanley initially denied doing any such thing, but he quickly confessed to running the game because he was interested in impressing a girl from the other side of town, a girl from a family much better off than Stanley's.

Alfred's mind downshifted and he quickly hatched a plan. Rather than approach the girl and violate class lines, Stanley should approach one of his buddies and offer to pay for a night out. He could bring along some friends—especially female friends. The young lady in question would inevitably turn up at some point, and she would take notice of Stanley's bankroll and generosity.

"But how do I get away from this place?" Stanley wanted to know, explaining that Sam Moscow turned up every night at closing time.

"I'll take over for you," Alfred volunteered. "I'll put your quarters in my pocket." All Stanley had to do, Alfred continued, was return to the station before Moscow arrived. Alfred would take Stanley's nightly dollar as remuneration for his efforts.

Stanley agreed. What he didn't realize was Alfred's own cunning: rather than short the customer by a quarter, Alfred was giving him fifty cents less than he ordered. He'd pocket a quarter for Stanley, a quarter for himself, and have the dollar salary at the end of the night. Stanley was too grateful to notice. He suddenly had all the friends he could handle, and he was still making money, even though he was nowhere near the gas station.

As Alfred would lament many years later, the scam might have worked indefinitely if he hadn't fallen victim to his own greed. What would happen, he wondered, if he shorted the customer seventy-five cents' worth of gas per order, putting a quarter in one pocket for Stanley and dropping two quarters in another pocket for himself? The answer, he realized, all too late, was somebody would notice. On the very first night that Alfred adjusted his pay scale, a customer drove in, ordered gas, and paid. But rather than leave, he pulled out of the station and met another car parked a short distance away. The car belonged to Sam Moscow. The customer and gas station owner held an animated conversation, pausing at one point to dip a stick into the customer's gas tank.

It was at this point that Stanley, unaware of any problem, turned up to close out his shift. Rather than fill him in on what was going on, Alfred gave Stanley his take in quarters and hightailed it out of the station. When he was a safe distance away, Alfred turned back to see what was happening. Sam Moscow had driven into the gas station lot and jumped out of his car and was punching Stanley repeatedly. Stanley was big enough to take the punishment, and guilty enough not to turn Alfred in.

As Alfred would remember it, Stanley didn't return to school for a week. When he did, Alfred was nowhere to be found. Summer vacation was on the horizon, and Alfred simply began his vacation a little early.

3 THE HILLS

The gas station misadventure was still fresh in Alfred's mind, and summer was just beginning, when a legitimate job opportunity popped up. Alfred's Aunt Barbara, married to Tillie's brother Louis, worked as the personnel director at St. Raphael's Hospital in New Haven, and she called Tillie to say that the hospital was about to lose its third-shift switchboard operator. Barbara, a friend of the shift supervisor, had spoken glowingly about Alfred, praising his intelligence and reliability. Alfred, Barbara told her sister-in-law, should drop by and talk to the supervisor.

Alfred couldn't help but make a strong first impression: he told the supervisor that he was eighteen, a high school graduate, and about to enter Yale. He was hired on the spot.

The job, Alfred would recall when retelling the story, didn't require a great deal of vigilance or work. The hospital received only a handful of calls at that time of night, and when one did come in, all Alfred had to do was see that he made the proper connection on the switchboard. It was boring work, but it paid fifteen dollars a week.

Alfred's deception might have worked on the person hiring him, but he didn't fool any of the young nurses dropping by to check out the hospital's new hire. He certainly wasn't a Yale candidate, and his poor grooming and dressing gave him away as just another teenage kid trying to pass himself off as older than he was. They'd see him once and never return.

The head nurse was the sole exception, taking an unlikely interest in the boy. As Alfred would describe her, "she was quite old, thirty or better, and she looked exactly like President Woodrow Wilson, not only in face, but in figure, which was tall, erect, unbending."

Although not initially attracted to her, Alfred enjoyed her visits, which relieved some of the tedium of sitting around and doing nothing. He was

25

also, since the loss of his leg, unaccustomed to sustained interest from the opposite sex. She grew bolder (and more attractive to Alfred) as the days went by, until one night the nurse appeared at Alfred's station and soon they were making out and pawing at one another. Unfortunately, Alfred was finished before she could get his trousers open. Disappointed but unbowed, the nurse promised to return in an hour.

When she did, she led him to a bathroom and asked him to pull down his pants and sit on the toilet. This made little sense to Alfred, and his confusion gave him away: this was his first time. Still undaunted, the head nurse lowered herself onto him.

Capp's account of his first sexual experience from here takes a wild turn—and not in an erotic way.

"I don't know how long it lasted [or] how long I passed out," he admitted, in his autobiography, "but when I came to, it was daylight outside, the door was open, and a mob of people were boiling around the room."

Alfred learned that there had been an accident during the night, and he hadn't been at the switchboard to take the emergency call. This, coupled with his transgression in the bathroom, was more than grounds for dismissal. He was given sixteen dollars and told to never return.

For Alfred, this was okay. It was early summer and he had money in his pocket.

Alfred knew better than to head straight home after being fired from his hospital job. He didn't doubt that his aunt would be contacting his mother and providing her with the lurid details, such as she knew them, of his final night on the job. His mother would not take the news well. This wasn't the worst she had heard in her lifetime of worries and disappointments, but it was pretty bad, and Alfred knew that she would cut loose on him as soon as she saw him. He didn't need the tongue-lashing—not today, not in the immediate future. He needed to get away for a while.

He decided to visit a friend named Gus Levy, whom he'd known since he was twelve, and while he walked to Gus's parents' house, he came up with a plan. He and Gus would hitchhike to Memphis, where Alfred's Uncle George, an Orthodox rabbi, and Aunt Minnie lived. His sixteen dollars would finance the trip. He and Gus would visit with his aunt and uncle for several days before heading back home. At some point along the way, he'd send a postcard to his mother, just so she wouldn't worry too much.

Gus was a year older than Alfred and, according to Alfred, a first-rate hustler. It was Gus who introduced Alfred to cigarettes, and to the idea that sneaking into the movies was better than paying for a ticket. He was effective because he didn't look or act the part of a scammer. He was well built, with broad shoulders and a slender waist, and he was good-looking, with a head of thick black hair. He was intelligent, and from the moment he and Alfred met, Gus filled Alfred with stories about how he was going to be the next great American novelist. Writing seemed like the best way to make a lot of money for very little work. Gus loved working outside the margins: if the deal was shady, he was all for it.

"If it [was] simple, honest, [and] straight forward, he was bored by it and wouldn't touch it," Alfred wrote in his characterization of his friend. To Gus, "any shifty way was better than any other kind."

Gus, already a veteran hitchhiker, was on board as soon as he learned that Alfred was bankrolling the trip. They set off with nothing but the clothes on their backs and Alfred's money. They had little difficulty finding rides—a couple of young people bumming their way across the country was common enough in the Roaring Twenties—but the going was much slower than Alfred had anticipated. There were no expressways or superhighways in those days, just two-lane roads or, worse yet, dirt roads that were barely wider than paths. It didn't matter to the boys. They were in no rush. They were more than content to sit back and see America from the comforts of a car. They could fill their bellies with food they picked up in roadside diners and restaurants, and make their way south and west at a leisurely pace.

They reached Washington, D.C., at the end of their second day on the road. They were riding with an elderly gentleman who asked them where they intended to spend the night. When they answered that they figured they'd be staying at a hotel, he informed them that hotels in the nation's capital could be expensive. They would be better off, he suggested, if they stayed in a rooming house. He knew of a good one and took them there.

The two slept in the next morning, and after cleaning up and dressing, they found the woman who ran the rooming house and asked where they might find a good restaurant nearby. They ate huge breakfasts, and when it came time to pay, Alfred learned that he and Gus had a big problem on their hands. They had blown through their money the first few days of their journey, and after paying for their meals, Alfred had thirty-five cents left from his original sixteen dollars.

Gus felt that it might be best if they just returned to Connecticut, but Alfred strongly disagreed. He wasn't yet ready to face his mother. He was determined to continue to Memphis. He'd find some way to make it.

They agreed to split up and go their separate ways. They walked to a highway and, after shaking hands and wishing each other well, took places on opposite sides of the road. A car stopped for Alfred. Gus ran across the street. "What the hell," he said, jumping in the car with Alfred.

The following twenty days—the time Alfred claimed it took to reach Memphis—were tough but eye-opening. The traveling companions found ways to stay fed. Gus would sneak up to porches and filch the milkman's deliveries. On other occasions, farmers or sympathetic drivers picking them up would set them up with a meal. They usually slept under the stars, but every so often someone would offer them an overnight stay in a cabin or house.

For Alfred, who had never strayed from the East Coast, the trip was an education. He'd heard all kinds of stories about how poorly people from the North were treated by southerners, but he found it to be quite the opposite. There was no way that he and Gus, with their New England accents, could have passed themselves off as anything but northerners, but they had no problems with the people picking them up or in the towns they visited. They were treated well regardless of where they went.

The two eventually arrived in Memphis. Aside from the surprise of having two uninvited guests at her door, both in need of a place to stay, Alfred's aunt was shocked to learn that he had taken such a long trip without any money. She demanded that both of her visitors contact their parents for the money needed for fare back to the East Coast.

Gus informed her that he couldn't write his folks; he was an orphan. His father had been a drunk and his mother had died when he was two. He was the youngest of eight kids. All had been brought up in different orphanages.

Alfred listened, stunned by what he was hearing. He could tell a tall tale with the best of them, but Gus made him look like an amateur. In reality, Gus was the eldest of three brothers, and both of his parents were alive. They owned a candy store, and their two younger sons worked there. They wouldn't let Gus hang around because he stole from them. He was laying it on thick, even by Alfred's standards.

This wasn't the first time Alfred had seen Gus in action. Earlier on this trip, just outside of Nashville, a woman in a Cadillac had picked them up and driven them to her home, where she promised to put them up for the night. It was apparent to Alfred that she had her eye on Gus, even though neither of the travelers had bathed in two weeks. Her husband, the woman told Gus, left for work very early in the morning but, in a line intended for Alfred, they could feel free to sleep in as late as they pleased.

Gus had other ideas. Early the following morning, before anyone was awake, he shook Alfred out of his sleep and told him they were leaving. He was carrying a big paper bag. They snuck out of the house and hit the road. After they had been picked up by a truck and were safely out of town, Gus opened the bag. He'd stolen the family's silverware. "This must be worth a hundred dollars," he told Alfred.

There was no point in arguing the theft on moral grounds; Gus was beyond that. Alfred made a weak attempt at it before changing his approach. What did Gus think would happen when the two of them, grubby-looking teenage boys, walked into a pawn shop and tried to sell silverware embossed with the owners' initials? There was little doubt about where the pawnbroker would be placing his next phone call. Gus could grasp this logic, and when they reached Nashville, they visited a place that polished silver, dropped off the silverware, and instructed the proprietor to call the owner when he was finished polishing.

Now here he was, in Memphis, listening to Gus feed his aunt a cock-and-bull story about being an orphan. Gus had even managed to work up a few tears while he narrated his story.

Later, when they were alone, Alfred chided Gus for lying to his aunt. There was no way he was writing his mother and asking for money, he told Gus. He'd be leaving before dawn the following morning. Gus could tag along if he wished, or he could stay with Alfred's relatives, who'd bought his story and were probably willing to adopt him themselves at this point.

"In Greenwich Village later, between wondering where the next meal was coming from, I tore my hair searching for a comic strip idea."

"One youngster—I guess he was the real Abner—said, when I showed him his picture, 'The picture ain't as good-lookin' as me. Looks more like you."

"I sketched the hillbilly people there, the prototypes of Li'l Abner and the folks of his world. My skill amazed them—till they saw the drawings."

"About the time my first crop of whiskers began to come up. I took a walking trip through the Kentucky mountains. Take it from me, it was thumb experience!"

"But I guess it wasn't. I came out lugging a contract and more money than I ever believed existed. I'd have pinched myself, only I had both hands full."

"Loud laughter ensued—so loud as to have me worried Li'l Abner couldn't be as funny as all that. I suddenly concluded the cause must be me."

"But would it sell itself? With all my strips and my hat in hand, I set siege to United Features. They put up a game fight, mom, but I got in."

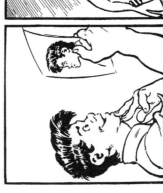

"I remembered my hillbilly. And I knew nobody had ever built a comic around one. So I did. Once started, the strip seemed just to write and draw itself."

In these panels drawn many years later, Al Capp told the condensed story of his first trip to the South in the 1920s, and its impact on the creation of "Li'l Abner."

The trip home, which took even longer than their journey to Memphis, proved to be invaluable to Alfred's future. As before, they relied on the hospitality of the people they met along the way, and in Kentucky, in the hills country of the Cumberland Mountains, they slept on haystacks and were often helped along by people unlike any Alfred had seen or heard of before. These people were desperately poor, living in tarpaper shacks and eking out day-to-day existences the best they could, oblivious to big-city ways, back-room politics, or Wall Street finances. They had their own colloquial language, and their customs were far from anything Alfred knew. Alfred was amused by their innocence, which contrasted with the phoniness he loathed in modern, sophisticated society. They treated him and Gus very well, and Alfred would never forget them.

"These people had a simple, appealing humanity that fascinated me," he said.

The traveling was beginning to wear him out. One of the motivating factors setting him on his journey in the first place had been a need to prove that he could do whatever a two-legged traveler could do, but he struggled on those days when the rides were few and the walking was long. One such day in southern Kentucky proved to be beneficial in the future.

"It was a hot day," he recalled, "and my thumb had no takers. So to break the monotony and postpone some weary hours of trudging I started to sketch."

He was in the midst of sketching a country landscape when a young boy approached him.

"Whatcha doing?" the kid asked.

"Embalming the landscape for posterity," Alfred told him.

The boy thought about it for a few moments. "That don't make sense," he finally said.

Alfred glanced down at his drawing and had to agree. He asked the kid if he wanted to pose for him, promising him the picture. When he saw the sketch, the young hillbilly wanted no part of it. It didn't look anything like him, he said. Alfred kept the sketch. He would refer to it later, when he was thinking of a subject for a comic strip. The sketch, a loosely drawn self-portrait dressed in hillbilly clothes, was similar to Li'l Abner.

The trip home took nearly a month. Alfred ran into his mother, who was out with his sister, Madeline, for a walk, before he made it to his front door.

"Hello, Mom," he began.

"Your brother Bence is at home," she answered. "He'll show you where the food is. We'll be back in later."

She never uttered a word, then or in the future, about the time her son had been away. She had been worried to death about him, but she refused to address Alfred's nearly two months away from home, or the pain and concern his absence had caused her.

"It was just as well," Alfred concluded, decades later. "I wouldn't have understood."

His family had no idea what to make of the trip. Neither Otto nor Tillie seemed angry; that had been the reaction of the early days of Alfred's absence, when they'd searched frantically for his whereabouts, only to come up empty. When they received his first postcard, they ceased worrying and resigned themselves to the latest example of Alfred's individualism. When he returned, they were relieved and curious. What could a young man, walking about and hitchhiking around the country on one good leg, have possibly done?

Alfred was full of stories, but, as always, they were heavily embellished. Otto Caplin didn't know what to think of them, but he was skeptical of much of what he heard.

"No one was able to get a coherent account of their trip," he noted in his memoir. "At various times Alfred hinted at being lost in the mountainous regions of Tennessee and of being first regarded with suspicion, then fed and entertained by the hill people. He told about being picked up by questionable-looking men who ran them for miles in high-powered cars, and about disputes with local sheriffs. He claimed they always emerged triumphant from these adventures."

Alfred might have told tall tales, bald-faced lies, and embellished truths, but he never wavered, then or later, on his reason for hitchhiking as much as he did in his youth: he needed to prove to himself that he could do whatever a boy with two strong legs could do.

There would be other hitchhiking episodes in the years ahead, but nothing rivaling the trip to Memphis. Alfred and his friend Don Munson hitchhiked regularly, often to New York City. Don, another aspiring writer, would explore the town while Al, as he was now calling himself, planted himself on a corner near Times Square and spent hours just watching everything going on around him. He loved observing people, elegantly dressed and walking about with a sense of purpose, making their way to the many playhouses in the area. He'd revered the theater since he was a boy, especially after he'd seen a performance of *Romeo and Juliet* with an aunt. He'd even done a little writing of his own, first as a boy, when he staged little productions in the neighborhood, and later in high school, where he won a prize for a play he had written. But writing plays, he decided, was not for him. He treasured the classics too much to even consider trying to compete in the field.

Cartooning seemed more reachable. He was supremely confident in his ability, believing that he was every bit as good as some comic strip artists he saw in the newspaper or illustrators featured in magazines. Al's guidance counselor, though, didn't know how to advise him. There were schools for serious artists and illustrators, but none that he knew of specialized in classes for people interested in creating comics. Al knew of correspondence schools, but they required prepayment, and that would have been out of the question, even if he had trust in their worth. A decade later, he would say, "Cartooning is something to do, not to study."

His formal education was slipping badly. He habitually skipped classes, and Otto Caplin spent more time than he cared to remember with the high school principal, who always seemed to be on the verge of expelling Al for his truancy. Father and son would quarrel over it, but Al knew that soon enough his father, now working again for the old paint company, would be on the road and away from his day-to-day life.

He spent most of his time with Gus Levy, Don Munson, and several others sharing their disdain for the classroom. One day, Al, Don, and four others decided to steal a car and take it on a joyride. They made it as far as Norwalk, where they were stopped by the police and taken into custody. For Tillie, this was the ultimate humiliation—a rabbi's daughter going to spring her son from jail. Otto tried to reassure her. What kind of actual trouble could he be in? After all, he couldn't drive a car. Besides, they were all just kids and not professional car thieves. Fortunately for all, the car had not been damaged in any way, and its owner refused to press charges.

Otto finally lost his patience when he returned from a sales trip and learned that Al, Bence, Don, and Gus had taken off for Asbury Park, New Jersey, where they'd somehow managed to find summer jobs. Otto found Don on the Boardwalk, working as a carnival barker for a shady character selling a fruit and vegetable slicer called the "Wonder Slicer." Al was hanging around with an alcoholic portrait sketcher. Otto blew up when Al told him that he was enthusiastic about doing this kind of work.

"So it's your ambition to become a street-corner faker and carnival tramp!" Otto shouted at Al, predicting that he would wind up on a corner, tin cup and pencils in hand. "A beggar," he continued. "A filthy, dirty bum, sleeping in flop houses, eating scum out of garbage pails! You say you don't like drink, but you'll drink whenever you can get it, just to get away from yourself, and finally end up on Skid Row."

The boys weren't that far removed from the life Otto was describing. Gus had found a flophouse hotel, and the four had stayed there, two sleeping on a mattress and two on the floor, until they had been evicted. They wound up sleeping under the Boardwalk. Food had been scarce.

Despite the hardship, Al preferred it to the prospects of returning to school. High school, he concluded, was a waste of time. Why sit in a classroom pretending to apply yourself to studies you had little use for, when you and your buddy could be thumbing rides to more exciting places, such as Montreal, where you could tour the city's whorehouses?

He never did graduate from high school, mainly because he couldn't pass geometry, a required course. He excelled in English and history, but Latin and geometry made no sense at all to him. He couldn't fathom how he would ever apply anything he learned from these disciplines to real life. Latin was a dead language, never heard except in Roman Catholic churches; geometry was equally useless unless you aspired to be a mathematician or scientist. After becoming a celebrity cartoonist, Al would boast that he flunked geometry nine times—a school record.

He decided that any future education would have to focus on art. If he was going to be a cartoonist, he required classical training. The nearby Yale

Art School offered such training. Al scheduled an appointment with the dean of admissions and assembled a portfolio of the best of his drawings.

The dean didn't examine a single sheet of his work. The visit was over as soon as he asked Al where he had graduated from high school. Al, perhaps remembering the debacle at the hospital two years before, told the truth: that he hadn't actually graduated. The dean immediately handed back the portfolio and told him to return when he had a diploma in hand.

Al stewed over the rejection. He wouldn't make the mistake of honesty again.

4 UNCLE BOB'S GENEROSITY

The failure to be accepted into the Yale Art School taught Al Caplin all he needed to know about his primary disadvantages: he had no money for tuition and no high school diploma. He knew he had the talent to grab the attention of an art school's director of admissions, but he'd have to be much smoother during his interviews if he ever expected to get into a school.

In other words, he'd have to manufacture a good story and stick to it.

Handling the diploma issue didn't require a lot of thought. He would simply tell the administrator that he had forgotten to bring it with him but would show it to him as soon as possible. He guessed, quite correctly as it turned out, that no one was especially interested in seeing proof of his graduation. These were busy men.

The money issue demanded a plausible story. The schools asked for at least a partial tuition payment at the time of enrollment; Al didn't have enough money to pay for a sack of groceries, let alone tuition at a good school. There had to be a convincing promise of money, and for this Al invented a new family member, a wealthy "Uncle Bob" who supposedly sent him a substantial amount of cash—more than enough to cover tuition— every Christmas. It was here that the young Al Caplin's enviable gift for storytelling paid off. He was so convincing that no one questioned the validity of his story or demanded any proof of Uncle Bob's existence.

His first stop was the Pennsylvania Academy of the Fine Arts. Not only was the Academy one of the most prestigious art schools in the East; it also happened that Otto Caplin, back on the road after another failed business, was now in Philadelphia. As Al perceived it, his father would be happy to see him and provide him with a place to stay.

Ironically, all this was predicated on Al's belief in a less than truthful story that his father was telling his family. Everything was going swimmingly, according to Otto's letters. He was living at the Clinton Hotel, a huge apartment/hotel complex, chock-full of little old ladies and young students from the Jefferson Medical School. Within a matter of months, he promised, he'd be finding a place and moving the family to Philadelphia.

Otto was on one of his sales trips when Al arrived in Philadelphia, but the hotel's manager supplied Al with a key to his father's room. Al visited the school and sold his Uncle Bob story to the unsuspecting director of admissions, meaning Al would get nearly a full semester of classes before he was expected to cough up his tuition. Encouraged by the turn his life was taking, Al dashed off a note to his old traveling companion, Don Munson. The city, he told Don, was just like Paris.

Otto Caplin showed Al around the Clinton Hotel neighborhood, and Al quickly developed a routine for attending classes, finding cheap meals in nearby eateries, and hanging around the hotel lobby. He displayed some of his early charcoal sketches and basked in the praise of the hotel residents.

Not long after moving into the Clinton, Al stopped by a neighborhood tailor and laundry shop called Dubinsky's. He'd seen Morris Dubinsky, the shop's owner, and his wife working late in the evenings, their store lights on long after every other business in the area was closed. The older couple took a liking to Al. They were impressed when he showed them his art, and even more impressed when they learned that he was the grandson of Rabbi Davidson. During one of his visits, Al met the Dubinskys' daughter, Esther, who, though still in high school, was as attracted to Al as he was to her. On their first date, they attended a local production of Rodgers and Hart's *A Connecticut Yankee*. In no time, they were seeing each other every day.

Esther played violin and dreamed of studying music in Europe. Al told her he wanted to study art in Paris. Esther drove him around Philadelphia, showing him the historical sites, and the two began plotting a future. The following summer, Al promised, he would hold down a job in Asbury Park, drawing caricatures and saving his money; she could find work there, too, perhaps performing in a local orchestra or, more likely, waiting tables. They would save their money for their move to Europe.

But their relationship ended one evening in a very sudden and unexpected way. Esther was in an especially ebullient mood, and without thinking about what she was saying, she told Al that she wanted to go dancing.

"I want to dance all night!" she said. "If only you could—"

The unintended insult tore through its victim. Al pulled away from her and sulked; he would have nothing of her apologies. When she dropped him off at the hotel, it marked the last time they would see each other.

It was probably just as well. His attendance at school had dropped off, and he had a new friend in town: Gus Levy had dropped in, unannounced, at the hotel. Otto Caplin was unhappy with the intrusion. Leaving on another sales trip, he said he wanted Gus out of the hotel when he returned, but the living arrangements grew even more complicated in Otto's absence when Don Munson turned up, motivated by Al's earlier letter and the talk of Paris.

Gus fully intended to move on, but Don hoped to stay. He had designs on enrolling in a business school. Like Al, he had not graduated high school, but this tiny detail did not concern him in the least. As Al might have expected, Don had put together a scam of his own: he'd paid a shady high school administrator a hundred dollars for a diploma bearing his name. He could go to the college of his choice.

In this confederacy of well-intentioned sleight-of-handers, Otto Caplin presided as chief. Al depended upon him for his room and a small weekly stipend, and believed he would continue to provide with Don staying on. Otto suggested that his room was much too small for three men; it would be much better if the two boys had a place of their own. He managed to find them a small suite on another floor, in a different wing of the building, and Al and Don moved in, scheming almost immediately about the parties and young women they would be hosting. Within a week, Otto was gone— permanently. Al and Don thought he was coming back, and the landlady certainly believed he would be returning, but as the weeks passed and no one heard a word from him, the truth sank in. The landlady would run into Al and ask if he'd heard from his father, but after a while, she quit inquiring. And she never asked for rent.

Al would say that he learned a great deal from the time he spent attending the Academy and other schools. His drawing improved, though he didn't see it at the time.

"The Academy was a daily defeat for me," he'd remember. "We would draw figures from life or a plaster cast . . . My figures looked worse and worse. I grew so ashamed of them [that] I stopped greeting or saying good-bye to my fellow students. I didn't want to give them any chance to say anything about my work. Fifty years later, I look back at these drawings. If they weren't first rate, they were at least a gallant if tormented effort to be first rate."

Al knew all along that each day brought him closer to the end. He'd leave to return home for the holiday season, the school would eagerly await its share of the money Al would be receiving from his wealthy and generous Uncle Bob, and Al, like his father at the rooming house, would become a ghost.

While on vacation, Al wrote the director of the Academy with the sad news that Uncle Bob had suffered a regrettable reversal of fortune, and for the first Christmas, he had been unable to send him money. It was all very tragic, of course. Al would have liked to continue his education at the school, but he couldn't expect officials there to trust him any longer. He promised to pay the tuition one day, but for the time being, it was probably best to part ways.

Despite his struggles the previous summer, Al had every intention of re-turning to Asbury Park and pursuing a job as a Boardwalk caricaturist. The same four would be going, and before he left for New Jersey, he understood that it was going to be even tougher this time around. He had no guarantee that he would be able to compete with the sketch artist he'd met the previous summer and scratch out enough money to get by. Don was returning to his job barking for the salesman, but Bence and Gus had no idea what they would be doing.

This time, however, they didn't have enough money between them for a flophouse room. On their first night in Asbury Park, they slept under the Boardwalk. Al was mortified when he awoke the following morning. He had sand in his hair and on his clothes, and he was in desperate need of a shower and shave. The best he was going to be able to manage was to sneak into a hotel and use one of the men's rooms to clean up. He couldn't be assured that this would help: it was overcast and looked as if it might rain at any minute.

On his way to a hotel, he ran across Anderson, the Boardwalk sketch artist he'd met the previous summer, who informed him, first, that he looked awful, and, second, that rain would most assuredly wash out their day's work. Anderson suggested that Al drop by his rented room and wash up, an offer that Al gratefully accepted. Once there, Anderson offered Al a drink, but Al, a conscious teetotaler, declined. Anderson's room was a dive, and Al quickly retreated to the bathroom for a shower. By the time he'd showered, dried off, and redressed, it was pouring rain and Anderson was prepared to cancel his workday. Nobody would be out and about, he told Al. He might as well stay in and have a few drinks.

Dispirited, Al left Anderson and walked back to the Boardwalk in the rain. This wasn't at all what he'd planned, and to witness how Anderson lived put him face-to-face with a grim reality. Al had envisioned Asbury Park as a place where he could use his art to earn money. Instead, he'd seen how pathetic that existence could be—if Anderson was any indication. He couldn't see himself walking around like Anderson, smelling like a combination of booze and cheap cologne, hanging out on the Boardwalk and hoping he might earn enough scratch to afford a room and food, only to slip home at the end of the day and take slugs directly from a quart bottle of liquor. The thought depressed him.

His father had been correct when he suggested that Al was only pushing himself for the life of a bum.

The news was no better for Bence and the others. Don's job fell through when the salesman decided that Asbury Park could survive without his brand of vegetable slicers. Don had dropped by a few places and found work at a soda fountain in a drugstore. Bence and Gus had come up empty in their job searches. They couldn't count on Otto to look for them, chew them out, and take them home, as he had the previous summer.

Al concluded then that he'd have to find a way to attend an art school the forthcoming term. The starving artist's life, Boardwalk style, wasn't for him.

The four lasted three weeks before returning home, broke and hungry, defeated by their latest efforts to head out on their own. Bence quickly found a job similar to the one Don had in New Jersey, but Al had nothing. He was trapped in the house, forced to listen to his mother's lectures about the uncertainty of an artist's life. Al would quarrel with her on occasion, but most of his time was spent skulking in his room, where he could at least be alone with his black moods.

Uncle Bob surfaced again the following fall, this time in Boston. Otto Caplin had started up another business and moved his family to 96 Wellington Hill Street in the Mattapan section of the city, and after investigating the art school availability and discovering that the city boasted of a huge selection, Al decided to try the Museum School, another prestigious institution developing young artists. He visited the school, reprised his Uncle Bob performance, and showed the officials his portfolio.

This time around, Uncle Bob had a wife, Aunt Diana, who had passed away at a very young age. Bob and Diana had been unable to have children, and Uncle Bob treated Al as a sort of surrogate. Moved by the story, the admissions director told Al that she would really like to give Uncle Bob the grand tour of the campus, in the event that he ever found himself in Boston.

Al loved the city and would be connected to it, in one way or another, for most of the rest of his life. His experience at the Museum School, however, was no different than his earlier experiences in Philadelphia. He took in everything his instructors had to offer, worked hard and suffered from a lack of self-confidence, and dropped out when Uncle Bob had another downturn in his business fortunes.

Fortunately for Al, the schools didn't trade information about their former students. Al found another school, the Vesper George School of Art, before the next term began. He had to adjust his story about Uncle Bob—he'd now be getting his check in May—but otherwise he was learning that he could get an education in art, a little bit at a time, for no financial investment.

His time at the Vesper George School ended suddenly and unexpectedly. For reasons he would never be able to explain, he had been working on a sketch of a hideous woman—"the most awful woman I could imagine," as he'd later say—and he left it on his easel when he stepped out for lunch and a smoke. When he returned, the sketch was gone. He was ordered to report to the office of Miss George, the ancient daughter of Vesper George. She had the sketch and she was very unhappy. The gift of caricature, she informed him, was a blessing, but—

She couldn't continue. She broke down in tears, returned his drawing, and expelled him from the school with no further explanation.

Al didn't understand the reason for his expulsion until he was out in the corridor and glanced back down at his drawing. The sketch bore a close resemblance to Miss George. Al would never admit to creating the caricature on purpose, but it didn't matter. He was barely nineteen and he'd managed to be tossed out of three art schools.

The fourth would be the charm.

When Al Caplin ran into Catherine Wingate Cameron, he knew almost instantly that this was his type of woman. She was bright, attractive, cre-

Catherine Cameron and Alfred Caplin at Seabrook Beach, New Hampshire, in 1931, during their courting days as art students.

ative, fiercely individualistic, and one of the few people he'd ever met who could match wits with him.

The meeting would have never taken place if Caplin hadn't enrolled in still another school, the Designers Art School in Boston, where Catherine also happened to be a student. As he would learn, her family was from Amesbury, a town about an hour away, and while attending school, she lived in Brooke House, a girls' dormitory. He'd noticed her in one of his classes, and he hoped he would find an occasion to talk to her.

"She was so beautiful," he wrote, "and I wanted so painfully to know her, I acknowledged her not by an indifferent grunt but by a menacing growl. Yet she smiled a radiant smile at me every day as if she knew what I really meant."

Al Caplin and Catherine Cameron did not become a couple immediately, despite Caplin's yearnings. They maintained a distance you might expect from two co-workers who smile and nod as they pass in the hall. He was either too shy or too intimidated to ask her on a proper date.

All that changed dramatically when Al accidentally tore the seat of his pants on the way to school one morning. He would later claim that this was his only pair of pants, which seems unlikely, but in any event, he ripped his trousers, and rather than return home and miss a class, he continued on to school and took a smock from the locker of a student who rarely attended class. He had already taken his place in the classroom when the normally absent student, angry about the missing smock, made his appearance. Rather than hand the smock over in front of everyone in the room, Al asked his fellow student to follow him out to the hall. As he was returning the smock, he felt someone slipping another one over his shoulder. It was Catherine. She had followed the two into the hall.

Al was moved by this act of kindness.

"I resolved, that morning, to marry her," he wrote, "and I did."

When retelling the story in "Al Capp, by Li'l Abner," the autobiographical comic book he created for the Red Cross during World War II, Capp concluded this episode with a romanticized scene involving Catherine actually sewing a patch on his pants while he stood modestly behind a dressing screen. This might or might not have happened—he fudged the truth on

In his 1946 booklet for the Red Cross, Al Capp recalled a meaningful incident in his early relationship with Catherine at art school. (These panels and others throughout the text have been modified from original strip configuration for clearer reproduction in this space.)

more than one occasion in the comic—but there is no question that Caplin, accustomed to having the upper hand on those rare occasions when he actually spent any time with a woman, was thoroughly smitten.

From there on, their relationship developed very quickly. Caplin quipped that his mother's sandwiches were as responsible as anything for the progression of their romance. Catherine had no more money than Al, and they'd split Tillie Caplin's potato sandwiches over lunch. ("My mother could make symphonies of potatoes," he'd joke. This was a nice humorous touch to the story, although Catherine and Elliott Caplin both remembered the sandwiches as being chopped liver.) To Caplin's delight, Catherine had a devilish streak, and they worked out a scheme in which they'd manipulate a meal-ticket machine at a local cafeteria, buying their meals for a fraction of their cost and using the savings to go to the movies together. In no time, the two were virtually inseparable. With money so scarce, they spent hours just walking and talking, enjoying one another's company, each learning as much as possible about the other. For the first time in his life, Caplin was deeply in love.

As the school term wound down, Caplin faced another expulsion. With summer ahead, and no intentions to attend classes anywhere during that period, he and Catherine made plans for their immediate futures. Catherine dropped out of school and returned home to live with her parents and look for work in Amesbury. Caplin, satisfied that he had learned all he needed to work in the world of newspaper comics, decided to end his formal education and take his talents to the Land of Dreams—at least for artists. With only a portfolio of drawings and six dollars in his pocket, no job prospects, no connections, and no place to stay, he caught a train to New York City. He and Catherine would reunite when the time was right.

5 BREAKING INTO THE BUSINESS

Al Caplin did some fast talking to secure an apartment on 12th Street in Greenwich Village, a place run by a Mrs. Ford, the widow of a New York City police officer. The landlady was willing to allow Caplin to stay rent-free in the apartment until he received his first paycheck, which, he assured her, would be forthcoming the following Friday. That he had no job didn't deter Caplin from risking eviction with a lie. To endear himself to the lonely landlady, he did a charcoal sketch of her late husband. Creating the portrait, Caplin trimmed substantial weight from Officer Ford's frame and gave him a youthful appearance. In Capp's version of the tale, the landlady was overwhelmed. She never again brought up the topic of rent. In fact, she even gave him urgently needed money and left food and treats for him in his apartment.

This was fortuitous, because in Depression-era New York, there wasn't much demand for young cartoonists with no prior experience. Caplin found a job doing hackwork for a small advertising firm marketing comic strips for newspapers. The strips were nothing but ads, but they were worth two dollars each. Although he hated the work, Caplin could crank out two strips a day, which meant that he cleared about $3.60 per day after he deducted his expenses for paper, ink, and round-trip subway fare to the agency's offices. He would hole up in his apartment and work into the wee hours of the morning, deliver the strip early the next day, and spend much of the remainder of the daylight hours hoofing from newspaper syndicate to newspaper syndicate, trying to impress editors with his portfolio.

By his own admission, most of the work in his portfolio was derivative—Al Caplin versions of the popular comic strip artists of the day. He hoped to impress editors with his artistic range, but the drawings did nothing for the syndicates. They already had "Little Orphan Annie." Why would they be interested in someone who drew like Harold Gray?

The imitations did eventually pay off. Caplin's uncle Harry Resnick contacted an editor he knew at the Associated Press and arranged an interview. Wilson Hicks, an assistant features editor, liked Caplin's imitation of Thomas Aloysius "Tad" Dorgan, the renowned cartoonist and journalist, whose boxing comics set an industry standard. His brother, Dick Dorgan, was contributing a one-panel comic for Associated Press, an "Our Boarding House" knockoff called "Colonel Gilfeather," using a style closely resembling his brother's. Hicks examined Caplin's samples, including his Tad Dorgan imitations, and though he would concede that the kid had talent, Caplin was, in Hicks's opinion, "a long way from being a finished cartoonist." Hicks thanked Caplin for dropping by. He wouldn't be needing another artist imitating Tad Dorgan or anyone else.

On the way out, Caplin, unaware of the blood connection between the two artists involved with "Colonel Gilfeather," saw some of the proofs for upcoming "Gilfeathers," which he later dismissed as "sort of ruptured, blind Tad." The poor quality set him off enough to return to the editor's office.

"You said you had an imitation of Tad," he told Wilson Hicks. "I hope you don't mean this guy. He's never seen Tad."

"Look at the signature," Hicks shot back.

Caplin looked but held his ground.

"I've got a brother, but he doesn't draw like me," he argued. "He doesn't draw at all. That's the kind of brother you've got."

Hicks sent Caplin packing, but he contacted him a few weeks later. Dick Dorgan wasn't satisfied with the salary that Associated Press was paying him, and he was bolting to the King Features Syndicate, which paid twice what Dorgan was earning at AP. If Caplin was willing to work for fifty-two dollars a week, the job was his.

This represented a hefty salary hike—more than double what he was earning at the advertising agency. Caplin took the job, making him the country's youngest syndicated comic strip artist. In a joyful letter home, Caplin promised his mother that he would be sending her twenty-five dollars a week. He then wrote Catherine and proposed that she come to New York and marry him.

Catherine wasn't so sure. She was all for getting married, but she had just started a job as a substitute music and art teacher in Amesbury and couldn't see quitting it. Perhaps it would be better if they met in Connecticut, got married, and returned to their respective jobs. They would keep their marriage a secret until their future was more stable.

For the time being, they did nothing. Caplin applied himself to his new job without retaining anything recognizable from Dick Dorgan's daily panel. He was making more money than he'd ever earned in his life, and the future looked hopeful. The nuptials could wait.

Caplin, signing his work "A. G. Caplin," added his own distinct touches to "Mister Gilfeather," as the comic was now called. He shifted the focus of the feature from the colonel, who, as far as Caplin was concerned, too closely resembled Major Hoople, the crusty main character of "Our Boarding House," to the colonel's equally obnoxious younger brother. He adjusted the style of artwork as well, from Tad Dorgan to Phil May, an underappreciated English cartoonist that Caplin greatly admired. Caplin had checked out a copy of May's *London* from the Boston Library and was thunderstruck by May's ability to combine great writing with equally compelling art. Caplin studied May's work with more enthusiasm than he had felt when studying any artist during his formal schooling, and he struggled to bring elements of May's style to "Mister Gilfeather." May's work was tinged with dark humor, which might have been acceptable from a creative standpoint, but not from a newspaper perspective. After all, these were the funnies. Subscribing newspapers began dumping the strip to the tune of one cancellation per week—a figure that added up to an unacceptable loss over the months.

Caplin's days on "Gilfeather" were numbered, and he knew it. His colleagues advised him to return to the strip's earlier style, when the comic was funny but, to Caplin, disappointing. "Gilfeather" had never been his idea, and he hated continuing someone else's work. He liked the money, but as the months passed, he wondered how much longer he could hang on.

As he discovered, there was other talent in the room.

An unfinished "Mr. Gilfeather" panel by Alfred Caplin, ca. 1932. His title character is on the left. The lettering and background have not been inked, suggesting that this panel was either rejected midway through or abandoned when Caplin left to return to art school.

He had taken to working nights, occupying a desk on the thirteenth floor of the Associated Press building, enjoying the solitude and quiet that came after the day shift left and life slowed down in the big newsroom. Caplin's desk was near the windows overlooking Madison Avenue, and he generally kept to himself, working on a "Gilfeather" and occasionally staring out into the night. In the middle of the room, another artist worked away, oblivious to everything going on around him. AP had hired him to retouch photographs, which he did during the daylight hours, but in the evening, after the newsroom had emptied out, he'd pull out what Caplin believed to be comic strip work.

The young man's name was Milton Caniff, and in the years to come, he would become one of the brightest luminaries among newspaper comic strip artists. He would also become one of Al Capp's lifelong friends.

The future creator of "Terry and the Pirates" and "Steve Canyon" could not have been more different from Caplin. He was two years older, hailed from Ohio, and had been an Eagle Scout. He had attended Ohio State University and, for a while, considered a career in acting. His gifts as an artist were apparent at a very early age. At fourteen, he enrolled in a correspondence art course and took a job as an apprentice at the *Dayton Journal*. A year later, he was drawing a comic strip, "Chic and Noodles," for his high school paper. While in college, he worked part-time (and eventually, after graduation, full-time) for the *Columbus Dispatch*, adding to a developing résumé that would help him later, in March 1932, when he took a job in the art department at the Associated Press. He began on April 1 and met Caplin on that same day.

Caniff and Caplin were initially very formal toward one another, both willing to grunt a hello if they passed each other in the halls or newsroom, but neither enthusiastic about volunteering any insight into his work or ambitions in comics. Caplin, accustomed to being on the receiving end of the older AP artists' scorn, appreciated Caniff's showing him any interest or respect, though he did maintain his gruff manner around the new hire. Caniff had dropped by Caplin's drawing board on his first night on the job and looked at Caplin's yet-to-be-completed "Gilfeathers." He uttered a few words of praise and returned to his own drawing board. They would chat from time to time in the nearly deserted newsroom, but both held their distance.

Their real friendship began in an offbeat way—at least in the strange story that Al Capp would tell.

The AP building stood across the street from the Ritz Hotel, and to pass the time, Caplin would turn off the light at his desk and stare into the lighted hotel windows. One drama in particular caught his eye. Every evening, always at the same time, a young, attractive woman would prepare herself for her husband's return from work. She'd stand in the bedroom and try on a variety of provocative negligees until she found what she wanted to be wearing when her husband arrived. For Caplin, this was the peep show of his young life. He'd watch as the woman's husband walked through the door, his body language indicating nothing but defeat and depression. The man would sit on the edge of the bed, open his briefcase, and shuffle through papers while his sympathetic wife tried to seduce him, first by what she was wearing, and then by kissing and caressing him. They usually wound up making love. Caplin, utterly transfixed, as he would later put it, made this a part of his nightly routine at the Associated Press.

One night, to get a better look, Caplin attempted to climb out on the window ledge. Suddenly, someone was grabbing him from behind.

It was Milton Caniff.

"Don't," he implored, fearing that Caplin, like so many during the Depression, was about to jump.

"Quiet," Caplin admonished. He directed Caniff's attention to the action taking place in the room across the way. For the next half hour, the two stared silently at the spectacle unfolding before them.

"How long has this been going on?" Caniff finally asked.

Caplin explained that it had been going on for some time, but he hadn't said anything to Caniff because he didn't want to disrupt his work.

"No work is more important than the life study," Caniff scoffed.

"I always thought so," Caplin said, "but I wasn't sure anyone else did."

"I do," Caniff responded, "and don't you forget it."

The story reached the unhappy conclusion that Caplin feared it might. One evening, while preparing for her husband's return from work, the young woman answered a knock on the hotel door. Two men with grim expressions entered the room and spoke to her. The woman fainted. Caplin and Caniff never saw the woman or her husband again, and both quit watching the hotel. It took no imagination to see that these two young people, locked in a daily survival battle in a pitiless city, had become the Depression's latest victims.

* * *

Caniff's version of the early days of his friendship with Caplin was, as one might expect, much tamer. He never mentioned the episode about the young woman in the Ritz, and his accounts in interviews toned down Al Capp's blustery talk about how he took the novice cartoonist under his wing. Not that Capp's talk about helping out Caniff would have been accepted by those who knew him: acting as a father figure would not have been typical Capp behavior.

As Caniff remembered it, he had checked out the comics talent at AP, as one would size up the competition in the room. Caplin, he determined, was gifted, but he was turned off by Caplin's loud, bloviating manner. Caplin seemed determined to gain the approval of the veteran cartoonists, even if doing so involved his constantly talking up the caliber of his own work.

Milton Caniff, left, the creator of "Terry and the Pirates" and "Steve Canyon," shares a laugh with Al Capp in this undated photo. The two met at the Associated Press in 1932 and remained close friends for life.

Caniff, by nature, wasn't anything at all like this, and, as he wrote in a 1959 memoir for *Life* magazine, Caplin's swagger might have arisen as a way to disguise the struggles he was having with "Mister Gilfeather." Caplin worked at a painfully slow pace, sketching and erasing, sketching and erasing, until he had nearly worn through the paper on his drawing board. Unlike the other cartoonists, who methodically cranked out material with very little effort, Caplin was learning on the job, with virtually no encouragement, and it did nothing to ease an already disagreeable disposition. Despite his earnings being the greatest of his life thus far, he was obviously a kid with no money: he wore shabby clothes, and when leaving the office at lunchtime, he would peer into the windows of nearby restaurants, looking at menus and selecting his dinner by his meager ability to pay. Caniff claimed that on one occasion an old woman selling newspapers on the street took pity on Caplin and gave him the change he needed to eat.

"He was kind of a sad sack in those days," Caniff told his biographer, R. C. Harvey.

Their friendship, he told Harvey, might not have happened at all if they hadn't been working nights. "In an empty office like that, you talk about things you wouldn't talk about if other people were there," he said.

Perhaps their conversations would turn to a drama taking place in the hotel across the street—Caniff didn't volunteer that information—but both agreed in their retelling of the story that they spent a lot of time discussing their hopes for the future. Both dreamed of having a syndicated comic strip, and both were confident in their ability to do so.

In a 1948 *Cosmopolitan* article about those early AP days, Capp said: "[Caniff] knew many theatrical people and agents in New York, and people like that are always throwing parties. The first time Milt took me along, I met Jean Harlow, Kay Francis and Jean Muir . . . In return for this kind of hospitality, I began giving Milt free lectures on art."

Caniff disputed this claim. Years after Capp's death, Caniff noted, "Al used to write about me—these wonderful exaggerations—that he used to advise me how to draw . . . Invariably the opposite of what happened. That I introduced him to movie actresses, none of which was true . . . He just forgot about facts whenever he was writing. He considered it promotion."

Caniff was only mildly surprised in the fall of 1932 when Wilson Hicks plopped an envelope containing Caplin's unfinished cartoons on his desk, informed him that Caplin had quit, and asked him to take over the strip. Caplin, Caniff learned, had returned to Boston.

Caniff continued the panel until the following spring, but he had no more enthusiasm for "Gilfeather" than Caplin. The panel went unsigned until November 7, 1932, and even then, some newspapers preferred to title the panel "Colonel Gilfeather by Dick Dorgan." Caniff would rework the comic into a panel called "The Gay Thirties," even as he privately developed what would become his seminal strip, "Terry and the Pirates." He would resume his friendship with Al Caplin at a later date, when Caplin was working under the name of Al Capp and they both had attained some of the goals they had discussed while working for AP.

Al Caplin and Catherine Cameron married on August 16, 1932, while Caplin was still working for the AP. Caplin met her in Connecticut, as planned, and they followed through on their decision not to say a word to their parents about the wedding. For their "honeymoon," they returned to Caplin's New York apartment, where they hung out for what Caplin would call "a fairy tale week." He showed her his "Gilfeather" cartoons, and she agreed with his assessments of their value. The early Dorgan imitations were amusing but uninspired; the more recent Phil May–influenced work, while more cerebral, was not the kind of work that would please readers eager for a chuckle during hard times.

Caplin felt like he was mired in quicksand; the more he struggled, the deeper he sank. He reached the end two weeks after Catherine returned to Amesbury, when his editor received a letter from the managing editor of the *Brockton Enterprise*. "Mister Gilfeather," the managing editor complained, was the worst cartoon on the market. Caplin's editor showed the letter to Caplin and told him not to fret, but Caplin knew the letter's accusation was on the mark. He left a note of resignation on Wilson Hicks's desk, picked up his belongings from his apartment, and caught a train back to Massachusetts. The last "Gilfeather" with Caplin's signature appeared on September 10, 1932.

In all likelihood, Wilson Hicks was greatly relieved to rid himself of Alfred Caplin. As far as he was concerned, Caplin had been a burden from the beginning.

"Never have I worked with a more difficult person than Alfred Caplin," he declared in 1959. "He rarely met deadlines. He would disappear for days. He was often gruff. It took me a while to figure out what was wrong. It was simply that he loathed and despised 'Mister Gilfeather.' It was not his—and more than anything else he wanted his own cartoon."

Caplin had no inclination of what he should do once he reached Boston. It certainly was not the time to tell the world that he and Catherine were married. Living at home would be a step backward; his brothers were now of college age and seemed to have their immediate futures better planned. There were no long-term jobs in comics, yet he gave little thought to doing any other kind of work.

His mother came to his rescue, promising to find a way to send him back to school. She sympathized with the artistic dilemma he faced at the Associated Press, though her understanding might have been tempered by the fact that Otto Caplin was enjoying what, for him, would have been a lucrative work period. He was still out on the road, selling oil, but he was sending money home regularly. The money still wasn't enough to make all of the bills on time, but the ax of eviction and starvation wasn't hanging quite as precariously over the Caplin family's head, either.

Maybe Tillie Caplin supported her eldest son because she saw so much of Otto in him. Maybe she felt the special bonding between a mother and her firstborn. Maybe she truly believed in his talent. Whatever the reason, she approached one of her brothers and secured a "loan" for her son's tuition.

If any of this bothered Al Caplin, he never indicated it, not then and not in future interviews or his autobiography. He attended classes, hitchhiked to Amesbury on Saturdays, stayed overnight, and returned home on Sundays. He managed to get by when he could barely scrape together the loose change needed for a pack of Camels. He found occasional freelance work, illustrating articles for the *Boston Post*, but his main focus was on school. He enjoyed knowing that, for once, he was attending classes on a real uncle's money, that he wouldn't be obligated to go through the humiliating explanations when it came time to pay tuition and he had to explain that Uncle Bob had just gone through a bad turn in his business.

He wound up dropping out of school for another reason. Catherine had been feeling poorly, and when she visited her physician, she learned she was a couple of months pregnant. She and Al had no choice but to confess their secret marriage. They came clean to Catherine's parents, who were surprised to learn that their daughter had married a Jew. Caplin shrugged it off. They could raise their grandchild under the religious banner of their choice; he had no objection.

"The Camerons took it well for a family who had never met a Jew," he quipped decades later, when looking back at the conversation.

With a family soon to support, Caplin left school, packed his bags, and headed back to New York City for one last shot at earning a living as an artist.

Caplin detested the entire process of peddling his wares. He was convinced that he was as gifted as anyone earning a living in comics, yet no one in New York, including his old boss at AP, would hire him. Every day was a repeat of the previous day: lug a portfolio around the city, watch an editor shuffle through the art, listen to the same story about how he had talent but there just wasn't any work for him, and move on. Caplin had managed to secure his old apartment with Mrs. Ford, and life became unrelentingly repetitive.

His run of bad luck ended one day as he was leaving another of these rejections. In his version of the story, he was crossing Eighth Avenue, carrying his portfolio, when he paused to admire a fancy sports car headed in his direction. Two people occupied the car—a man, who was driving, and a woman seated next to him. Seeing that Caplin wasn't about to move out of his way, the driver slammed on his brakes, narrowly missing Caplin, who had dropped his portfolio in the street. The angry driver jumped out of his car.

"You damned idiot!" he shouted at Caplin.

"Oh, balls," Caplin muttered in response.

The man turned away as if he intended to return to his car. One of Caplin's drawings lay at his feet. The man picked it up and looked at it.

"You a cartoonist?" he asked.

Caplin snatched his drawing and prepared to leave.

"I am Ham Fisher, the creator of 'Joe Palooka,'" the man declared.

Caplin stared at the short, pudgy, red-faced man. He had very little use for "Joe Palooka," but he knew success when it was standing in front of him. Fisher's comic strip was one of the most popular of the syndicated dailies.

"You don't know what a thrill it is to meet you, sir," he said, pumping Fisher's hand.

Fisher glanced at a couple more of Caplin's drawings.

"You got a job?" he asked.

"No sir, I don't," Caplin said.

"Hop in," Fisher said, leading Caplin to his car.

Both would come to bitterly regret the day they ever crossed paths.

6 HATFIELD AND McCOY

Al Capp and Ham Fisher would never agree on much of anything, including the circumstances swirling around their initial meeting that late-summer day in 1933. Fisher claimed that he saw Al Caplin walking down the sidewalk, carrying the samples of his art wrapped in the kind of heavy blue paper used by some syndicates of the day for returning rejections. Feeling sorry for what he perceived to be a down-and-outer, Fisher called out to him from his car window, inquiring if he was a comic strip artist. As Fisher remembered, Caplin had about a nickel to his name. He offered him a job because Caplin looked so utterly dejected.

Capp vigorously disputed Fisher's account, though he told several different versions of their meeting. In his unpublished autobiography, he presented the account of Fisher's almost running him over with his car, although the story seems dubious. It's unlikely that Fisher would have stopped his car on a busy New York street, jumped out to yell at Caplin, paused long enough to look over his art, and then offer him a ride. Caplin apparently told his brother a story very similar to Ham Fisher's, because Elliott Caplin's retelling in his book, *Al Capp Remembered*, echoes Fisher's account almost to the letter. Capp modified Fisher's story when talking to a *New Yorker* writer in 1947, long after "Li'l Abner" had risen to the height of the comic strip world, although in this later permutation Capp said that Fisher mistook him for a McNaught Syndicate errand boy.

The two did agree on several details: Ham Fisher was driving his car, Fisher's sister was seated in the car next to him, Caplin was somewhere outside, the two did exchange words, and Caplin wound up riding with Fisher to his plush apartment in the Parc Vendome.

Fisher, a man who knew his limitations, needed help on his strip. He could work up a good storyline for "Joe Palooka," but on his very best day, he was only a marginally talented artist. He had a taste for beautiful women, fashionable clothing, good liquor, expensive cars, and high-end vacations, all easily within his reach due to the fortune he was earning from his syndicated strip. Finding a young talent to help him with the art for "Joe Palooka" would only make his life easier and his comic strip better, especially if he could secure this kind of assistant for a modest wage.

When they arrived at his apartment, Fisher showed Caplin several penciled strips of future "Joe Palooka" entries. Caplin judged the boxing scenes to be excellently rendered, but he cringed at Fisher's female characters, which, he felt, "seemed to [have been] drawn by a man who had never met one." Caplin kept his thoughts to himself, even when Fisher confessed that the strips needed a lot of work.

"Think you can fix 'em up?" he asked Caplin.

This was an amazing question. Here was Caplin, desperately broke, with no immediate prospects of employment, being asked to improve the work of one of the most highly regarded names in the comic strip business. Caplin kept his composure and allowed that he could probably do a few things to improve the drawings.

Later in the afternoon—around five o'clock, as Caplin would recall—Fisher left Caplin alone with the work and went out for the evening. When he returned nine hours later, a little overserved at the local saloon, the improved strips were awaiting him. Fisher loved them.

"You doing anything tomorrow?" he asked.

When Caplin informed him that his schedule was clear, Fisher told him to report back at the apartment at nine o'clock the following morning. He'd be working all night on new material and would be sleeping when Caplin arrived, so Al should just go about his business on his own. New strips would be waiting on the table. He handed Caplin a ten-dollar bill—the first money Caplin had earned in a long while.

Caplin was elated. He was back in business.

Hammond Edward Fisher ranked among the lucky ones. In a move that would have made his protégé proud, he'd scammed his way into a syndicated comic strip, and he had taken full advantage of the opportunity. His

Ham Fisher, creator of "Joe Palooka."

rise in the business was swift and lucrative. For someone who liked to play, there was plenty of fame and fortune to exploit—when he chose to do so. He lived alone and, as Caplin learned early during his tenure with Fisher, he could be very parsimonious with his money, if it was being spent on someone other than himself.

Fisher had been born thirty-three years earlier, on September 24, 1900, in Wilkes-Barre, Pennsylvania, and, like so many other artists in the business, he had displayed a gift for writing and drawing at a young age. He toyed with the idea of a career in journalism, in which he might have done quite nicely, but he preferred drawing the sports comics that were popular features in newspapers around the country. He'd come up with the idea for his boxing strip, "Joe Palooka," while working as a sports cartoonist for a paper when he was still in his teens, but his editor had no interest in it. Fisher never gave up on the idea. It took him seven years to find a taker for the strip, and even then, it took a slick bit of deception to make it happen.

Fisher had approached the McNaught Syndicate with the strip, but the editor there, like those before him, rejected it. However, the editor was impressed enough by Fisher's knowledge of comics to offer him a job as a comic strip salesman. Fisher was resourceful enough to recognize the opportunity in front of him. He would be traveling around the country, hawking other cartoonists' work, but he would also have the eyes and ears of editors who might be willing to take a look at his "Joe Palooka" samples and listen to his sales pitch for the strip. He took the job.

It worked. In 1928 Fisher lined up "Palooka" clients, one paper at a time, until he'd rung up twenty newspapers interested in picking up his strip. It's uncertain whether Fisher presented "Joe Palooka" as a fait accompli, as a definite part of the syndicate's future list, or if he ran the idea past editors as a possibility for something in months to come, but however he sold it, he reached a level of success that forced McNaught to reconsider its original rejection. "Joe Palooka" was in.

By the time he and Al Caplin met, the strip was one of the top five comic strips in syndication, perhaps as a result of its message delivered during the Depression: there was hope for the average Joe, if he was willing to punch his way through adversity.

Caplin had a scam of his own that he ran on Fisher. The afternoon after he had given Caplin his initial ten-dollar bill, Fisher got up, examined Caplin's work from that morning, and offered him another five dollars. The ten dollars from the previous night had been a generous offering from a drunken man; the five offered the next day represented the tightwad intentions of a sober boss. Caplin pocketed the five without mentioning the earlier payment. This, he was delighted to discover in days to come, would be the norm. Fisher would come in bombed from a night on the town, pay Caplin, and promptly forget about it. He'd offer more the next day, believing he was getting exceptional work at a bargain price when, instead of being underpaid for his work, Caplin was actually enjoying a windfall profit. When they finally settled on a $22.50 weekly salary to produce the Sunday Palooka strip, Caplin was confident he'd see more than that.

Caplin found the early days of working on the strip "exhilarating." He reveled in the knowledge that he was contributing to a comic strip reaching millions of readers, and his relationship with Fisher was cordial. He discussed story and character ideas with Fisher, who insisted that Caplin draw humane, rather than grotesque, characters. Caplin soaked up Fisher's advice. Comic strip artists often relied on the humor in outlandish-looking characters to get their laughs, but under Fisher, Caplin began to see the value of strong storytelling. Despite the acrimonious split and years of backstabbing that would mark their future, Caplin was content with his working arrangement with Fisher. Had Fisher paid him more, he claimed later, he might have stayed with him for his entire career.

The Caplins' first child, a daughter, was born on May 21, 1933. According to Catherine, she and her husband referred to their unborn baby as "Abner" through Catherine's pregnancy. When she was born a girl, they named her Julie.

Al Caplin would return to the "Abner" name later.

Catherine and Julie Caplin joined Al in New York as planned. Caplin had found a two-room apartment at 20 West 69th Street on New York's Upper West Side. Remembering how rough his mother had it when trying to raise her children without help at home, Caplin hired a part-time maid for six dollars a week. They weren't living the high life by anyone's definition, but, between his salary and the overages he enjoyed whenever Fisher paid him while drunk, Caplin was pulling in enough to support his family, pay the maid, send money to his mother, and mail six dollars a week to his brother Elliott, who was attending Ohio State University and living on scratch.

Sometime soon after settling in New York, Al and Catherine attended a vaudeville performance at a theater near Columbus Circle, where they witnessed a performance by a small group of hillbilly musicians and singers. Caplin sat entranced as the troupe, accompanied by fiddles, Jew's harps, and other instruments, sang and danced with deadpan expressions that added elements of innocence and humor to their performances. The Caplins loved it. Catherine believed the performance might have been the catalyst for the creation of the comic strip that made her husband famous.

"We thought they were just hilarious," she said. "We walked back to the apartment that evening, becoming more and more excited with the idea of a hillbilly comic strip. Something like it must have always been in the back of Al's mind, ever since he thumbed his way through the Southern hills as a teenager, but that vaudeville act seemed to crystallize it for him."

These were the types of characters that Caplin and Ham Fisher had batted around in their discussions about what could make comics funny yet humane. Fisher had no interest in creating the kind of biting social commentary for which his young assistant would become so well known, but in their discussions about character and story, Caplin asserted a strong influence on the development of characters found in "Joe Palooka," including some that came as a result of the hillbilly show.

Not that there was anything visionary about any of this: as comics historian M. Thomas Inge noted in "Al Capp's South: Appalachian Culture in Li'l Abner," "culture in the United States, high and low, had been obsessed with things Southern and Appalachian since the turn of the century." Mountain music, integrated into bluegrass and country and western music, as heard in the work of Jimmie Rodgers and the Carter Family, enjoyed steadily growing popularity. Depression-era novels such as Erskine Caldwell's *Tobacco Road*, published in 1932, and *God's Little Acre*, published a year later, and William Faulkner's *Light in August* (1932), were set in horribly impoverished rural southern communities. At the time when Al Caplin was developing his hillbilly characters, Laurel and Hardy were in production on their film *Them Thar Hills*. Caplin's keen understanding of popular culture, blended with the memories of his own experiences in Kentucky, Tennessee, and West Virginia, amounted to nothing less than a creative stewpot for a young cartoonist seeking a subject and setting for his work.

Out of all of this rose a legend, a myth created by Capp and perpetuated until his dying day, a story so convincing that comics scholars and critics would repeat it for more than three decades after Capp was gone.

It was a legend that would lead to great bitterness and hostility, and would indirectly lead to one man's death.

Here is how Al Capp, then Al Caplin, would have you believe it happened.

As the result of his and Ham Fisher's discussions, new characters for "Joe Palooka" were developed. These characters were as backwoods as you

Al Capp and his eldest daughter, Julie, ca. 1938.

could get, and they lived in the hills, far away from the city. They would appear in "Joe Palooka" from time to time, setting the stage for Caplin's comic strip, "Li'l Abner."

"One of the characters we created was a fat, flannel-mouthed orator and crook who Fisher named Congressman Weidebottom," Capp would recall. "We gave him a home district in the Southern Hills."

Out of these same hills—and Caplin's fertile imagination—rose a character who, in a different context, might have been the Missing Link: a hairy, dim-witted, incredibly powerful oaf and would-be boxer named Big Leviticus. Caplin discussed his idea with Fisher, but nothing ever came of it. After seeing the hillbilly vaudeville revue, Caplin began thinking about scenarios in which the character might be brought into "Joe Palooka."

Caplin believed that it might be interesting to have Joe Palooka and Big Leviticus cross paths, maybe in the ring. The possibilities were wide open. What would happen if a character, beloved by readers who believed in goodness, justice, and all that is decent about working your way to the top, met a primitive fighting machine with no noticeable ideologies? When and how would such a fight be staged?

Caplin was too smart to press such a storyline on a boss who wouldn't allow him to so much as ink the faces of the strip's major characters.

Then the unthinkable occurred: Ham Fisher went on vacation and Al Caplin took over as ghostwriter of the Sunday edition of the strip. It was the start of something new.

Not surprisingly, both had different recollections of what happened. Fisher, like all other comic strip artists, typically submitted his work to the syndicate four weeks before it ran, and six to eight weeks for the color Sunday strips, which had to be prepared by specialty engravers and printed on off-site presses. This practice gave editors the opportunity to examine content well in advance of publication, and production departments plenty of leeway in seeing that the pages came out exactly as planned. It also allowed comic strip artists the opportunity to plan their vacations.

Fisher liked his time off, and he was accustomed to planning ahead. According to his version of events, when he took his vacation early in the fall of 1933, he submitted plenty of material to last his entire vacation. But in Caplin's version of the story, in his absence, there weren't enough strips. Without consulting with Fisher, he began a new series of "Joe Palooka" Sunday strips—the new story featuring Big Leviticus. The first strip ran on October 22.

The storyline was fairly straightforward—one Fisher himself might have invented. Knobby Walsh, Palooka's manager, brings his fighter to the hills country of Kentucky, supposedly to fight Big Leviticus in an exhibition bout. The fight, of course, has been stacked heavily in Big Leviticus's favor, with his gun-toting father acting as the referee. The champ, believing that he could use the exhibition to teach Leviticus a few of his tricks, is stunned when the behemoth, rather than pull punches, hits him with a series of haymakers that drops him to the canvas. Palooka gathers his wits and is prepared to fight for keeps, but Leviticus kicks him in the head, ending the fight. To even the score, Walsh convinces Leviticus and his family that, with proper training and management, he can mold him into a world champion boxer. The title would be worth millions. Leviticus agrees, but in their first sparring session, Joe Palooka gets his revenge, knocking the much bigger fighter senseless before he and his manager beat a hasty retreat from the hills. The story took five Sundays to tell.

Ham Fisher was not amused by the story. As soon as he returned from his extended vacation, he angrily confronted Caplin, the two quarreled, and Caplin was sent packing.

In interviews over the years, on those rare occasions when he agreed to address questions about Fisher and the terrible feud that festered between them, Al Capp was asked by "thousands of interviewers" about the origins of "Li'l Abner," and, by his own account, he offered thousands of answers. Fisher, of course, once "Li'l Abner' became a success, had protested that the hillbilly characters he had objected to in his own strip were nonetheless created while Al Caplin was his employee, and therefore they were his intellectual property. Capp, however, denied any connection between the "Abner" characters and those in the Big Leviticus episodes of "Joe Palooka"—aside from their residence in the hills country. But he disputed, too, the origin story of Big Leviticus. He was not the product of an ambitious renegade assistant, but the product of necessity, when a negligent comics artist abandoned his strip.

According to Capp, it all began when Fisher became obsessed with Marlene Dietrich. She was the rising star in the movie business, and Fisher, after a brief meeting, believed that he could woo her with bountiful flower arrangements, flashes of his wealth, and his charm. Unfortunately, she was set to sail to Europe the day after he met her in New York, and Fisher reasoned that he had no other way to reach her than to jump on board her ship. This came at a steep price. The ship was booked solid except for a $200-a-day suite, which Fisher snapped up just before the gangplanks were pulled and the ship set sail.

It didn't go well. Dietrich became seasick and stayed in her cabin. Fisher bided his time, going so far as to tell some passengers that he intended to marry her. Finally, after several days, she made an appearance, surrounded by publicity men, but she didn't remember Fisher from their previous meeting. When one of her publicists recognized him as a cartoonist, he mistakenly introduced him as "Bud Fisher" to Dietrich, who was pleased to meet the creator of "Mutt and Jeff." Fisher tried to explain that he was the artist behind "Joe Palooka," not "Mutt and Jeff," but Dietrich had no idea what "Joe Palooka" was about. Fisher, smoldering from the encounter, wound up retreating to his suite.

Meanwhile, back in New York, Al Caplin faced two growing problems: he was running out of money, and the syndicate had exhausted its supply of "Joe Palooka" Sunday strips. Caplin could do nothing about his dwindling cash, but he was wise enough to know that something had to be done about the "Joe Palooka" material. Rather than tell the syndicate that his boss was chasing an internationally acclaimed film star to God only knew where, he started the Big Leviticus series on his own.

One day, in the midst of all this, the Parc Vendome doorman knocked on Fisher's door and told Caplin that Ham Fisher had a visitor who urgently needed to see the artist. Caplin tried to dismiss the doorman with the excuse he was using on everyone calling on Fisher—he was extremely busy and couldn't be interrupted—but the visitor, a man named Phil Boyle, adamantly insisted that he meet with Fisher. Boyle, the doorman explained, was Fisher's assistant. This was news to Caplin. He instructed the doorman to send him up.

The two had a fascinating meeting. Boyle, it turned out, worked with Fisher on the "Joe Palooka" daily strip. He and Fisher had known each other back when Fisher was a salesman and Boyle an artist for the same newspaper in Youngstown, Ohio. Fisher had never forgotten Boyle, who had done some work on early prototype sketches for "Joe Palooka," and after he'd sold his comic strip to the syndicate, he contacted Boyle about moving to New York and working as his assistant. Fisher offered him seventy-five dollars per week—half again what Boyle was earning at the newspaper in Ohio—and Boyle packed up and moved. He was in his forties, single, and supported his invalid mother.

Boyle knew of Caplin's existence, not because Ham Fisher had mentioned him, but because he knew somebody had to be drawing the women in "Joe Palooka." Fisher sure as hell couldn't do it. Boyle and Caplin hit it off and decided to team up on the daily and Sunday strips. They'd keep "Joe Palooka" running until Ham Fisher returned.

"The story wasn't as sentimental as Fisher's," Al Capp would remark of his collaboration with Boyle, "but it was funny."

When Fisher returned, he gave Caplin his back pay but their conversation deteriorated when Caplin mentioned that he'd met Boyle and that the two of them had worked together on the strip. Caplin put an end to the conversation when Fisher berated his efforts.

"If you can get anyone more loyal than us," he shouted at Fisher, "get 'em!"

The two were finished as employer and employee. Their feud, however, was just beginning.*

Capp's account is an interesting story, but the facts do not support it. A close examination of the Sunday "Joe Palooka" strips indicates that the first with Caplin's distinctive style appeared on October 15, 1933, although Caplin's contribution to that October 15 strip was minimal.

The hillbillies turned up in "Joe Palooka" one week later, on October 22, and that was the very first strip drawn entirely by Caplin. Big Leviticus appeared one week after that, on October 29. All told, there would be five consecutive weeks of this continuity, beginning on October 15 and ending on November 19, 1933. That Fisher's brand-new assistant immediately drew the Big Leviticus debut supports the theory that a script already existed for the episode. Fisher, then, was present for the first run of hillbilly strips, and not on vacation, as Capp had people believing in all of his retellings of the story after the birth of "Li'l Abner."

The next Leviticus continuity began on February 11, 1934, and ran for five weeks, through March 11. It could very well be that Fisher was chasing Marlene Dietrich at this time, and that Caplin was reviving and writing Big Leviticus on his own in Fisher's absence. But it is almost unthinkable that Fisher fired Capp almost immediately after his return. The last "Joe Pa-

---

* A week after firing Caplin, Fisher spoke to another young artist who hoped to work as his assistant. Although the meeting had been arranged, Fisher angrily dismissed the would-be collaborator, saying he'd just fired a similar assistant and wanted nothing to do with hiring another one. The young artist's name was Will Eisner, and he would become one of the most influential comics and graphic novel artists in comics history.

looka" with Caplin as a contributor ran on July 8, nearly four months after the final Leviticus Sunday strip.

Phil Boyle did, indeed, ghost Ham Fisher's "Joe Palooka" dailies, and it is likely that Caplin met him at one point or another, and that the two shared the experiences with Fisher. It is even possible that the two worked together on some of the strips, as Capp said they did in his autobiography. There is, however, one untold story that bears noting: Al Capp always complained about how Ham Fisher stole one of his assistants, Moe Leff, in the early days of "Li'l Abner." Before that occurred, Capp lured Phil Boyle away from Fisher for a very brief period of time, sending off another volley in their escalating feud.

In light of all of these events, Ham Fisher seems justified in some of his claims against Capp, though there is no way of knowing who exactly created Big Leviticus. Fisher had no corner on the hillbilly market, of course, and much of his anger undoubtedly originated from professional jealousy—"Li'l Abner" eventually bypassed "Joe Palooka" in popularity—but Capp's story about the vacation and his taking over the strip with his hills people is typical Capp: part truth, part fiction.

With a wife and child to support, Caplin had to find another job in a hurry. It was time, he decided, to strike out on his own as a comic strip artist. At a recent cocktail party thrown by Ham Fisher, he'd been encouraged by the cartoonist, illustrator, and animator Milt Gross, who recognized his talent and urged him to draw his own strip. In considering a subject for this strip, Caplin kept returning to the hillbillies he had created for Fisher, and he decided there was great potential for a comic strip set in rural Kentucky and focusing on a family unlike anything on the market. The main character would be in his late teens, good-looking, and powerfully built, but far from the smartest young man on the planet—or even in the hills. His parents, with whom he lived, would be rather similar to Caplin's own parents: the father a sort of bumbling, incapable, henpecked character who was more of a presence than a provider; the mother a tough, pipe-smoking, dominating woman who kept the family together and trouble at bay. The young man— Abner Yokum—would be chased around by a gorgeous, shapely, love-starved blonde who, despite her best efforts, never seemed to be able to turn Abner's head. Caplin sketched the characters until he was satisfied with their appearances, and then he drew up a few weeks of sample strips to display to potential buyers.

He set his sights high. His first visit was to William Randolph Hearst's King Features Syndicate, the leading comic strip syndicate in the business, and rather than present himself to a lower-level editor, he marched up to the office of Joseph Connolly, the head of the syndicate. In the outer office, he jotted down a brief note telling Connolly that a well-known cartoonist said he, Al Caplin, was the best young cartoonist around. He bribed an office boy with a quarter, and the kid brought the note to Connolly. Caplin waited, confident that Connolly would be unable to resist such a brash introduction.

Connolly eventually emerged from his office and invited him in. He looked over Caplin's samples and listened to his plans for the strip. He liked much of what he saw and heard, and, according to Al Capp's account, he was prepared to offer him a generous $250 a week for the strip—on the condition that he make a few changes.

"'Great strip, great art, yes sir,'" Al Capp remembered, quoting Connolly in a 1979 *Comics Journal* interview with Richard Marschall. "'That Abner's an idiot. Make him a nice kid, with some saddle-stripe shoes on him. And Daisy Mae's pretty, but how about some pretty clothes? As a matter of fact, why not forget the mountain bit and move this all to New Jersey.'"

In Al Capp's version of the story, he told Connolly that he'd have something ready for him in a week, then escaped Connolly's office feeling that "it was my biggest triumph and I felt sick." He left the King Features Syndicate building and took "Li'l Abner" to the United Feature Syndicate offices. After hanging around for a couple of days, politely but unsuccessfully awaiting an audience with Monte Bourjaily, the general manager, he elbowed his way into his office. Bourjaily loved the strip and vowed to publish it as Caplin presented it. He offered Caplin fifty dollars a week for it—a paltry figure compared to the earlier offer from King, but Caplin was satisfied and closed the deal.

Capp's story was one of artistic integrity winning a rare victory over the unholy dollar, and Capp would stick to the story throughout his life. But others disputed the account, including his uncle Harry Resnick, Capp's earliest business advisor, who claimed that Caplin took the United Feature offer because Joseph Connolly, rather than make the generous offer that Caplin claimed, had vacillated on his decision and taken too long to say anything. Caplin had simply accepted the first decent offer coming his way.

There was, however, one major issue to contend with: immediate money. Before leaving the United Feature offices, Caplin inquired about when he might expect his first paycheck. In four weeks, he was told. Caplin didn't have four weeks. He was almost out of money. He needed to find some way to fill the four-week gap—some kind of temporary job, preferably in cartooning. He'd met a few comic strip artists while working for Ham Fisher; maybe one of them could use a temporary assistant.

Caplin saw Frank Godwin first. The creator of the popular "Connie" cartoon strip greeted Caplin warmly and appeared to be receptive to hiring him as an assistant, but he was buried in work and unable to talk at length. Instead, he asked Caplin to return the next day. Encouraged by Godwin's response, Caplin went home and told Catherine he was fairly certain their money problems had been addressed. He went as far as to invite her to accompany him to the next day's meeting, wanting, as he later recalled, to show her that all comic strip artists weren't as horrible as Ham Fisher. To his great surprise, his reception the next day was disappointing and shocking. Godwin not only changed his mind about hiring Caplin; he refused to even look at his two visitors. "I don't think we have anything to discuss," he said.

Bud Fisher came next. The cartoonist was famously reclusive, but Caplin showed up at his apartment unannounced and pushed his way past a valet to get inside. Once he did, unbelievably, he found Fisher willing to look at his portfolio. Fisher was impressed enough to give Caplin an unfinished "Mutt and Jeff" strip to complete and bring back the following day. However, when Caplin arrived at Fisher's apartment at the appointed time, freshly completed "Mutt and Jeff" in hand, the doorman at the apartment turned him away. "Mr. Fisher is not interested in your drawings," he informed Caplin.

This second rejection raised more than a little suspicion. Something was wrong. Two well-known cartoonists had received him warmly, examined his work, and all but guaranteed him a job, only to back away without explanation.

Capp finally learned the reason for this when he visited Rube Goldberg. The comics icon had hit a downturn in his career. The strip that established his reputation, "Mike and Ike," had ended in 1929, and "Boob McNutt," another strip that he'd created during the "Mike and Ike" salad days, was on the way out. Younger readers weren't amused by the material that had brought big laughs in the pre-Depression 1920s. Goldberg, whose comic inventions of complicated machines designed to accomplish simple tasks had made his name part of the American idiom, had been reduced to following trends rather than setting them.

Caplin's arrival at his door came at an opportune time. Maybe a fresh perspective might infuse some life into the strips. Caplin outlined his background, took out his samples, talked about some of his ideas for Goldberg, and, as before, left with work that he was to complete and bring back the next day. This time, however, there was an unexpected wrinkle. Caplin was walking down the stairs to leave the building when he realized that he'd left his drawings behind. When he arrived back at Goldberg's door, he could hear the cartoonist talking loudly on the phone.

"He stole money from you, Ham?" Goldberg asked. "Why didn't you have the little bastard arrested?" He had called Ham Fisher for verification of Caplin's story about working for Fisher.

Caplin listened with mounting anger as Fisher apparently waved off any thought of prosecuting the thief, presenting himself as a magnanimous human being in the process. When the call ended, Caplin knocked on the door and handed back the strips he was to work on. They were too hopeless to improve, he explained to Goldberg as he picked up his own samples and left.

The Frank Godwin and Bud Fisher rejections suddenly made a lot of sense. New York was home to a number of the most successful artists in the business, and Caplin had no doubt that Ham Fisher would be talking to each and every one of them. The feud was on, and Fisher was firing the first shots.

Capp's plan for counterattack was brilliantly nasty, even by his standards. It began with an almost tearful, regret-filled meeting with Fisher at the Parc Vendome. Capp told Fisher that he'd made a terrible mistake, and now, unable to find work in New York, he had no choice but to move back to Massachusetts.

Fisher, as Caplin anticipated, took pity and offered him his old job back—at a reduced salary, of course, and on the condition that Caplin sign a one-year contract agreeing to a ten-hour workday, a relinquishing of all rights to anything he created on the job or at home, and total secrecy about his employment. Caplin might not have predicted Fisher's exact terms, but he'd worked for him long enough to know that, first, Fisher still needed him as an assistant, and, second, he would make Caplin pay dearly for what Fisher considered to be nothing less than insubordination when he quit the first time around. Still, even more importantly, Caplin knew that Fisher was too tightfisted to pay an attorney to draft a legally binding contract.

It worked precisely as planned. A young attorney stopped by Fisher's apartment, drew up a boilerplate as dictated by Fisher, and agreed to have the contract prepared in short order. The cost, he assured Fisher, would not be too high. Fisher exploded, as Caplin knew he would, and weeks passed without his consulting another attorney. In the meantime, Caplin worked and collected his pay. When, later, the first "Li'l Abner" strips appeared in the papers, Fisher voiced no objection. "Li'l Abner" was excellent, and Fisher could see himself as part of its future success. After all, hillbillies had initially been part of his "Joe Palooka" strip, even if they weren't the same hillbillies, and this new strip's talented creator was still his assistant, ostensibly under his guidance.

It was now time for Caplin to break the bad news. When a contract from Ham Fisher hadn't materialized, he explained, he'd gone to United Feature and agreed to an exclusive contract with them. He had no alternative but to leave Fisher and focus solely on "Li'l Abner."

If Fisher had any inkling that he'd been taken, he didn't let on. "Li'l

Abner," as he saw it, was no threat to him. If the kid wanted to strike out on his own, that was fine with him. He wished Caplin well, and the two parted ways.

Fisher's goodwill would last only so long—until "Li'l Abner" became a sensation and boasted a larger circulation than "Joe Palooka."

Then the real war would begin.

7 LI'L ABNER

When giving the background of "Li'l Abner," Al Capp would have preferred that people believe that his comic strip came close to being an overnight success. There was a rather slow introductory period, he claimed, during which readers learned what they needed to know about the characters and subscribing newspapers learned what they needed to know about the comic strip's commercial potential. The timeline on this period, however, was longer than Capp wanted to remember. The first daily strip appeared on August 8, 1934, and the first Sunday strip appeared half a year later, on February 24, 1935. Only eight newspapers carried it in the beginning, well below any minimal threshold of success, but the numbers rose steadily until, as Capp boasted, "all hell broke loose."

He began signing the strip "Al G. Cap," a shortened version of his given name. By the twenty-fifth daily he changed it to "Al G. Capp," and by the second week of January 1935 he permanently dropped the initial and settled on "Al Capp."

The early strips bore little resemblance to the outrageously funny satires and parodies of the future. For all the personal and professional animosity that he'd worked up against Ham Fisher, Capp had learned a great deal from him, and he borrowed heavily from this knowledge when he created "Li'l Abner." Capp wanted nothing to do with writing material for kids and adolescents, nor did he wish to create the joke-a-day strips that took up so much room on the comics pages of newspapers. He aimed for a large adult audience, the kind that would almost anxiously turn to "Li'l Abner" every day, wondering what was going to happen next to the characters from Dogpatch. For this, he needed strong, continuing stories.

Ham Fisher and "Joe Palooka" had provided him with the model for continuity and technique. Each strip would stretch out for a period of several weeks, carefully plotted in a way that guaranteed the readers' return to the strip. Cliffhangers brought them back after a weekend away; action sequences kept them returning from weekday to weekday. Other popular strips, such as "Dick Tracy" and "Little Orphan Annie," which featured extended, continuing stories known as continuities, with idiosyncratic nonrealistic styles, served as additional models. "Li'l Abner," although humorous, began more as a typical adventure strip placed in an unusual setting.

Looking back on his early "Li'l Abner" entries, Capp would state, with obvious irritation, that he wasn't interested in creating serious material, that he was more or less pushed into the mainstream of the times. Adventure and suspense strips were becoming the next big thing, and Capp complained that he had no choice but to follow the trend.

"Suspense was what editors wanted when I was ready to create my own comic strip," he'd say, "but all I wanted to do was fun and fantasy."

The problem, he'd insist, was that suspense characters were one-dimensional, dualistic good guys vs. bad guys, and that he saw the human race in much different terms.

"I simply couldn't believe in good guys and bad guys—as I drew them," he said. "I discovered good things in the bad guys, and vice versa. So my hero turned out to be big and strong like the suspense-strip heroes, but he also turned out to be stupid, as big, strong heroes sometimes are."

There was no doubting the growing popularity of the adventure or suspense strip. In the three-year period between 1931, when Chester Gould introduced "Dick Tracy" to the world, and 1934, when "Li'l Abner" made its first appearance, Martha Orr's melodramatic "Apple Mary" (which, under new writers and artists, would become "Mary Worth"), Alex Raymond's "Flash Gordon," Lee Falk and Phil Davis's "Mandrake the Magician," and "Secret Agent X-9," written by Dashiell Hammett and illustrated by Alex Raymond, made their initial appearances as syndicated comic strips. Milton Caniff, Capp's former colleague at Associated Press, was already working on "Dickie Dare" before his landmark strip, "Terry and the Pirates," hit the newspapers in 1934. There was plenty of funny stuff to read, like the enormously popular "Blondie" (1930), but change was in the air. A new creation—the comic book—joined the comics market the year "Li'l Abner" hit the newsstands, and while the early going was slow and plodding, at first essentially just reprinting newspaper strips, the upstart cousin hung on and slowly gained in popularity until Superman blew the lid off the market with the superhero's appearance in *Action Comics #1* in 1938.

Capp would grumble that he had to cut some of his humorous material from his early "Li'l Abner" strips, and there might be no contesting that, though he did manage to add strong elements of humor to those early entries. The main characters in "Li'l Abner," including Abner Yokum, his parents, and Daisy Mae Scragg, were with the strip from the beginning. Their physical appearances would change as the strip evolved, with Mammy and Pappy Yokum becoming half-pints rather than the average-sized people they were in the beginning, and Daisy Mae becoming much more voluptuous, but they changed very little as characters over the strip's forty-three-year run. Their backwoods ways would be a constant source of humor.

The first story cycles are strong examples. Mammy Yokum hears from her long-lost sister, Bessie, who ran away from home and, unlikely as it seems, met and married a wealthy duke, who left her a fortune when he passed away. "The Duchess of Bopshire," as she is called, never had children, and she wants to spend some of her fortune on cultivating Li'l Abner. All he needs to do is move into her Park Avenue apartment in New York. Everyone is thrilled by the news—except, that is, Daisy Mae, who's madly in love with Li'l Abner, despite the fact that he'd rather spend time with Salomey, the family pig, than court any woman.

The hillbilly-in-New-York setup offered Al Capp almost endless material for both drama and humor. Bessie, a pretentious gasbag, tries to introduce her nephew to the finer points of the high life, including its wealthy, available young women, but Abner bumbles along: it's a successful setup, similar to that of the popular *Beverly Hillbillies* television program, which would appear three decades later.

When Li'l Abner becomes unwittingly engaged to a young socialite, the announcement of the pending nuptials draws the attention of a couple of thugs, who hatch a kidnapping plan. They succeed in "kidnapping" Abner, but only because he views it as a means of freeing himself from the clutches of his engagement; he disarms his two captors and winds up trussing the two up while he goes out for sandwiches for all of them.

LI'L ABNER   News From Town

It took a while for the style and characters of "Li'l Abner" to fully develop. In this second strip (August 14, 1934), Capp's pen strokes are thinner, Mammy and Pappy Yokum are relatively tall, Mammy's bonnet has not yet acquired its trademark squared-off visor and shape, and Abner is not yet the robust youth with the arching shock of hair readers came to know. The signature, "Al G. Cap," quickly became "Al Capp."

The kidnapping is big news, and when it makes its way back to Dogpatch, Mammy Yokum decides to head to New York and rescue her son, leading to a series of funny misadventures, from Mammy's beating up a train conductor because he has the audacity to ask for fare, to a similar altercation with a New York cabdriver taking her to her sister's Park Avenue digs. Mammy eventually conjures up a vision and finds Li'l Abner, not in the clutches of villains but working as a dishwasher in an upscale restaurant. Unfortunately, he has run up a big bill and is trying to work it off, but he can't stop eating the restaurant's food and is now the captive of his appetite, dishwashing by day and sleeping in the restaurant at night. The story reaches its happy ending when Abner is freed and Mammy confronts his fiancée and sees to it, in her inimitable way, that the engagement is broken off.

The story cycle ran six days a week, from Monday through Saturday, from August 13 to October 29, 1934. The strip became a family affair, with Al Capp penciling and inking the principal action and Catherine filling in a lot of the backgrounds. They kept it as simple as possible. As Catherine would note, neither could draw vehicles or machines of any sort, so most of the panels from each day's entry focused on the characters and dialogue balloons. Catherine lettered on the early strips, but Al wasn't satisfied with it and soon took over. A slow, deliberate artist, Capp managed to hit his deadlines, but it didn't come easy.

It became even more challenging when Catherine announced that she was pregnant with their second child. As before, she returned to Amesbury to stay with her parents during her pregnancy, leaving Al on his own in New York City, creating the strip and wondering what he had to do to boost its lagging circulation figures.

Worried that "Li'l Abner" wasn't being picked up by enough newspapers to justify its existence, Capp asked for permission to personally pitch his strip to newspapers. He'd visit offices in New York, Massachusetts, and Connecticut, often on side trips when visiting Catherine in Amesbury. Capp proved himself to be a good salesman: his critical first sale was to the *Boston Globe*, which became his flagship paper. He was encouraged by a steady if modest increase in subscribing newspapers. United Feature ballyhooed "Abner's" spike in popularity in trade publication ads. The word was getting out.

The syndicate, encouraged by the growing response to the strip, awarded Capp with a full-color Sunday entry beginning on February 24, 1935. Accompanying the strip, as was customary when Sunday strips filled an entire page, was a smaller substrip called "Washable Jones," featuring the title character, a young hillbilly boy, and a ghost he accidentally pulls from the water while fishing. Both ran independent of the "Li'l Abner" weekday continuity, and both featured stories that continued from Sunday to Sunday, though sometimes the Sunday "Li'l Abners" were completed in just one segment. Syndicate sales of the strip accelerated, and by August, the first anniversary of "Li'l Abner," over one hundred newspapers were on board, a truly meteoric rise for a new feature.

According to Capp, one unintended offshoot of this new development was the renewal of hostilities with Ham Fisher—or, perhaps more accurately, new stakes being brought to a feud that Capp believed had long ended. Fisher had offered nothing but encouragement for him after the first appearance of "Li'l Abner"—or so Capp claimed—but when the Yokum family turned up in the Sunday papers, including a paper in New York, the "Joe Palooka" creator resumed his efforts at discrediting Capp whenever and wherever possible. Capp would inevitably get wind of Fisher's badmouthing him to a features editor in Detroit or some other city removed from New York, Fisher would always deny it when Capp confronted him with what he'd heard, and then it would happen again. Capp couldn't understand why Fisher didn't seem to realize that there was plenty of room for both strips in the comics universe, and he did his best to ignore him.

He had other concerns on his mind. He wanted to get out of New York City, and with the *Globe* representing his most prestigious subscriber, he began planning a move to Boston. He'd always loved the city, which had a strong artistic community and offered the benefits of large-city life without the stifling population and daily grind of Manhattan. The city was steeped in history, and with Harvard nearby he would be living in proximity of an Ivy League school. After Catherine delivered their second child, Cathie, on September 19, 1936, he moved his family to Beantown.

He also hired an assistant, a young but experienced cartoonist named Moe Leff, to assure that he'd still meet deadlines and continue the high standards he'd set for "Li'l Abner." The "Washable Jones" strips demanded more time and attention than the black-and-white "Abner" dailies, and while Capp had little difficulty in coming up with storylines for both strips, which he recorded meticulously on yellow legal paper, his mind raced ahead of his ability to draw and ink the art. Leff, who had worked as an assistant on various strips over the years, became an invaluable assistant until he, too, was eventually sucked into the vortex of the Al Capp/Ham Fisher storm.

Al Capp took great pride in his abilities as an artist and a writer.

"No artist who can write should avoid words," he'd say. "No author who can draw should avoid drawing."

This wasn't just the typical pontificating on Capp's part. He strongly believed from the very beginning that his comic strip required more than good art and a passable story, and he viewed his identity in the business as something more than an artist illustrating gags for readers looking for a daily laugh.

"I don't think of myself as a cartoonist, or of 'Li'l Abner' as a cartoon," he stated. "I think of myself as a novelist and of 'Abner' as a novel, a page of which is published every day. At the end of the year, I've written 365 pages, fully illustrated."

Capp mined the literary world when he shaped his new comic strip, turning to one of his childhood favorites. Charles Dickens had created memorable characters that appealed to the masses, if not his harshest critics, and Capp used Dickens as a model for his Appalachian characters. The strip, he realized, would not rise to the level that he desired unless his characters were the type of people his readers might identify with. The early continuities, designed to familiarize readers with the Yokum clan, Daisy Mae, and a handful of others, were deliberately kept simple, but as time passed and more characters—and humor—were added to "Li'l Abner," the storylines became more complex, taking a meandering path.

"At times," he explained in 1935, "I fall in love with some secondary character in the Li'l Abner story and I feature him or her for days, neglecting the principal of the tale. Then I will get a wire from my syndicate editor, something like this: 'Sequence O.K., but don't forget that Li'l Abner is the hero.' Then I realize I must get down to earth and give the strip the focus which is consistent with its title."

In future years, "Li'l Abner" would be recognized as much for its memorably named secondary characters—Moonbeam McSwine, J. Roaringham Fatback, Evil-Eye Fleegle, Joe Btfsplk, Lena the Hyena, Available

Jones—as for the Yokum family. Capp would return to his favorites from time to time, featuring them in new stories, sometimes with altered names and appearances. Being exact was never his main concern. The goal was to entertain.

The characters' unique names also owed something to Dickens.

"We work damned hard on them," Capp said. "We'll spend four hours to come up with just the right name for a character who will pass in and out of the strip and never be seen again. I want a name to describe the character, as Dickens does. So when I name a girl Moonbeam McSwine, you don't need to be told that she's a beautiful and unsanitary character."

Then there were the words he put into his characters' mouths. Capp's characters spoke their own language, rooted in English but enunciated in choppy syllables, like the uneven whack of an ax splitting wood. It was the sound of the hills, as Capp remembered it. Over the years, journalists and breathless scholars would insist that the language was straight-on accurate, but Capp never made a claim to it. The dialect was simply intended for humor. Later, when he was surrounded by assistants, everyone spoke the language nonstop in the studio until it rolled off their tongues with the ease of any native language. Even if it was fabricated, it had its own natural rhythm.

It was also very funny. Readers in Philadelphia or New York or Kansas City could look at the strip, work their way through the mangled dialogue, issue their belly laughs, and feel superior to the knotheads from Dogpatch—until they realized, as happened on so many occasions, that the joke was on them.

United Feature and Capp worried, at least in the strip's early days, how those calling the South their home might react to the bastardization of their idiom and lampooning of their culture, so no attempts were made to market the strip in the southern states. But after a southern editor, while on a trip to the North, saw "Li'l Abner" in a newspaper, judged it to be unbearably funny, and signed on for the strip in his own paper, the floodgates opened. Papers from all over the South started subscribing, and, to Capp's surprise, there were no letters threatening his good health. The South, he surmised with great pleasure, found the strip as funny as readers elsewhere. Encouraged by the response, he invented even more outrageous new words and expressions.

His characters' faces were also unforgettable. Capp had a keen interest in faces from his earliest days as an art student, and when he drew them he more than adequately compensated for whatever he lacked as a draftsman drawing backgrounds, machinery, animals, or even human figures. He molded them carefully and thoughtfully. Capp openly admitted that the models for some of his characters were actual people, some of them celebrities, some just people he saw on the street. Their expressions, however, came from an almost scientific understanding of the connection between facial muscles and emotion. Even with first-rate assistants, Capp insisted on drawing his characters' faces. He kept a mirror affixed to his drawing table, and whenever in doubt about how to capture a facial expression, he'd look in the mirror and contort his face to reach the desired effect.

Capp improved as an artist over the long run of the strip, and he was always his own best audience: if he could laugh at what he created, he felt confident that others would, too. The strip's rapid rise toward the top in circulation numbers convinced him that he was correct.

One syndicated comic strip was not enough for Capp. Ideas rampaged through his mind; "Li'l Abner" could not accommodate all the stories and adventures. Capp and his staff stayed busy with the daily and Sunday strips, but Capp's ambitions would not be harnessed. In 1936 he ghostwrote scripts for "Joe Jinks," a strip originated in 1918 but abandoned in the early 1930s by Vic Forsythe. Capp's earnings from that freelance assignment for United Feature Syndicate augmented his growing revenue from "Li'l Abner," but "Joe Jinks" was not a property he was emotionally invested in, nor did his ghosting give him any meaningful leverage with United Feature. He wondered what kind of money he might be earning if he created another successful, nationally distributed strip of his own. He began plotting ideas.

In 1936 Capp had also hired a trio of assistants, Walter Johnston, Andy Amato, and Harvey Curtis. Johnston's salary started at forty dollars a week, Amato received thirty-five, and Curtis, whose role was much more limited, started at ten. They would remain loyal to Capp for decades, both because close relationships developed between them, and because Capp, unlike

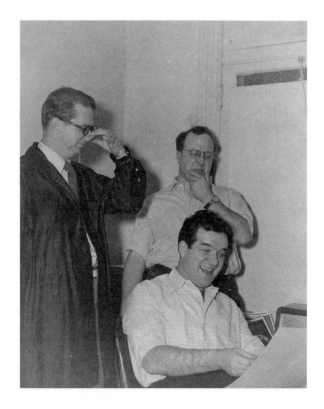

Key assistants Walter Johnston, left, *and Andy Amato mockingly disapprove their boss's gag in this posed photo. Al Capp was relatively generous with his core staff, and they remained loyal for many years.*

many other bosses of the day, provided incentives and bonuses for his key employees.

All three were the kind of characters Capp might have created for "Li'l Abner." Amato was the most versatile of the group, and he had the storytelling ability to have created his own strip, if he had been so inclined. Always armed with an inexpensive cigar, a quip for any occasion, and the ability to add wild details to Capp's stories, Amato became Capp's right-hand man. Johnston, the best pure draftsman, was invaluable because of his ability to draw nearly any kind of machine, vehicle, or gadget. Unlike Amato, whose manic energy fueled the studio, Johnston was quiet and serious. Curtis, who lived with his mother and had a gun fetish, had a skepticism that Capp could admire; his job was to work on backgrounds, do the lettering, draw borders, fill in blacks, and sign Capp's name to the strip. Capp always wrote the scripts, penciled the preliminary layouts, stressing the primary bodies, and inked the main characters' heads. He had the final say on the continuities.

Even with the three new men on board, Capp was realistic enough to admit that he and his assistants would not be able to produce yet another feature running daily and Sundays. It was simply too much work. He had to find someone else to team up with.

Capp pondered the possibility of dividing the duties: he would provide the scripts, and someone else could produce the art. He put together several weeks' worth of scripts and contacted Raeburn Van Buren, a first-rate magazine illustrator living on Long Island. Capp had seen Van Buren's work in the *Saturday Evening Post*, and it captured both the humor and the drama that he envisioned for the strip. The two agreed to meet in New York City.

Van Buren had grown up in Kansas City, Missouri, and had worked as a sketch artist for the *Kansas City Star*. The demands of the job forced him to learn to sketch very quickly, whether he was depicting a courtroom scene or a raging industrial fire. In a half hour, he could do a pen-and-ink sketch that would take others hours to finish. In addition to this, the *Star*'s art director, Harry Wood, had taught him how to draw comics.

This was not how Van Buren hoped to use his artistic talents, though. He moved to New York and attended the Art Students League, but soon discovered that, because of his time at the *Kansas City Star*, he was much further along in his education than his fellow students. He found freelance work illustrating for the pulp magazines, earning a pittance but gaining a fortune in experience. He then moved on to more prestigious publications such as *Red Book* and *Collier's*, and eventually found regular assignments with the *Saturday Evening Post*, *Life*, and other magazines. It was a living, but a tough one requiring a lot of hustling in a very competitive field. He yearned for a single, stable source of income.

Still, when he met Al Capp, he wanted nothing to do with his comic strip proposal. Capp tried to persuade him that moving away from magazine illustration would be an intelligent decision.

"He emphasized that radio and eventually TV would kill the fiction magazines that I'd been working for," Van Buren explained in a 1980 interview.

"He claimed that now was the time to get into something that wouldn't be hurt by the coming changes."

Unfazed by Van Buren's initial rejection, Capp continued to develop the strip, hoping to impress him with more material. His premise for the strip was simple: Aubrey Eustace Scrapple—"Slats"—was a tough, streetwise kid from New York, recently orphaned and shipped to the small, fictitious town of Crabtree Corners, where he would be living with his much older cousin, Abigail "Abbie" Scrapple. Capp wrote the scripts for fourteen weeks' worth of strips and shipped them to Van Buren.

Van Buren liked what he read. He returned a batch of sketches of the primary characters, and over the next couple of months, he and Capp honed the artwork, characters, and storyline into something they could present to a syndicate editor. The two exchanged letters about the strip's direction and the way the characters should look, but Capp left most of the decisions about the art to Van Buren. Capp told Van Buren that he initially intended the strip to focus on the Abbie character, but the longer he worked on the script, the more appealing the Slats character had become. This, he claimed, was the way it had gone with "Li'l Abner."

"When the idea for working on the strip 'Li'l Abner' first dawned on me," Capp wrote in a letter to Van Buren, "there was no Li'l Abner at all. The central character was 'Daisy Mae'—a dumb, beautiful blonde hillbilly. Li'l Abner himself was injected to provide love interest."

Capp never repeated this account in any interviews or other letters, so it very well could be that he was fabricating a story to give Van Buren the feeling that the strip, which he was calling "Abbie an' Slats," could evolve into something as successful as "Li'l Abner."

Neither Capp nor Van Buren was satisfied with the length of time the development process took, but they were eventually confident that their proposed strip was ready to show to one of the syndicates.

"We took them over to King Features, where we asked to see the legendary Joe Connolly," Van Buren recalled. "However, he was out so Al said, 'United Feature has been pretty good to me with "Li'l Abner"'—let's go over there.' Fortunately, United gobbled it up right away."

"Abbie an' Slats," running Monday through Saturday, hit the newspapers on July 7, 1937, to very enthusiastic response. The strip carried only

Alfred G. Caplin, before changing his name to Al Capp, age twenty-two, is drawing a "Mr. Gilfeather" panel cartoon at the Associated Press in New York in 1932. The mustache was short-lived and Capp never again sported facial hair.

Though he could afford to eat in fancy restaurants and often did, Al Capp also enjoyed diners and roadside cafes, as captured in this undated photo from the 1930s.

Undeterred by the early loss of his left leg, Al Capp loved to drive and was especially fond of new convertibles. In this photo from the early 1940s, he chauffeurs his daughters and their friends.

Capp assumed this jaunty pose around 1939. He was a chain smoker virtually his entire adult life, but the ciga-rette holder shown here was just a passing fad.

In mid-1940, during the shooting of the first *Li'l Abner* movie in Hollywood, Catherine (l), Al, and Al's sister, Madeline, enjoyed a side trip to Yosemite National Park. While in California, Capp began a torrid love affair with singer Nina Luce, an affair that Madeline helped her brother keep secret.

While in Hollywood for the filming, Al Capp met many celebrities, including Lucille Ball. At a party that year thrown by composer George Antheil, Ball was flirting with Capp and repeatedly put her hand on his leg. Nina Luce, Capp's lover at the time, disapprovingly looked on, then said to Antheil, "I hope she doesn't get a splinter!"

Nina Luce and Al Capp in 1941. The two fell deeply in love in 1940 in Hollywood. Soon afterward, Nina left her singing career to be near Capp in Boston. Three months later, she fled to Texas, but Capp assiduously pursued her for another full year.

Tillie Caplin in 1943, with her four children and two oldest granddaughters. Back row: Elliot, Jerome (Bence), and Alfred. Bottom: Julie, Tillie, Madeline, and Cathie.

Actress Dorothy Lamour poses for Capp in this 1943 publicity shot.

During World War II, Al Capp provided a variety of public services. This 1943 photo shows him with an army poster in which Li'l Abner teaches soldiers the importance of saluting.

Capp, ever the voracious reader, at a New York City newsstand in 1949.

Al Capp (r) and his brothers, Elliot (l) and Bence, formed Capp Enterprises, Inc. in the late 1940s to market the shmoo and other "Li'l Abner" trademarks. In this 1950 publicity photo, they examine samples of licensed merchandise.

At a 1950 publicity shoot for a March of Dimes crusade against polio, Al Capp balances on his prosthetic leg to simulate kicking an inflatable kigmy toy.

Capp strikes a pensive pose in this 1950 publicity photo.

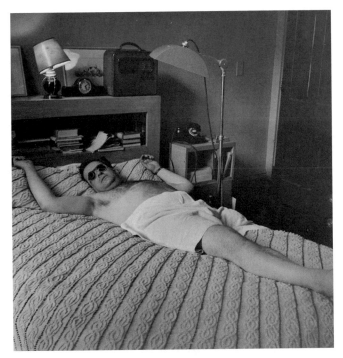

This undated and previously unpublished photo is the only known example where Al Capp's single bare leg is visible.

Catherine, Al, and his daughters, Cathie and Julie, relaxing aboard a transatlantic cruise ship, likely the *Isle de France*, in the mid-1940s.

Al Capp often self-referentially placed himself into "Li'l Abner" strips, something almost no other cartoonist of his era did. (But then, no other cartoonist had his high public profile, either.) These previously unpublished and unfinished self-caricatures show how he roughly penciled an image before adding inked line work with pen and brush.

Publicity photo of Capp to promote the ABC-TV program *Do Blondes Have More Fun?*, which aired in August 1967.

His grandchildren were the emotional core of Al Capp's later years, as epitomized by this 1964 image taken by Michael Pierce, a professional photographer who was married to the Capps' youngest daughter, Cathie.

In April 1964, Otto Caplin's children threw a surprise eightieth birthday party for him in New Haven, Connecticut. From left: Bence, Madeline, Alfred, Otto, and Elliot. Four months later Otto died.

After a career of overwhelmingly adulatory publicity, Capp's last hurrah in the press was his lampooning of folk singer Joan Baez as the repulsive Joanie Phoanie in 1967. Capp's increasingly strident political remarks and an eruption of sex scandals soon permanently turned public opinion against him.

Vice President Spiro Agnew shakes Al Capp's hands in Washington, D.C., in November 1970 as Martha Mitchell, wife of Attorney General John Mitchell, looks on. Within three years, all three men fell hard: Agnew resigned in disgrace, John Mitchell was caught up in the Watergate scandal (later serving prison time), and Capp never recovered from headlines exposing his secret sex life.

President Richard Nixon shares a laugh with Al Capp in the White House in November 1970.

Capp (top left) and his attorneys leave the Eau Claire, Wisconsin, courthouse on February 1, 1972, after Capp pled guilty to reduced charges of attempted adultery. Though he received only a $500 fine, the satirist never recovered from the cumulative bad press and the moral hypocrisy the case exposed. Hundreds of newspapers soon dropped "Li'l Abner."

Van Buren's name, at the demand of United Feature. The syndicate wanted two separate entities, and would complain from time to time when storylines in the two strips were too similar to each other. The new strip was a success in its own right, and the number of subscribing newspapers grew. A Sunday version of "Abbie an' Slats" debuted on January 15, 1939.

Capp would stay with "Abbie an' Slats" until 1945, writing all the continuities for the daily and Sunday strips, though he was chronically late getting scripts to an increasingly irritated Van Buren. "Li'l Abner" always came first. When he finally stepped away from "Abbie an' Slats," he turned his writing duties over to someone he already knew and trusted: he handed the job to his brother Elliott. After college, Elliott was constantly trying to break into the comics business, with little success. "Abbie an' Slats" offered him an entry.

On Saturday, November 13, 1937, Capp ended his week of "Li'l Abner" strips with the customary cliffhanger. In this case, it also signaled the beginning of a new story cycle. Capp promised a story about a "strange mountain custom— Sadie Hawkins Day." Li'l Abner, away from Dogpatch through the last story cycle, felt honor-bound to return to his home for the event.

"I would always begin my stories with 'What if . . . ?'" Capp explained later. "What if there were a special day in Dogpatch in which any bachelor, caught by any lady before sundown, must marry her (except for ladies over a hundred, who are entitled to any boy they want)? What if we all know that Daisy Mae is incurably smitten with Abner and will die if anyone else nabs him?"

Capp offered the history of the tradition in six panels, beginning in the Monday, November 17, strip and concluding the following day. According to the legend, Sadie Hawkins had been the extremely plain, if not downright ugly, daughter of Hekzebiah Hawkins, one of the first settlers in Dogpatch.

As the years passed and Sadie was still living at home, with no prospects of dating, let alone marrying, Hekzebiah hatched a plan: all the single men in Dogpatch would gather in the town square, and a race would be staged. The men would be given a fair head start, and then Sadie would be allowed to pursue them. If she caught one of the eligible bachelors, she could

The Sadie Hawkins Day tradition debuted in "Li'l Abner" in November 1937. This fictional event immediately spawned hundreds of actual Sadie Hawkins Day celebrations across America.

marry him. Sadie Hawkins had snared her man, and the event became an annual affair, staged every November for all single men and women.

Readers loved it. These were days long before women's liberation, when custom largely dictated that a woman should passively wait for a man to express interest in her; the idea of turning the tables on the men was enormously appealing. Letters poured in, with readers demanding to know more about the Dogpatch festivities. The University of Tennessee staged its own event, based on the strip, in which students, dressed up like "Li'l Abner" characters, participated in a foot race, and if a coed caught a young man, he was obliged to take her to the newly minted Sadie Hawkins dance. Such events soon spread to other schools.

In the years ahead, Capp would reprise the Sadie Hawkins race in "Li'l Abner" at about the same time every November, though there was never a specific date assigned to the festivities. Li'l Abner had his close calls, but he always managed to escape Daisy Mae's clutches.

"We would always find a way to get him out of it," he said, "but one time there was no way to get him out. No human way. We sat around, paralyzed—until it came to me. 'This is our world,' I cried. 'We can do anything we want. If human ways won't work—let's try a SUPERHUMAN way!' From there our endings came a lot easier."

Over the years, the Sadie Hawkins parties grew larger and more complex, and expanded to include high schools and church groups. *Life* magazine noted that 201 colleges in 188 cities held Sadie Hawkins Day in 1939, a mere two years after the original comic strip was published. The numbers grew from there. United Feature Syndicate, recognizing the marketing possibilities, offered Sadie Hawkins kits and handouts suggesting ways of making the parties more successful.

Capp found it all very "amoozin' and confoozin'," to borrow one of his favorite "Li'l Abner" expressions. Every year, he would be invited to participate in Sadie Hawkins events on campuses across the country. He would be asked to act as master of ceremonies at the dance or serve as a judge at the Sadie Hawkins beauty pageant. One such contest gave Capp his favorite Sadie Hawkins story—another tale that's as entertaining as it is unlikely.

As he told it, it happened at a large midwestern university—he'd never say which one. Among the winner's prizes donated by local merchants were a full wardrobe, a modeling job, and a mink coat; the mayor would be giving her the keys to the city. At the ceremonies in the university's gym, Capp looked over the five finalists and privately selected the winner. Just as he was about to announce her name and present her with her trophy, the state's new governor-elect, a bit tipsy from the drinking throughout the festival, rushed up and put Capp on the spot by asking if could make the presentation. Capp told him the winner and watched as the politician walked across the stage. Flashbulbs went off, the assembly roared its approval, and the mayor presented the lucky girl with the keys to the city.

"I was so ashamed of myself I wanted to hide," Capp recalled. "There wasn't a single thing for me to do. I couldn't tell the truth and humiliate the winner. I could only promise myself never to forget what had happened when I let another man do my job.

"He had given the trophy to the wrong girl."

The Sadie Hawkins story represented a breakthrough for Capp, solid proof that he had a powerful understanding of what his readers would appreciate. In the early days of "Li'l Abner," the strip's storylines had been touch and go. Capp would come up with an idea for a specific continuity, submit it to United Feature for approval, rework it if the editors deemed it necessary, and finally get around to creating the actual art. He had been given more leeway as the strip's popularity grew, but he was still closely supervised, mainly because nothing like "Li'l Abner" had ever been attempted before, and there were no established guidelines for how to present satire and adult material on a page usually devoted to adventure or humor. United Feature monitored readers' and subscribing papers' responses. Editors were particularly sensitive about sexual or violent content in the strip, especially as Capp and his assistants became bolder in the content of their stories.

"Let's keep the strip free of degenerate or vicious elements, no matter how funny they may strike you at the time," William Lamb, Capp's managing editor at United Feature, wrote in a letter typical of his attempts to placate readers' and editors' objections to material in "Li'l Abner." "Make it burlesque, but not risqué," he admonished Capp on another occasion.

Capp reacted to these letters by backing off—but only for a short period. If United Feature complained that the action in the strip was too intense or violent, he would create an especially soft story for the strip's next continuity, but soon enough he would be pushing his limits once again, if for no other reason than to avoid becoming too predictable or, often as not, to amuse himself and avoid becoming bored with his work.

There would be occasions during the strip's long life when a newspaper refused to publish a strip or series of strips, perhaps the best known taking place in 1947, when Capp was needling corrupt politicians in one of his more pointed sequences. Capp had lampooned politics through the portrayal of Jack S. Fogbound, the senator from Dogpatch, and in this continuity, he had the senator offering to sell his deciding vote on a piece of legislation to the person willing to pay for the erection of a university in his name. In the past, Capp had presented the senator as "Fogbound," but in order to achieve a quick laugh and have the university known as "P.U.," he changed the spelling to "Phogbound." The senator's first name and middle initial were another joke, meaning "jackass." In his artistic renderings of the politician, Capp really cut loose, picturing him with a racing form peeking out of one of his coat pockets and a sleazy magazine, *French Models*, poking out of the other.

The *Pittsburgh Press*, irked by what the editors believed was a tone too disrespectful of those serving in Congress, refused to run the story.

"They said I implied that some U.S. Senators are ignorant, boorish, and dishonest," Capp said. "Me, all I ever knew about Senators came from reading the columns of the *Pittsburgh Press*."

Capp responded to the widely reported rejection by consulting with his friend Drew Pearson, the muckraking syndicated columnist ("Washington Merry-Go-Round") and radio commentator (for whom Capp would occasionally substitute over the years when Pearson vacationed). After hearing Capp's story, Pearson went on the air and talked about this case of censorship; if any listeners in Pittsburgh wondered what was happening in "Li'l Abner" during its absence from the *Pittsburgh Press*, all they had to do was send Capp a letter and he would supply the missing strips.

Capp loved it, especially when the letters started pouring in.

"Who ever would have thought that so many people who like my strip are actually able to write?" he quipped.

8 NINA

In 1939, Capp received word that there was interest in making a feature-length movie adaptation of "Li'l Abner." He was delighted. There was a rumor that Buddy Ebsen would be brought in to play the lead, and Capp, who had seen Ebsen onstage, was all for it. Ebsen, who would eventually play Jed Clampett in the television situation comedy *The Beverly Hillbillies*, a "Li'l Abner" knockoff, did not appear in the movie, and given the way the film turned out, it was probably just as well.

Capp's bosses at United Feature were far less enthusiastic about Hollywood's stated interest in "Li'l Abner," especially when Capp began making noises about driving or flying out to the West Coast to become more actively involved in the project. Hollywood, they cautioned Capp, was a town of disposable ideas, a place where today's shiny object became tomorrow's rusted junk. Movie options lapsed, contracts stalled; projects were lost in development hell.

United Feature general manager George A. Carlin expressed his worries in a letter to Capp. "While, if it ever comes to happen, a Hollywood trip might be fun, or at least a new and exciting experience, I look forward with no pleasure to your participation in the screen version," Carlin informed Capp. "I am really afraid of your reaching a saturation point on your output and I think the movie trip might not do the newspaper feature any good. However, if a definite offer comes to you, I am not going to stand in your way."

There was good reason for such concern. Raeburn Van Buren consistently complained to the syndicate about Capp's habit of delivering his scripts for "Abbie an' Slats" at the last possible moment, forcing Van Buren to hurry his artwork to meet deadlines. Van Buren saw this as a matter of Capp's devotion to "Li'l Abner" at the cost of less attention to "Abbie." The syndicate thought Capp was taking on more work than he could handle.

None of this concerned Capp in the least. But once contract negotiations had been finalized, he caught a train for the West Coast. He brought along Andy Amato for help on "Li'l Abner" while he was away, and the plan called for Catherine and Madeline, Al's sister, to join him later. There would be a brief vacation to go with all the work.

Hollywood might have been created for someone like Capp. It was energetic, glitzy, full of beautiful people, conspicuous in its consumption, and seductive in what it promised to someone bold enough to dream. Capp's extroverted personality, coupled with the nationwide popularity of "Li'l Abner," made him a welcome guest at A-list house parties and posh nightclubs where the glamour crowd congregated. It was at Don the Beachcomber in Hollywood that he first set eyes on Nina Luce, a twenty-five-year-old singer and part-time model trying to break through in Southern California's ultra-competitive nightclub scene.

Capp was smitten the moment he and Nina met. He autographed a drink coaster and had it delivered to her, and she joined him after she was finished singing. Nina was beautiful, intelligent, feisty, and talented.

Nina Luce was born on February 1, 1915, in Waco, Texas. Her father played fiddle, and Nina sang at family gatherings from a very early age. She loved attention, and her natural good looks and talent saw that she wasn't short of it. As a junior in high school in Baird, Texas, she won the "Headlight Queen" crown, the equivalent of Homecoming Queen elsewhere. A year later, her family moved to Riverside, California, where she finished her schooling. Immediately after her graduation, she moved to Hollywood.

By the time Al Capp met her in 1940, Nina (who spelled her own name Niña and pronounced it like the Spanish word), had kicked around the Los Angeles area long enough to make connections. She often sang at the shows of such bandleaders as Jimmy and Tommy Dorsey. She and Rita Hayworth modeled together and became good friends—enough so that, years later, Nina would name her daughter after the actress. She dated actor Victor Mature, director Sam Fuller, and even Mohammad Rezā Shāh Pahlavi, the future Shah of Iran. Her career opportunities expanded when she met George Antheil, the self-proclaimed Bad Boy of Music, who seemed to know everyone on the West Coast—and far beyond.

Antheil was fifteen years older than Nina. He'd been a musical prodigy

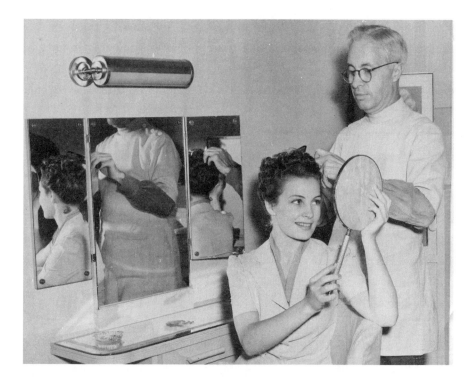

This publicity photo of Nina Luce in a Sunset Boulevard hair salon appeared in print in August 1938, less than two years before her intense affair with Al Capp began.

in New Jersey, studying piano from the age of six and composing his own work while still a teenager. He moved to Europe in 1922, where he enjoyed enormous success and befriended the likes of Igor Stravinsky, James Joyce, Pablo Picasso, and Ezra Pound, but the rise of Hitler convinced him that he might do best back in the United States. He wound up in Hollywood, applying his talents to film scores.

Antheil had seen Luce at one of her nightclub performances and had taken her under his guidance. He introduced her to club owners and record producers, advised her on her career, and eventually took her in to live with him and his wife, Boski Markus. Antheil described Nina in his autobiography as "one of the most extraordinary yet utterly lovable characters [he'd] ever met"; someone who "played poker like a gangster" and whose observations on life were "invariably brilliantly illuminative."

The attraction between Capp and Luce was immediate and very intense. Marital fidelity had never placed high on Capp's list of priorities, but this was something special. He felt he'd found an intellectual equal.

"There are lots of moonstruck gals who will follow me to and fro because I can do things for 'em," he told her bluntly. "[But] you are the most independent li'l cuss of all li'l cusses," he said, meaning it as a compliment.

Nina, like Capp, was a night owl. She loved socializing and making the after-hours rounds. She was unattached, with no children, and showed no inclination toward getting married and settling down. To Capp, she was some of what he'd lost, some of what he'd never had, but mostly something fresh, exhilarating, and unknown.

When asked what he was doing in Hollywood, Capp would say that he was researching for a future "Li'l Abner" story—perhaps because it soon became clear that the movie would not be a huge source of pride. "Li'l Abner" received the same treatment that many other comic strips suffered in Hollywood adaptation: a small budget, a breakneck production schedule, unimaginative writing, and a creative malaise that kept the film from rising above B-movie status.

Ham Fisher had seen "Joe Palooka" pummeled into submission in the 1934 adaptation of his popular strip. Beginning in 1938, Columbia Pictures cranked out a series of full-length features based on Chic Young's "Blondie"— six formulaic films in two years. No one pretended that these movies were designed to be high art or anything more than happy diversions from difficult times.

Albert S. Rogell, Li'l Abner's director, didn't have full comprehension of what made the comic strip work. He understood Dogpatch and did a credible job re-creating it for the big screen, and he grasped what Capp was trying to do with the Li'l Abner/Daisy Mae relationship and the Sadie Hawkins race. Too often, however, writers Charles Kerr and Tyler Johnson played for the cheap laugh, whether it was the Dogpatch community's southern affectations and butchering of the English language, or the slapstick comedy, which might have worked more effectively if handled with a lighter hand. Capp received onscreen credit as the creator of the comic strip and the story upon which the screenplay was based, but despite his presence in California, he had very little to do with the film's production. For future movie trivia fanatics, a couple of major show business names crossed paths with the picture, although not in any memorable way. Comedian Milton Berle shared a songwriting credit for the film's title song, and silent film and silver screen star Buster Keaton, his career in such a downswing that he didn't even earn a mention on the movie's posters, played the role of Lonesome Polecat, a recurring character in the comic strip.

The movie, released on November 1, 1940, was ignored by the Hollywood trade journals, and none of the major newspapers bothered to review it. The comic strip's popularity didn't translate into acceptable box office figures, and the movie, designed for release during the busy holiday season,

A scene from the 1940 RKO movie adaptation of "Li'l Abner." Left to right: *Johnny Morris as Pappy Yokum, Martha O'Driscoll as Daisy Mae, Granville Owen as Li'l Abner, and Mona Ray as Mammy Yokum.*

slipped from sight before the Christmas decorations had been pulled from department store windows.

All of this might have been harder on Capp if he hadn't been so wrapped up in his affair with Nina Luce. The relationship became no less intense when Catherine and Madeline arrived in California. Catherine had never interfered with Capp's work, and since Capp was ostensibly in Hollywood on business, he was able to sneak out without arousing her suspicions. It also helped that Catherine preferred to avoid the party scene—and Madeline managed to keep her occupied. Capp had a strong bond with Madeline, whom he described to Nina as "a swell and straight-thinking gal," and he enlisted her help in keeping his affair a secret. More boldly, he confided his plans to move Nina to Boston when his time in California ended. Madeline disapproved of the plan, mainly because Nina's health was not the best.

In a hastily written letter sent while he was preparing to leave the Beverly Wilshire Hotel in Beverly Hills, Capp told Nina that "my sister gave me whooping hell for dragging you off with your throat in bad shape." In another, written while he was in transit on his way home, he wrote of how he and Madeline had "talked and talked," and of how she had admonished him for being "brutish and selfish" in trying to pressure Nina into flying to Boston when she was ailing.

Nina's tonsils needed to be removed, which concerned her, first, because she had no money to pay for the procedure, and, second, because she would require recovery time before she could resume her singing career. Capp had no interest in the latter. He was convinced that their love was true, and he selfishly hoped she would cancel her commitments on the West Coast and move to Boston as soon as possible.

He aggressively pursued the plan. He would buy Nina's plane ticket. She could stay at the YWCA until she found a suitable apartment and a job, and they could pick up where they'd left off in Hollywood. Capp pressured Nina whenever she sounded like she was having second thoughts about leaving California. It didn't matter that she had a contract to perform in a club; Capp assured her that he could use his position to free her of that obligation. When she told him that she needed to have her tonsils removed,

Capp lost his temper. He'd purchased an airline ticket for her, he declared, and he insisted on her giving him a date of arrival.

"NO BACKSLIDING!!" he wrote in a letter illustrated with an angry self-portrait. "NO MINDCHANGING!! GET THOSE DAMN TONSILS OUT AND WIRE ME!! You mustn't let me down—or I'll come here and drag you back by the hair!!"

Not all his letters were so angry. Once home, Capp had established a routine that often found him leaving the house as early as three o'clock in the morning. In the total silence of an office customarily loud and busy, Capp's thoughts soon turned to Nina, and in no time he'd be seated at his typewriter, rolling in a sheet of letterhead paper decorated with a drawing of Li'l Abner on the left margin. He'd pour out his feelings in letter after letter, addressing Nina by his pet name for her, "Gaye," and always signing off as "Al," unless he was angry or anxious; in those letters, he'd sign off as "Bullsh"—short, no doubt, for "Bullshit" or "Bullshitter." On other occasions he'd sign his letters "Beast."

The letters could be sad, testy, sentimental, imploring, or demanding, depending upon how often she wrote him and what she said when she did. Capp wrote frankly—with more emotion than he would permit himself at any other time, with any other person. He'd write about the events in his personal and professional life, of how his wealth and fame meant nothing in comparison to how fortunate he felt about just being with her.

"I feel like suddenly rising and roaring—NOTHING important happened to me in Hollywood—except I met Gaye!!!" he wrote in his first letter after his return to Boston, Since that time, he complained, he had been inundated by interview requests, but journalists asked the same maddening questions. He'd once enjoyed being Al Capp and dealing with the press, he told her, but it hadn't been much fun since his return from California. His attention was elsewhere.

Capp's candor, placed in the context of his being thirty years old, married, and the father of two daughters, was disarming. He sounded as if he were sixteen years old again, enjoying his first taste of something other than puppy love, and trying to express himself in a manner that was honest and adult; yet, as he admitted, it always came out corny. He'd been racked with anxiety and the fear that they were through from the moment he left California.

"It was a sweet thing, wasn't it, Gaye?" he wrote wistfully. "Ordinarily, I have no truck with love stories, because most love stories are dishonest. So I've never read 'em—never lived 'em. Ours was an honest one, and a sweet one. If it's over, that doesn't change it. It was honest and sweet and good."

"I've never wanted anyone else—but you," he told her in another letter. "You're always with me now—whether I ever see you again or not—you always will be with me, Gaye. You are my kind of gal. I hope that, after you've read this far—I will still be your kind of guy."

Nina struggled with a decision. She had sent a letter in late July, in which she stated that she had been giving Capp's proposal a lot of serious thought but would not be coming to Boston. She still remembered the good times they'd had in California, but she had to face reality. "My heart has not changed tho my mind has taken control," she wrote.

Capp reacted bitterly.

"Why did you have to do it, Gaye?" he asked. "Why did you mess up something so good?" Mired in self-pity, he instructed her to gather his letters, bind them in blue ribbon, and put them away. "You've been loved, Gaye," he concluded, "much more than you loved in return."

His anger was short-lived. The next day, he sent a conciliatory letter restating his position, admitting that he struggled with her independent spirit. He'd balked at sending her money when she'd asked in an early letter, mainly because he wanted to preserve that independence: he couldn't bear the thought of her coming to Boston out of a sense of obligation.

In the midst of all this drama, Capp was offered a scriptwriting job— and the chance to return to Hollywood.

Somehow, "Li'l Abner" thrived during this stormy period. Capp complained to Nina that the emotional strain of this back-and-forth was exacting a toll on his work, but there is little evidence of it. The "Li'l Abner" stories of 1940 showed Capp and his assistants at the top of their game. John Ford's film adaptation of John Steinbeck's *The Grapes of Wrath* promised to be one of the motion picture events of 1940, and Capp used the occasion to create a parody, which wound up becoming one of the lengthiest continuities in the strip's history.

The "Li'l Abner" version of the Steinbeck classic began as little more than an excuse to relocate the strip to the big city. Capp decided to dispatch all of Dogpatch to Boston. Hard times had fallen on Dogpatch. The dreaded turnip termite had wiped out the turnip crop, and since "presarved turnips" were the town's sole source of support, something had to be done to stave off starvation. After hearing about migrant farm workers, the Dogpatchers decided to migrate to Boston, where they planned to make their way back to financial solvency by picking oranges—in the middle of winter. From such ignorance sprang a convoluted series of adventures, including a skirmish between the feuding Yokum and Scragg families in a fractured re-creation of the Battle of Bunker Hill.

Another story, written around the time Capp was meeting Nina, probably had a deeper personal connection to Capp than the typical "Li'l Abner." In this story, a couple of con men visiting Dogpatch overheard Daisy Mae singing a sad song, inspired by Li'l Abner's disinterest in her. After drying their tears, they came up with a scam that involved secretly broadcasting her on the radio, introduced to the world as Sorrowful Sue. Li'l Abner, listening to the program, fell in love with the voice and decided he had to meet the singer, later steadfastly refusing to believe the real identity of the Sorrowful Sue he loved. Capp used the continuity for a running commentary on the shallowness of celebrity and the shady dealings in show business—at the same time he was rubbing elbows with Hollywood celebrities.

The year's other noteworthy story involved a new Capp character: Adam Lazonga, formerly of Dogpatch, now renowned as the world's greatest wooer of women. Lazonga, getting on in years, was seeking a protégé, someone to teach the six main secrets of his successful method of making love, "Dogpatch style." Li'l Abner became his unwitting student.

In telling the story, Capp risked stepping into material unsuitable for young readers. Comic strips generally avoided the slightest hint of sexual behavior, but Capp, who had been testing limits for a long time, stacked his story with double entendres and barely concealed sexual references—even the hint, Dogpatch style, that sex was performed in a manner other than the standard missionary position. Capp modeled Lazonga's physical appearance after George Bernard Shaw, the playwright and novelist, whose play *Pygmalion* was built on a similar teacher/student theme, but Lazonga's eccentric views and behavior were based on English philosopher and mathematician Bertrand Russell, recently in Boston's local news because he had accepted a position as a lecturer at Harvard after having been dismissed from the City College of New York.

In interviews, Capp refused to connect Russell to his comic strip character, saying only that Shaw had been the model for the way Adam Lazonga looked. In the end, it didn't matter. Lazonga had become a vehicle for another lighthearted romp.

Nina was in San Antonio when Capp arrived in California for his latest attempt at screenwriting, but they continued to exchange letters. Her stance on moving to Boston was softening, catching Capp a little by surprise—enough to give him his own second thoughts about what things might be like if she followed through. He had to admit that the arrangement was very one-sided, with Nina sacrificing a lot in exchange for very little in return. In a brutally frank letter to Nina, Capp listed the downside of a move to Boston in such plain, unfavorable terms that Nina must have wondered why she was ever considering it. Boston, Capp wrote her, was "a grim city," populated by unfriendly people and offering very little excitement; the people she would be meeting at the Y would differ significantly from the type of people she hung around with at the Antheils'. Because their relationship had to remain a strict secret, she would be isolated, stuck working a job lacking the glamour of singing in a nightclub.

"You'll be chucking your career," he warned. "You'll chuck everything but me. That's all there will be, Gaye—just me."

Nevertheless, when he and Nina finally saw each other in Hollywood, they moved forward with making plans.

Nina flew to Boston on August 19, 1940, but lasted less than three months in the city. She moved into the YWCA and found a job at a retail store. She registered for a class at the Boston Conservatory and Capp spent as much time with her as possible, but between his time at the studio and his family obligations, he wasn't around nearly as much as either of them would have liked. By the time the temperatures were starting to drop and autumn was fading into winter, Nina was ready to move back to California.

A disagreement over money precipitated Nina's final decision to move back. Nina required emergency dental work costing $310, and that, along with her tuition fee at the Conservatory of Music, was more than she could afford. She had left for Boston with $150 in her purse; $100 of it went to the dentist. When she asked Capp for help, he was reluctant. He gave her a small amount, but when she asked for more, he turned her down, saying he wanted to preserve the independence he loved in her—he didn't want her to have any obligation to him. Capp paid her bills after she left Boston, but, as he wrote her, he felt humiliated by the letter she'd sent him two weeks after leaving Boston and heading to San Antonio.

"It was all about money," he said in the letter, not even attempting to hide his disgust. "Maybe it was never you I loved," he continued. "Maybe you never existed—maybe you were just a character I created. Whatever it was—there is so much left that, however much you destroy it from now on—you cannot wholly destroy the lovely thing you were to me."

Nina fired back in a strongly worded letter of her own.

"I came to you against my better judgment," she confessed. "I should have listened to my intuition, which told me to settle up my affairs before coming. But I wanted you so much and I didn't think the expense I was to you would be so important. I'm so sorry that came between us—I'm humiliated that I had to need anything but your love, which was plenty. If you really think I used you for a good thing you can dismiss the thought . . .

"I'm going to take a year out," she continued, "buckle down and try to get my house in order . . . Then I'm going to find someone who can make me happy and I'm going to marry—I won't pretend that I can go through life alone—but the next time I love I'll leave no chance for the object of my affection to feel he has been taken, for I won't need anything."

9 MERRY-GO-ROUND

Capp made his way back to Hollywood shortly after Nina left Boston. He would spend slightly more than two months away from home, caught up in the Hollywood "merrygoround," as he wrote it, working on projects that never saw the light of day. Nina was again in San Antonio, and Capp missed her desperately. The ghosts of their past haunted him wherever he went.

He wrote a flurry of letters, a few of which he mailed to Nina in San Antonio, most of which he destroyed. He would start a letter, often late at night, only to abandon it, start fresh the next day, and send them together when he was satisfied with what he'd written. The Al Capp self-assurance, a personal trademark dating back to his youth, had disappeared. In one letter he'd say that he realized they'd reached the end as a couple, then in another he'd write of all the times he'd wept over memories of their time together, and he'd insist that they were far from finished. Nina, by all indications, remained silent.

Capp also wrote letters to Catherine and the girls, but he wasn't eager to rejoin them. Despite his mournful, pleading letters to Nina, he was anything but a hermit while in Los Angeles. He socialized, and, as he would shamelessly admit to Nina, he spent nights with beautiful women drawn to his money and celebrity.

Capp left Hollywood, unsure that he would ever return, on February 4. An hour before leaving, he dashed off one final letter to Nina—a frank, tender, heartfelt love letter that expressed, in no uncertain terms, his deep love for her, but that also conceded that they would never be together.

HAVERHILL EVENING GAZETTE — FRIDAY, AUGUST 23, 1940

IS THERE A DAISY MAE IN THIS CROWD? Al Capp looks over possibilities for his Dogpatch beauty in the screen version of "Li'l Abner", which is soon to be made, while visiting Hollywood to work with Vogue Pictures in preparing for the film production. Capp is shown here on the set of "Too Many Girls" at the R.K.O.-Radio studio.

This photo of Al Capp in the middle of ten Hollywood beauties appeared in at least one Boston-area newspaper just three days before Nina Luce secretly arrived in the city.

"Whatever my paths may be from now on, inevitably I will return home," he told her. "My ties are too strong, I know now, ever to break."

Capp unhappily resumed his familiar routine after his return from California. A new "Li'l Abner" featured Moonbeam McSwine, but he wasn't enthusiastic about it. The character, modeled after Catherine, gave him little pleasure at a time when Nina occupied his thoughts. Catherine, he felt, was living in a dream world, unaware of her husband's love for another woman, of the many one-night stands he'd had in the recent past. She believed he was living an ideal life focused on work, home, and family.

"I am trapped, darling," Capp wrote Nina three weeks after his return from California, "trapped by Catherine's faith in me, her love for me, trapped because if ever she was awakened from the dream she lives within—she would, I think, die."

At one time, Nina had accused Capp of wallowing in misery, of hanging on to the sadness in his life rather than embracing the joy that came his way. This was true in the early months of 1941. He and Catherine had hit a rough patch in their marriage, and Capp had moved out of the house and into his studio; Don Munson, in the midst of problems with his own love life, had moved in with him. Even the continuing growth of "Li'l Abner" offered no happiness, since Capp worried that he would slip from the top and suffer a blow to his vanity.

"I'm desperately unhappy," he told Nina, "and whereas, before, I could live a kind of cockeyed, funny, wish-fulfillment life in my comic strip—I can no longer. The joy has gone out of it. It is a job now."

Only his children seemed to make him happy.

"My kids are asleep in the next room to this studio. It's a sweet little room—it's all yellow and every inch of floor space and bureau space and chair space is covered with their things," he wrote in a wonderfully descriptive passage to Nina. "Julie's thick nut-brown hair is spread all over her pillow—it's long and wavy and beautiful. Cathie is blonde and her hair is all over the pillow—she wears her hair long because Julie does. Julie's very much like me, Nina—arrogant, and with a violent temper and ever-hungry for excitement, impatient, vain, desperately and absurdly melancholy and hilarious by turns. She's a difficult kid at times—but, because, in her, I see so much of myself, I love her best. Cathie is like her mother, mild, gentle, shy."

Although she was his most passionate and long-term dalliance, Nina would certainly not be the last. Capp was obsessed with sex. He would never be satisfied with one woman, not because he couldn't find one woman to satisfy him sexually, but because he was constantly driven to look elsewhere.

His obsession with women was evident in the voluptuous women he created for "Li'l Abner" over the years, in his randy shop talk with his assistants, and, most of all, in his pursuit of extramarital flings that began, by his own admission, not long after he and Catherine were married. His passionate letters to Nina Luce belied the fact that he was bedding still more women when they were apart.

At least he could be honest about it with Nina. In one letter, in which he spoke of his unwillingness to leave his family, and of his love for her, he also described in detail the different women he'd been with while he was in Hollywood.

"Inside of me there is a restlessness, a badness, that will never—I know that—give me peace," he wrote. "It's a restlessness that makes playing as vital to me as breathing. It is a restlessness that makes for episodes like my two months in Hollywood—two months of steeping myself in lechery, in insincerity, in insane wildness."

Capp offered no apology for his behavior. He recognized the dangers but was unwilling (or, as he would have Nina believe, unable) to harness his desires.

"The more I feed on it, the greater my appetite grows," he admitted in what, in the years ahead, would seem a prophetic letter. "Someday, perhaps, it will destroy me. Perhaps already I am being destroyed. Maybe that's my goal in living—to destroy myself."

After Capp finally conceded that he would never leave his wife, Nina eventually stopped responding to his letters. Her silence made Capp desperate.

"Your silence has made me wonder if everything is well with you," he wrote in a somewhat transparent attempt to force a response. "If in your wisdom you have determined to cut this dead thing down—don't do it with silence, dear Nina. Let me know. You may have gotten married up or you may be ill—or you may no longer be in Texas. Don't drop out of my life too suddenly, Nina—let a fella know."

Nina didn't answer.

Hollywood beckoned. Capp's natural ear for dialogue and his theatrical aptitude made him a valuable asset in the film business. Even with Nina gone,

Capp pushed himself to work ahead so he could afford to take a month away from "Li'l Abner." This time, he would be taking a car, riding with a young pianist and composer named Frank Glazer and a Romanian conductor, both of whom wanted to write music for motion pictures.

He left on July 2, 1941. The three men took their time driving out, enjoying a trip that, for Capp, was a brief vacation before another prolonged period of working on scripts and treatments. Capp enjoyed the work in Los Angeles. In letters home, he told Catherine about all the starlets he'd met, all the trendy, upscale restaurants he visited, and all the lavish parties he attended, sounding more like a starstruck tourist than someone working in the business. When he arrived in California, he'd failed to secure a room in the Beverly Wilshire, his favorite hotel in Beverly Hills; the management put him up in a small rooftop room that, Capp delighted in telling his wife, was usually reserved for a diamond smuggler and had been used in the past by Irving Berlin and Cole Porter. He was thrilled when he met Dorothy Lamour and posed for pictures with her.

Once again, Catherine planned to join him after he completed some work. This time, Capp looked forward to it, and he wrote home regularly, keeping Catherine informed on everything happening in his life.

"I've been working very hard and I was happy to get your letter," he told her at the top of a typically chatty letter. "You are a nice girl, a sweet and gentle wife, and a beautiful lady and a loving, patient momma."

The work went much more slowly than Capp anticipated, and to his dismay, the studio asked him to hang on and help develop a musical for Bert Lahr, fresh off his starring role as the Cowardly Lion in *The Wizard of Oz.* Rather than vacation with his wife, Capp made arrangements to have Don Munson drive Andy Amato cross-country so they could work on "Li'l Abner." In breaking the news to Catherine, Capp sounded truly apologetic. "You should have had my nut examined before you married me, darlin'," he said. "I loves yah."

Despite the warmth in his letters home, Capp still longed to see Nina. His letters to her were now only intermittent.

In mid-November, long after he had returned home and resumed his work routine, Capp finally heard back from Nina. He'd asked her to send a photograph of herself, which she did, along with a cautious letter. Encouraged, he suggested that he drive down to San Antonio to celebrate New Year's Eve with her. Nothing, he said, would stop him now. Nina reluctantly agreed.

History itself wound up coming between them. The Japanese attacked Pearl Harbor on December 7, 1941, and the United States declared war on Japan, Germany, and the Axis. These events had no immediate effect on Capp's plans until the very end of the year, when he heard from government officials wanting him to begin a wartime project for them. He was in Washington, D.C., rather than San Antonio, on New Year's Eve.

For Nina, this was just one last instance of Capp letting her down. Again, she asked him to leave her alone.

The rejection hurt Capp, but he was finally ready to abandon his pursuit.

"I won't intrude into your new and good and sane life again, Nina," he promised.

The affair, this time, was really over. Capp and Nina would meet in the months ahead, Capp traveling to San Antonio and Nina to Boston, but the visits were brief, with no chance of reconciliation. Both were ready to move on. Capp would contact Nina occasionally over the next two decades, and he would even visit her in Tennessee, where she was working and had met her future husband, but both realized that a sustained relationship was just not possible.

Capp had an important decision to make when the United States entered World War II. His missing leg would keep him out of active duty, but he would still be required to serve in some capacity. He expected this much. From an artistic standpoint, however, he had to decide what he would do with the title character of his comic strip. Abner Yokum, frozen in time at nineteen years of age, would be a prime candidate for the draft—if Capp chose to address the war in his strip.

Other comics artists, caught up in the patriotic riptide following Japan's bombing of Pearl Harbor and America's declaration of war against Germany, Japan, and their allies, quickly moved to include the war in their work. Ham Fisher, Milton Caniff, Chester Gould, Harold Gray, Frank King, and others found ways to involve their characters in the global conflict, whether at home or overseas. And the daily strips weren't alone in their patriotic zeal. A new comic book character, Captain America, created by Joe Simon and Jack Kirby, wore a red, white, and blue costume and was designed to be a symbol of democracy in the battle against fascism.

"Li'l Abner" proceeded through the early months of 1942 with no indication that a war was on. Life in Dogpatch continued as always. Capp stayed current in his satire and parodies, sending up Orson Welles's *Citizen Kane* in the first "Li'l Abner" story of the year, but he remained silent about his plans for the strip during wartime. Readers sent letters, some satisfied with the status quo, others wondering about how Capp planned to work Li'l Abner into the war.

Capp waited until July 4 to deliver his answer. He interrupted his ongoing continuity with a two-panel message, written and signed in his own hand, the panels bookended with Li'l Abner and Daisy Mae sitting on the ground, apparently without a care in the world.

"Dear Friends," the strip began,

This seems the right day to answer a question many of you have asked me—

"When is Li'l Abner going into the Army?"

Li'l Abner isn't going into the Army. And here is why.

Perhaps Li'l Abner and his friends, living through these terrible days in a peaceful, happy, free world will do their part by reminding us that this is what we are fighting for—to have that world again—a world where a fella can do pretty much as he pleases as long as he doesn't bother his neighbors—a world where a fella can worship God in his own way—and where the next fella's got the same right—a world where a fella and his gal can look up at the moon just for the foolishness of it—and not because there may be planes up there coming to blast 'em both off the earth—a world where a fella is free to be as wise or foolish as he pleases—but mainly—a world where a fella is free!!

That world has disappeared—until we win this war. Perhaps this small section of our daily newspaper can do its part best by helping us to remember that a free world once did exist—and will again!!

Al Capp

The next day, the "Li'l Abner" story continued where it had left off. Capp never used his strip to address the issue again.

Capp hated being second in circulation numbers or prestige to any other comic strip artist. It was, as he once told Nina, a "blow to my vanity." Ranking among the top five in circulation, he allowed, should have been sufficient, but he did anything within his power to push aside the competition and move to the top. Several strips near or at the top were gag strips, which threatened Capp less than the ones that, like "Li'l Abner," ran as continuing stories. "Dick Tracy" and "Little Orphan Annie" could bring out the warrior in Capp.

The fact that he liked a comic strip's creator meant nothing. Capp was on friendly terms with Chester Gould, whose "Dick Tracy" always occupied a spot near the top of the list of daily strips. Gould, Capp repeatedly told reporters, was an exceptional writer and artist, well deserving of his popularity; he had set a standard of excellence that other cartoonists aspired to achieve.

For all that he admired about the artistry of "Dick Tracy," Capp was galled by its success. "Li'l Abner," he felt, was every bit as entertaining and creative, and certainly as well drawn. Capp, by his own admission, had borrowed some of Gould's storytelling techniques in the early days of "Abner," but he believed that the injection of humor, absent in "Dick Tracy," and stronger characterization had moved him past Gould in overall quality.

As if to prove his point, Capp created "Fearless Fosdick," a recurring "Dick Tracy" parody that would serve him well in years to come. Fosdick, Capp's version of the Dick Tracy character, turned up for the first time in the August 30, 1942, Sunday strip. Comics enthusiasts would have no trouble identifying the target of the parody. Fosdick had Tracy's lantern jaw, fedora hat, and impeccable suit; he was all business in his pursuit of such aptly and humorously named villains as Stoneface and Rattop, who, not at all coincidentally, bore monikers similar to Gould's Pruneface and Flattop. In time, Capp assigned Fosdick a love interest, the ever-suffering Prudence Pimpleton, a woman possessing an unfortunate jawline even more square and pronounced than Fosdick's, a totally devoted fiancée doomed to an eternal engagement with no wedding on the horizon. "His relations with

"Fearless Fosdick" ran for decades as a strip-within-a-strip in "Li'l Abner." It included a running gag about the long-suffering detective's meager salary of $22.50 per week—the same salary Capp earned as Ham Fisher's assistant.

Prudence Pimpleton, his veteran fiancée, are so Pure that to use the word 'relations' seems unnecessarily lurid," Capp joked in the preface to a 1956 book-length compilation of "Fosdick" episodes.

The first "Fearless Fosdick" continuity ran four consecutive Sundays. Capp employed a comic-strip-within-a-comic-strip format, which he would use to lead into the "Fosdick" stories for more than three decades. Lil' Abner would get a copy of the newspaper, usually dropped off in Dogpatch by train, and he'd feverishly search for the comics section. He'd begin reading "Fearless Fosdick," and from that point on, "Li'l Abner" readers would be treated to a strip alternating between the adventures of the world's most dim-witted detective and the reactions of his dim-witted hillbilly reader. Li'l Abner would emulate Fosdick to the extent that he would put his own life in peril if it reflected Fosdick's adventures.

In the first story, Fosdick was dropped from an airplane, tightly bound and free-falling headfirst toward the pavement ten thousand feet below. The inescapable situation baffled some of "Fosdick's" biggest fans, including President Franklin Roosevelt, Albert Einstein, and the strip's own mousy creator, Lester Gooch. They, like Li'l Abner when he reached the strip's weekly cliffhanger ending, could think of no way to save Fosdick from certain death.

The action in the strip reflected a common problem faced by Al Capp and his assistants. Quite often, they would discuss the ideal setup for a "Li'l Abner" story, only to run into an assortment of problems in following through to a suitable ending. A story could take a hilarious, meandering route, only to wind down to an illogical conclusion. In his initial "Fearless Fosdick" installments, Capp not only lampooned Chester Gould's famous detective; he created a wicked commentary on his own problems as a comics artist. If that weren't enough, Capp made a point of having one of his characters reading and ridiculing a strip peopled by "stoopid iggorant hill-billies."

In the first "Fearless Fosdick" sequence, Li'l Abner, fearful of his hero's fate, sent a letter to Lester Gooch, stating that he admired Fosdick and wished he could put himself in Fosdick's place in some of his adventures. Gooch, sensing a solution to his problems, hired a pilot to fly him to Dogpatch. Li'l Abner, Gooch discovered, was a man of his word. He allowed himself to be trussed up and dropped from a plane in the same manner as Fosdick. He escaped death and injury when he landed on his head, "whar nothin' kin harm me!!" Gooch adapted the same solution to Fosdick's plight, and the character—and fictitious comic strip—escaped to turn up at a later date.

The story set the tone for the future. Fosdick, Capp explained, was "without doubt the world's most idiotic detective. He shoots people for their own good, is pure beyond imagining, and fanatically loyal to a police department which exploits, starves and periodically fires him." More than willing to take a bullet for the cause, Fosdick was often pictured full of bullet holes of various sizes, making him look like a walking, talking, human-shaped block of Swiss cheese. Easily the world's worst marksman, Fosdick shot innocent bystanders in alarming numbers, but, as Capp explained, the loss of an unwitting civilian—or ten—was a small price to pay for a better world.

"Fosdick's duty, as he saw it," Capp quipped, "is not so much to maintain safety as to destroy crime, and it's too much to ask any law-enforcement officer to do both, I suppose."

"Fearless Fosdick" became immensely popular, especially among male readers of "Li'l Abner," and what began as a burlesque evolved into one of Capp's most enduring features. It gave Capp the opportunity to be sublimely absurd, such as in the episode in which a vicious but stupid crime gang is run by a chair. (The chair, in the continuity's conclusion, gets the chair.) Fosdick would be featured for years in Wildroot Cream-Oil advertisements, and for a brief period in the early 1950s he would have his own television program.

If Chester Gould objected to being the target of the longest-running parody in comics history, he kept it to himself. ("I'm getting quite a kick out of both," he told *Newsweek*, referring to seeing himself and his comic strip victimized in a competing strip.) Capp, enjoying the benefits of bolstering his own strip at the expense of another, praised Gould and "Dick Tracy" often enough to keep his readers from calling him mean-spirited.

"Because I am kidding Dick Tracy, I do not want to create the impression that I am not a Dick Tracy fan," he insisted. "I am a hell of a Dick Tracy fan."

Fearless Fosdick was not the only popular recurring character to make an initial appearance in "Li'l Abner" in 1942. Available Jones, whose motto, "If It's Too Unpleasant for You to Do—I'm Available," led him to every type of task imaginable, turned up on January 3, and Joe Btfsplk, the man with the perpetual rain cloud over his head and the biggest jinx to humankind, whose last name was best pronounced with a Bronx cheer, walked on in the July 11 strip. Both would rank among the most popular "Abner" characters during the strip's forty-three-year run.

In October 1942, Capp received a call from a John Marsh, an Atlanta attorney and advertising executive who took exception to a "Li'l Abner" story, "Gone wif the Wind," an obvious parody of the Margaret Mitchell bestseller, *Gone with the Wind*. In the Capp story, Li'l Abner played a character named Wreck Butler, and Daisy Mae appeared as Scallop O'Hara. Marsh informed Capp that he and his wife had seen the Sunday strip and had taken great exception to it. Capp, accustomed to calls and letters from disgruntled readers, tried to make light of the complaint. He suggested that the Marshes read "Rex Morgan, M.D.," a popular melodramatic strip, until the "Li'l Abner" sequence concluded.

Marsh was not disarmed by Capp's humorous response to his complaint. His wife, he insisted, would not be mollified unless Capp immediately canceled the remainder of the "Li'l Abner" story. Capp patiently tried to explain that this was not possible, that the rest of the strip was already submitted and prepared for publication.

In recalling the story, Capp embellished his account with typical bravado.

"He kept nagging," he said of Marsh, "but as I had to go back to work, I ended the conversation with a short Anglo-Saxon phrase of two words. It's very useful for getting rid of pests—and for the beginning of law suits."

Marsh, Capp learned later, was more than a mere pest; his perturbed wife was, in fact, Margaret Mitchell herself. After Capp's rude termination of their conversation, Marsh called United Feature Syndicate and reregistered his complaint, this time more emphatically. Mitchell was prepared to sue United Feature and Al Capp jointly for copyright infringement. The suit would demand a settlement of one dollar for every reader of every newspaper publishing the parody. This translated into roughly $76 million.

Capp couldn't understand what the fuss was all about. *Gone with the Wind* had been a phenomenal success, sitting atop the bestseller lists for what seemed like an eternity and winning the Pulitzer Prize in 1937. Two years later, a film adaptation of the book had set box office records, eventually winning an unprecedented ten Academy Awards. How could Mitchell feel remotely threatened by a comic strip parody?

United Feature examined copyright law and determined that there was a strong chance that Mitchell would win. This was years before Harvey Kurtzman's *Mad* and other publications stretched the boundaries and set broader legal precedents for satire. The comics syndicate struck a deal with the novelist: Al Capp would drop the story and issue a public apology in his strip, and Mitchell would drop the lawsuit. Capp reluctantly agreed and devoted two panels of the following Sunday's strip to his apology.

Capp would shrug it all off in future interviews, as if none of it mattered. He'd made sure that influential news sources knew about Mitchell's objections and lawsuit threat, and while it's unlikely that Margaret Mitchell's reputation and public appeal suffered as a result of an account published in *Time* magazine, Capp and his comic strip enjoyed a boost in publicity.

To Capp, this was of utmost importance. Few other comic artists in history craved attention the way Al Capp did. Creating a daily comic strip was a demanding occupation involving creativity and hard work under tight deadlines—work conditions that literally drove more than a few artists to

Al Capp and his syndicate would face the threat of an expensive lawsuit from Margaret Mitchell when he parodied Gone with the Wind in a series of 1942 Sunday strips. Capp was forced to apologize in a subsequent strip.

drink. Comic strip artists worked long hours and tended to be solitary figures, far removed from the publicity machine.

Capp differed greatly from this image. He was loud and aggressive; he
didn't drink; he worked relatively regular hours; he had a boisterous office
with at least three assistants at a time. He thrived in the spotlight, which
gave him the opportunity to expound on topics he found interesting and
hot-button issues in his strip. And he would employ any measure, including
the use of parodies and the creation of prearranged feuds, to haul in as much
publicity as he could muster.

Over the years, his competitive drive compelled him to take on Chester Gould ("Dick Tracy"), Harold Gray ("Little Orphan Annie"), Allen Saunders ("Mary Worth"), and Charles Schulz ("Peanuts"). His feuds might have
appeared to be friendly and light, but there was a darker, self-serving ele-
ment to them as well.

His 1947 "feud" with Will Eisner was a prime example. Although
slightly younger, Eisner had been in the business almost as long as Capp,
first as a comics packager and later as the creator of "The Spirit," a sort of
hybrid detective/superhero that was syndicated in the papers from 1940 to
1952. Eisner was greatly admired as an artist, and the Spirit stories, many
written by future Pulitzer Prize–winning cartoonist Jules Feiffer, ranked
among the most intelligent comics in the papers. Eisner and "The Spirit"
were not direct competition to Capp and "Li'l Abner," but that didn't prevent Capp from trying to find a way to sling a few arrows at Eisner while
generating publicity for himself.

"Sometime in late May or early June of 1947, the phone rang at the
studio, and the caller was, believe it nor not, Al Capp," Eisner recalled in an
interview forty years later. "He had this booming voice that came out of a
leonine head. He said, 'Hi, Will,' and after the preliminary compliments
about the work, he said, 'How about you and me having a little feud?'"

Eisner was game. He deeply admired "Li'l Abner," and by his own admission he was starstruck by Capp's call.

Capp set the terms for the feud. Eisner would fire the first shots by
creating a "Li'l Abner" parody in "The Spirit." Capp would feign anger at the
parody and respond in kind, with a parody of "The Spirit" in "Li'l Abner."
The press would eat it up, readers would be held in suspense over what

Will Eisner's The Spirit *was an unusual syndicated comic book insert in newspapers. Eisner was flattered when Capp suggested in 1947 that they parody each other's strips as a publicity stunt, and complied with "Li'l Adam, the Stupid Mountain Boy," by "Al Slapp." Capp never reciprocated.*

would happen next in the feud, and the two comic strips and their creators would benefit from a spike in publicity.

If nothing else, Eisner's contribution, "Li'l Adam," proved his mastery of the parody. In his "Spirit" Sunday newspaper insert published on July 20, 1947, Eisner told the story of the attempted murder of cartoonist Al Slapp, creator of "Li'l Adam: The Stupid Mountain Boy." The prime suspects were Elmer Hay (Harold Gray) and Hector Ghoul (Chester Gould). Eisner worked in a variety of inside jokes, known only to cartoonists working in the business, along with a biting commentary on the comics syndicates. He even worked in a comic strip within a comic strip, drawn by Feiffer—a funny parody of "Fearless Fosdick," Capp's own parody of "Dick Tracy."

In the period between Eisner's creating the story and its publication, a reporter from *Newsweek* called Eisner and asked what he was working on. Eisner told the reporter that he was feuding with Capp and had created a parody.

"When the article came out," Eisner said of the *Newsweek* piece, "I suddenly realized that Al had somehow heard about it and correctly figured it was a way to get a free ride. He had connections in all these places. But I was still so entranced by the fact that someone in his league had called me that I wasn't fully aware of what he was doing.

"What happened was he never honored the agreement. He never did anything in his strip about 'The Spirit.' I kept watching and waiting, and nothing happened. I then realized that he had euchred me into doing a parody of 'Li'l Abner' which *Newsweek* picked up, and he had been given a run of publicity. I was simply being used as a tool."

Thirty-nine years after the one-sided feud, Eisner continued to stew.

"I always harbored a kind of anger at him for doing something like that," the usually mild-mannered Eisner said. "He was always offering something interesting that never materialized."

10 GREETINGS FROM LOWER SLOBBOVIA

Capp might not have integrated the war into "Li'l Abner," but he was very active in the war effort. He managed to continue the strip without interruption, largely because of an agreement with the government. Although all three of his assistants were draft eligible, Capp used his influence to keep them stateside. He not only needed them for his own work, he argued, but he wanted to use them to help with all that he would be doing for the government.

The work was copious. When the United States entered the war, Capp joined the effort to promote war bonds. He and his staff developed a color Sunday feature initially called "Small Fry," after the diminutive lead character, but soon changed to "Small Change," a comic strip dedicated to publicizing war bonds. The public service strip ran on alternating Sundays for three years. As an honorarium for his efforts, Capp received an annual salary of one dollar.

He also contributed informational posters for those fighting the war. This proved to be more challenging than the weekly "Small Change" strip, not because Capp wasn't up to the art or the message, but because he was often dealing with serious matters that young soldiers, familiar with "Li'l Abner," might not take as seriously as the military brass intended. Capp breezed through a very large poster that explained why and how soldiers saluted one another, but a poster addressing venereal disease was shot down by the chief of chaplains for being racy.

As Capp and other cartoonists would learn, the military could be very squeamish about how sexuality was addressed. It would have been unrealistic to treat soldiers as an army of virgins, yet the depiction of condom use by comic strip artists was problematic. Nobody wanted the comics to become pornographic.

Physically handicapped, Al Capp could not serve in the military in World War II, but he provided considerable patriotic services. Here, in March 1943, he meets an army public relations staff.

Capp, who had used Li'l Abner—called "Private Li'l Abner"—in other army posters, struggled with using his comic strip's main character in a poster warning about the dangers of casual sex. In the strip, Li'l Abner could barely bring himself to kiss a woman.

"I couldn't very well point up the horrors of venereal disease without having somebody catch one," Capp recalled a few years later. "But I was damned if I'd destroy the technical perfection of my boy, even for my country."

Capp created another character, Bud Beargrease, to take Li'l Abner's place in the VD posters. Bud chased around an amply endowed woman named Anytime Annie, and the implications took off from there.

"It was wonderful," Capp remembered. "People who read it were as excited over whether Bud would or would not catch anything as they usually were over whether or not the buzz saw would cut Daisy Mae in half."

Capp's characters found their way into the war in other ways, too. Li'l Abner, Daisy Mae, Moonbeam McSwine, Wolf Gal, Sadie Hawkins, and others—even Fearless Fosdick—were painted on the noses of bombers, a tradition that would continue when the United States entered the Korean conflict.

Capp's biggest contribution was far more personal. Military hospitals in the United States housed countless soldiers seriously wounded overseas, many returning as amputees. Capp, having lost his leg at nine, knew of the anger and despair that these young men were just beginning to deal with. Capp had used the loss of his leg as motivation, and he wanted to motivate others.

By his own count, Capp visited nearly five hundred veteran hospitals throughout the war, always with the knowledge that he would have to win over each one of the amputees, none, under the circumstances, particularly caring about Capp's celebrity.

Capp's message—that the loss of a leg wouldn't prohibit you from doing almost anything a two-legged man could do—required him to address his own difficulties. He'd never learned to walk comfortably on his wooden leg; it was clear to anyone watching him that he was an amputee. He'd walk awkwardly, swinging his artificial limb forward in a manner that would embarrass him throughout his life. He couldn't very well convince others that they could look normal with artificial limbs if he staggered on his own.

So, during the wartime years, he forced himself to walk with a more natural gait that was actually quite painful for him. He would walk into an amputee ward, look at a group of silent, sullen faces, set up an easel, and begin drawing.

"I'm Al Capp," he'd say. "I draw 'Li'l Abner.' I'm supposed to entertain you slobs."

He would say very little while he sketched. Eventually, he would tell his own story about how he lost his leg as a boy, how it had been amputated far above his knee. He would pull up his pantleg and expose his wooden leg. Only then would he engage in any dialogue with the wounded soldiers. He'd ask each one which leg he'd lost. When he had finished this exercise, he'd go into his pitch.

"Everybody is worried about you slobs," he'd go on. "The Red Cross, your doctors, the Pentagon, all worried because you're just lying there. Well, I'm not worried because I know what they don't know and what you don't. I know you're men.

"M-E-N. That's what worries you guys. You're lying there, thinking you can't get the girl. Well, your worries are over. You're men, whether you've got one leg or two. I'm married. I've got two daughters and a son. Any questions?"

Capp would finish his speech, hand each man a drawing, and move on. He was convincing, especially when he walked away, confident and seemingly without effort. In his book, *Remembering Al Capp*, Al's brother Elliott wrote about how the veterans were inspired, unaware that Capp had to take a "rigorous course in walking" taught by an expert in the use of prosthetic legs.

As Elliott recalled, when the war ended, Al "resumed his starboard sway when he walked. He said he was vastly more comfortable that way."

Capp used his art to deliver a similar message to injured veterans when he created an autobiographical comic book, *Al Capp by Li'l Abner*. He took license in the telling—he portrayed himself as losing his leg as a teenager, for instance—but the story was entertaining and, more important, poignant. The comic book, distributed by the Red Cross, did not attempt to sell false hope to those whose lives had been permanently altered by the cruelty of war. Instead, by setting himself up as an example, Capp showed how one needn't be disabled by the loss of a limb. He was living proof.

Al and Catherine Capp completed their family late in 1944, when they adopted their son, Colin Cameron Capp. Named after Catherine's father but called "Kim" or "Kimmy" by the family, Colin was eight years younger than Cathie—to the day. Both had been born on September 19, Cathie in 1936, Kim in 1944. The Capps had wanted a son, but it wasn't going to happen after Catherine had to have a hysterectomy. They chose to adopt.

As an adult, Kim would speak fondly of his childhood, though he was never comfortable being the son of a celebrity, to such an extent that as a teenager he tried to keep his identity a secret.

The Capp family was easygoing, with Catherine and her staff running the household and Al acting as the reluctant disciplinarian. Every day, around five thirty, Al would return home from work, and the family would gather around the dinner table and eat their evening meal together. Catherine and the kids could almost immediately tell if Capp's work was going well: he could be moody and quiet if things were going poorly, but more often than not, he'd be boisterous and jovial.

"He would narrate what he had written for the day in Li'l Abner's dialect," Julie recalled, adding that he was "very theatrical in his presentation." He laughed uproariously at his own jokes; for the children, not yet old enough to understand the nuances of their father's satire, Capp's laughter was a cue for them to laugh along. As both Julie and Kim would recall, they thoroughly enjoyed the stories and their father's funny presentations. Family time, to all in the household, was invaluable.

This was the only aspect of his job that he brought home. Business deals and money were never discussed.

Capp encouraged his children to think freely, and he insisted that they treat their education very seriously. They were going to graduate from high school and go on to college—something Capp himself had never done. The Capp library housed all the classics, and Al would haunt the area's secondhand bookstores and antique shops for new additions. If the kids complained that there was nothing to do or, worse yet, that there was nothing on television, Capp ordered them to find a book.

Besides reading, Capp tried to pass along his love of classical music, movies, and the theater. He relished family vacations, especially those overseas, when the Capps took ocean liners to France or England. He tried to drag his kids through museums and churches, with only marginal success.

During the war years, this was still part of the future, at least for Kim. Capp might have impressed his readers as being cynical, but as a father he strove to provide his children with the type of childhood denied to him by poverty and the Depression. He bought a home, an elegant New England Georgian house surrounded by a white picket fence, a few blocks from Harvard Square, a short distance from the Harvard campus. Prior to the war he'd also purchased a sixty-five-acre farm in New Hampshire. The property was literally on the state line, a stone's throw from Amesbury, Massachusetts, where Catherine grew up. The two girls would be raised here, and in the 1950s, after the girls moved to Cambridge, it would be converted into a summer home.

As much as he doted on his family, Capp valued work above all else; other than his assistants, he had very few close friends, and, as evidenced by his lengthy trips away from home, he had no trouble picking work over family if he was forced to choose.

In its October 28, 1946, issue *Life* devoted a three-page spread to a contest in which Al Capp challenged artists to create the ugliest woman ever presented in a comic strip. The winner would receive five hundred dollars— a generous haul for the time—but it was Capp who would benefit most from what, even by his standards, would become a benchmark in product promotion.

Capp had no equal when it came to self-promotion and the promotion of his strip. For nearly a decade, he had basked in the publicity that Sadie Hawkins Day had brought "Li'l Abner." He reveled in public appearances. He was a master of working the phones and convincing magazine and newspaper editors that he had a story they needed to report. No other comic strip artist instinctively knew marketing as well. In an article devoted to Capp's contest in 1946, comics historian Rick Marschall labeled him "the most egomaniacal self-promoter in comics history. Capp "used every trick in the book to boost Li'l Abner and divert attention from other strips," Marschall explained, "and he dreamed up a promotion that was probably as duplicitous—certainly nefarious and rascally—as it was brilliant."

At the beginning of 1946, "Li'l Abner" still held its familiar position among the top five strips in the business, reaching an estimated twenty-five million readers in more than six hundred newspapers. Capp, never satisfied, wanted more, and to boost his numbers he came up with an extended project, beginning in March and ending in November. The scheme involved several loosely connected "Li'l Abner" continuities; promotion on radio and in newspapers and magazines; the writing of an "Abner"-related song, to be performed by some of the most popular recording artists of the day; a contest challenging artists to come up with a character for the strip; and, in one of his most ambitious moves to date, the creation of a fictitious nation that, in time, would become a treasured part of "Li'l Abner" lore. Capp's work during this period led comics scholar and editor Dave Schreiner to remark that "Li'l Abner" in 1946 was "possibly the strip's strongest run, period."

It began with a story about Lester Gooch, Capp's creator of "Fearless Fosdick." Gooch, in response to a fan letter from Li'l Abner, went searching for the world's ugliest woman. He traveled to a godforsaken country called Lower Slobbovia, a land encrusted in snow and ice, and populated by miserable people continually endangered by starvation and hungry wolves. Capp's Lower Slobbovia, as revealed over the weeks, had its own national anthem, its own strange dialect (that sounded like a fractured combination of English and Yiddish, with a dash of Russian), and its own unique laws and customs. Even after Lester Gooch was arrested and jailed for refusing to marry Lena the Hyena, the grotesquely ugly woman he'd been seeking to meet, Capp continued to roam free through this newly created country and offer his unique, satirical observations on a country so poor as to make Dogpatch look like an exemplar of the high life.

Capp took matters a step further in June, when he finally had Li'l Abner visit Lower Slobbovia and encounter Lena. The notoriously girl-shy Dogpatcher found himself caught in the same predicament that trapped Lester Gooch earlier in the story. Lower Slobbovians kept Lena locked away, lest horrible things happen to those innocents who actually set eyes on her, and according to the law, the first man who cast his eyes on her was obliged to marry her. This was not good news for Li'l Abner, whose hair literally stood on end when he got his first glimpse of her.

Capp was too clever to allow readers to see just how hideous Lena was. Instead, every time she appeared in a panel, he had her head concealed by a white box emblazoned with the message "Deleted by Editor." This form of censorship, Capp advised his readers, was imposed by subscribing newspaper editors who judged Lena's looks to be "too terrifying, depressing or nauseating for family readership."

Readers demanded a look at just how ugly this woman was—precisely the response Capp wanted. Lena, he announced to the public, was too hideous for him to draw, but if anyone out there cared to take a whack at it . . . thus the national contest was born. Artists were encouraged to submit their interpretation of what the world's ugliest woman might look like, with a

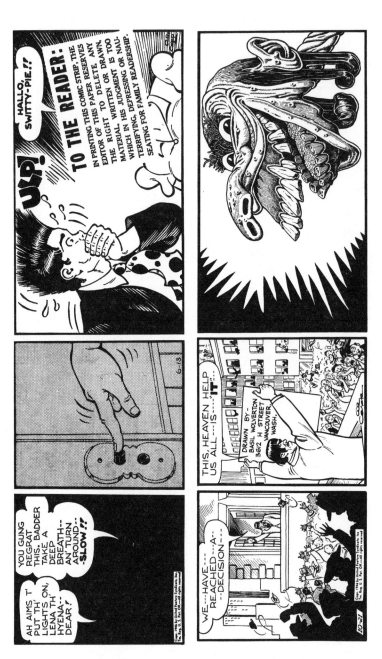

A 1946 "Li'l Abner" sequence focused on Lena the Hyena, the ugliest woman in the world. An image of her face purportedly had to be censored by newspaper editors, in fact leading to a highly publicized contest to imagine what she might look like. Cartoonist Basil Wolverton won with this monstrosity.

$500 prize going to the winner. A panel of three judges would make the final decision. Local newspapers got into the act as well, sponsoring their own contests and awarding prizes to subscribers.

But Capp was just getting started. Something had to save Li'l Abner from the forced marriage, and for this he came up with another unique form of self-promotion: he created a song, "Li'l Abner, Don't Marry That Girl"—to be sung on the radio, on programs that Li'l Abner was certain to hear, even in the outreaches of Lower Slobbovia. Capp wrote the lyrics and, through an acquaintance, found someone to write the music. The promotion then hit the airwaves in an unprecedented way. On successive nights, Frank Sinatra, Kate Smith, Jack Smith, Fred Waring, and Danny Kaye sang the song on their popular radio programs. Bob Hope also had the song performed on his show. When a recording of the song became available, "Li'l Abner" readers rushed to stores to purchase it.

Back in Lower Slobbovia, when Lena heard the song, along with Daisy Mae's plea for Li'l Abner to stay single, she volunteered to dump Li'l Abner so he would be free to marry the woman who truly loved him. Once again, Abner avoided marriage in the eleventh hour.

Contest entries flooded into the United Feature offices—a million, according to *Time* magazine, a half million, according to *Life*, though the figures were undoubtedly inflated. For his celebrity panel of judges, Capp persuaded Sinatra, actor Boris Karloff, and surrealist painter Salvador Dalí to subject themselves to the stacks of entries. All the women in Lower Slobbovia were homely, Capp instructed his trio of judges; their selection had to set a new standard for the word "ugly."

The winner, created by comic book artist Basil Wolverton, fit the description, bearing only the slightest trace of human facial characteristics.

Lena, of course, would have been the perfect candidate to enter the annual Sadie Hawkins Day festivities, and Capp devised a way to make it happen. Lena wound up visiting Dogpatch and staying as a guest of the Yokums, and she and the Wolf Gal entered the eagerly anticipated Sadie Hawkins race. Thus concluded one of Capp's most ambitious years in the strip.

11 THE SHMOO, THE KIGMY, AND ALL ONE CARTOONIST COULD EVER WANT

On November 29, 1947, the *New Yorker* presented the first installment of a two-part Al Capp profile. Taken as a whole, the biographical and professional retrospective was by far the lengthiest magazine piece to date about a cartoonist. Capp had recently won the prestigious Billy DeBeck Memorial Award (later renamed the Reuben Award, after one of Capp's heroes, Rube Goldberg), and the *New Yorker* was intrigued by the overwhelming popularity of the artist.

The *New Yorker*'s interest extended beyond Capp himself, to the idea of comics as a pop cultural phenomenon. Writer E. J. Kahn Jr. cited figures that were bound to impress—or alarm—even the stuffiest reader.

In the decade between 1937 and 1946, Kahn wrote, comics had supplanted motion pictures and radio as the most popular form of American entertainment. "Every month, nearly forty million comic books are bought and presumably read. Every day, seventy million people, or half the population of the country, are reported to read, openly or furtively, comic strips in the newspaper." Exact figures, Kahn added, were impossible to calculate, given the syndicates' habit of inflating the numbers of their readers, but in the end, "any analysis of such statistics is apt to bring on a headache."

Placed in the context of such a burgeoning business, Capp was an ideal profile subject. He was perceptive, thoughtful and, as always, funny. Capp, for a change, kept his stories within screaming distance of actual fact, although Kahn advised *New Yorker* readers, early in the profile's first installment, that Capp's imagination and memory were always at odds, with his imagination usually winning out at the end of the day.

"Capp regards himself as a storyteller, not a mere cartoonist," Kahn wrote, "and he is unable to tell any story, including that of his life, without embellishing his remarks with harmless and diverting fictions."

The profile caught Capp in fine form, moving smoothly from topic to topic, whether he was talking about the events of his youth or his fear of losing his hair, his suit with United Feature Syndicate or his background with Ham Fisher. He reflected on the origins of "Li'l Abner" and offered a bird's-eye view of how the strip was worked out in his studio. Capp would be the subject of many profiles and interviews in years to come, but he would never be as informative and entertaining as he was in this one.

Capp was well aware of the huge sums "Li'l Abner" was earning for United Feature Syndicate. His contract with the company was much more generous than most comic strip artists would dream of, with an escalating pay scale that made him the highest-compensated cartoonist in the business. Most comic strip artists took 50 percent of what the syndicates took in. By 1947, Capp commanded 65 percent of the take, with an additional 5 percent raise due in January 1949.

Capp still wasn't satisfied. The arrangement, he thought, was all wrong. Syndicates viewed comic strip artists as private contractors, but the syndicates held the copyrights on their creations, just as comic book companies owned the work of their artists. There were rare exceptions, such as Will Eisner, who owned all of his nongovernment work, including his popular feature "The Spirit," or Capp's old friend Milton Caniff, who quit producing his "Terry and the Pirates" strip over ownership disputes, only to start up "Steve Canyon," which he owned. For Capp, there were also merchandising perks that very few artists enjoyed: "Li'l Abner" had scored an impressive assortment of commercial endorsements, toys, clothing, comic books, and other merchandise, all of which brought in a substantial monetary reward to Capp and United Feature.

Capp resented paying the syndicate more than he felt it deserved. Syndicates, he felt, should be treated like agents, rather than owners, and their share of the profits should compare to the percentages taken in by literary agents, typically in the 10 to 20 percent range. After all, they were selling the work, not publishing it.

The comic book business offered its own examples of the sort of practices that Capp considered to be grossly unfair, most notably in the

case of Jerry Siegel and Joe Shuster, the young Cleveland duo who created Superman, who were struggling with ownership issues over their
creation. Siegel and Shuster found themselves trapped in a work-for-hire
arrangement that paid them a relative pittance while their publisher
earned a fortune on the comic book industry's most important creation of
all time.

Capp arrived at his conclusions after conducting considerable private
research—inquiries and research that went well beyond the usual cartoonists' kibitzing and complaining at National Cartoonists Society meetings.
Capp called publishers and editors of newspapers subscribing to "Li'l Abner" and asked about the terms of business. He haunted publishing parties
and conventions, where he talked shop with writers, editors, and agents.
When United Feature learned of these activities, it sent its own people to
intercept Capp and engage him in conversation before he got too far along
with his research. Capp battled back. He started attending these events with
a beautiful woman on each arm; their job was to distract the United Feature
people while Capp made his getaway.

The standard business practice, Capp learned, was that sales personnel would offer a comic strip to unsubscribing newspapers or, in the case
of exceptionally popular strips like "Li'l Abner," "Little Orphan Annie,"
"Blondie," and others, newspaper editors would approach United Feature
and request syndicate rates. The rates were based on a newspaper's circulation and location, with large-circulation papers in big cities paying premium
prices for the strips (often extracting exclusivity within a geographic radius
in the deal) and smaller-circulation papers getting the strips at lower rates.
Capp was curious about the sales tactics used by United Feature. Did the
syndicate's sales staff put as much effort into corralling small newspapers,
where the money would be relatively small, as they put into the larger circulation papers, where the payoff was substantially greater?

There was also the issue of the syndicates' expectations for the life and
success of any given strip. Comic strip artists were offered contracts based
on the belief that a strip had a limited life span.

"There was an unwritten law that a successful strip had a life span of
12 years," Capp explained in an interview late in his life. "I think that was
Bill Conselman's rule—he wrote 'Ella Cinders'—and it was figured that a

strip had had it after a dozen years. Of course after 10 years I was going better than ever."

Throughout his research, Capp was busy putting together a strategy for his next move. United Feature was aware of his querying editors, publishers, and salesmen about business practices, and the higher-ups at the syndicate had heard him voice at least halfhearted threats about withholding a couple of weeks' worth of strips until he was better compensated, so he had to develop a new approach if he expected to overcome the odds and wrest control of his creative work before his contract with United Feature expired in 1954.

Capp consulted with his attorneys and, on July 10, 1947, filed suit against the United Feature Syndicate and United Press International, the syndicate's parent company. In the suit, Capp charged the syndicate with failing to use its best efforts in selling the "Li'l Abner" strip and failing to obtain prices "consonant with its popularity and commercial value." The suit sought $14 million in compensation and damages and, more important, the reassignment to Capp of all rights to "Li'l Abner."

As daring as the lawsuit seemed—a syndicate might have removed a lesser-known artist from his strip and continued it, using a replacement artist—Capp was told that he had a good chance of winning the suit or at least settling it out of court. United Feature couldn't afford to take a $14 million hit, and even if it felt like gambling, the attendant publicity would be a public relations nightmare.

Capp went on the offensive in his strip, too. In two Sunday installments of "Li'l Abner," Capp struck back at the comics industry in a scalding parody of Siegel and Shuster's problems (and, to those in the know, his own trials at United Feature), in which two young comic strip artists, creators of the immensely popular "Jack Jawbreaker" comic strip, were being used and abused by the heartless Squeezeblood Syndicate.

It was either a courageous or foolhardy move. Capp was not only ripping his syndicate, but he was also expecting the syndicate to distribute his parody to its hundreds of subscribing newspapers and thus tens of millions of readers.

United Feature distributed the strips.

* * *

Comics, particularly comic books, were coming under attack at this time, largely due to the efforts of Fredric Wertham, a German-born psychiatrist whose anticomics crusade received widespread media attention. In 1948, he was just beginning a relentless attack that would culminate in the 1954 publication of *Seduction of the Innocent*, a book-length screed that attempted to connect comic books with juvenile crime. A natural storyteller, Wertham used anecdotes, rather than statistics and scientific methods, to underscore his points. In the March 27, 1948, issue of *Collier's*, journalist Judith Crist, in an article titled "Horror in the Nursery," gave Wertham his first significant forum in a mass-circulation periodical, and he spun his stories about how comics had influenced all kinds of delinquent behavior. Wertham was not interested in hearing from those in his profession who didn't share his feelings; he was a self-appointed opponent of comics, spokesman for concerned parents, and advocate for immediate action against those producing these offensive materials. "The time has come to legislate these books off the newsstands and out of the candy stores," he proclaimed.

This was hardly the first time that an individual or group called for government intervention against perceived dangers in comics. Opposition had been around since the advent of comic strips in newspapers and, more recently, the wide distribution of comic books. Because of careful scrutiny by cautious syndicates and the watchful eyes of subscribing newspaper editors, comic strips were largely sanitized. But the comic book industry, not subject to such screening, had managed to produce huge quantities of bold and unfettered content with impunity. By the late forties and early fifties America's newsstands proliferated with "true" crime and horror comic books replete with bloody and explicitly violent images, walking decomposing corpses, and similar content, which most parents, if they were paying attention, would have certainly found unsuitable for their children. But comic books retailed for only ten cents, there were no age restrictions on their sale, and children of any age had easy access to them.

While such comics had been a source of some concern for a while, Wertham was a skilled writer and pop psychiatrist, and his articles over the next few years, many appearing in popular magazines, touched off a national debate, leading to the 1954 establishment of a comics code that oversaw the content of every comic book appearing on the market.

On the evening of Tuesday, March 2, 1948, Capp appeared on *America's Town Meeting of the Air*, a weekly radio program broadcast by ABC. A four-member panel, moderated by George V. Denny, addressed the topic "What's Wrong with the Comics?" The audience packed into New York's Town Hall for the live broadcast, anticipating a spirited discussion, was not shortchanged.

John Mason Brown, a drama critic, author, and columnist for the *Saturday Review of Literature*, spoke first, and he minced no words.

"I deplore them and, to continue the understatement, I abhor them," he said of comics. He had read them, he conceded, and he'd gone as far as to permit his two sons to read them whenever it would "subdue" the boys on train rides, or when he needed peace and quiet at home. He hated doing this, he confessed, because reading comics was a poor substitute for reading books. Comics were a form of trash, and even if he had to allow that trash was "part of every healthy diet," comics were "the lowest, most despicable, and most harmful and unethical form of trash."

He was only warming up.

"Most comics, as I see them, are the marijuana of the nursery!" he exclaimed, to the merriment of his audience. "They are the bane of the bassinet! They are the horror of the home, the curse of the kids, and a threat to the future!"

George J. Hecht, publisher of *Parents* magazine, as well as several educational comics geared to young readers, followed Brown. Comics, he pointed out, were exceedingly popular: 91 percent of boys and girls between six and seventeen read comics. In a measured speech, he argued that comics had been used as educational tools for children and military personnel and that there were "good comic magazines and bad comics just as there are good books and bad books, good motion pictures and bad motion pictures." He suggested that the comics industry should police itself.

"There is nothing wrong with comics that good publishing cannot and will not correct," he concluded.

Hecht had already done his part to back his words. Back in 1941, he had launched his comic book series, *True Comics*, to offer an exciting yet wholesome alternative to the action and superhero comics that had burst on the market since the creation of such phenomenal superheroes as Superman and Batman. In its first issue, *True Comics* had offered stories of Simón Bolívar and Winston Churchill. But Hecht hadn't been satisfied with simply offering interesting content that parents would approve of: he created advisory boards for the comic book, with such child movie stars as Mickey Rooney and Shirley Temple on board to keep him informed as to what kind of materials kids wanted to see. Later that same year, another publisher started up *Classic Comics*, a series of comics adaptations of classic literature. The title would be changed to *Classics Illustrated* in 1947.

Journalist Marya Mannes was up next, with more fearmongering about the link between comics and juvenile delinquency, backed by outlandish statistics.

"Comic books are the addiction of three out of four American homes," she stated, without bothering to mention where she obtained this statistic. "In one out of three American homes they are virtually the only reading matter. Repeat, the ONLY reading matter."

Comics, in her mind, were killers: "I believe that a steady, uncontrolled and indiscriminate diet of comic books can stunt a child's mental and spiritual growth just as much as a steady malnutrition can stunt his physical growth."

This was familiar territory for Mannes. A year earlier, in "Junior Has a Craving," an essay published in the February 17, 1947, issue of *New Republic*, Mannes had submitted a similar approach in condemning the effects the growing interest in comics was having on young readers. Comics, she wrote, were "the greatest intellectual narcotic on the market," and the time that children spent reading them was time in which "all inner growth is stopped."

By the time Al Capp finally had his say, he was fully prepared for battle. He began by noting that, as a drama critic, Brown possessed no special qualifications to talk about comics.

What, Capp wondered, would kids say if the topic of the evening had been "What's Wrong with Drama Critics?"

"Drama critics are not only the bane of the bassinet," he suggested, mocking Brown's earlier statement, "they're the didey service of the nursery . . .

"Of course," he went on, "as any fool can plainly see, these kids would be wrong because kids just aren't the best judges of dramatic critics. And this point occurred to me during Mr. Brown's speech: dramatic critics just aren't the best judges of kids."

Capp asked the audience to envision a father, mother, and their eleven-year-old son sitting in a living room and discussing what they'd read in the day's newspaper. No one had to guess where Capp was heading with this anecdote. The parents, objecting to their son's reading comics, order him to look at the news.

"I did, Pop," the kid replies. "And oh boy, it's full of murder and crime and violence and S-E-X, too, Pop."

Perhaps, the father counters, it might be best if his son put down the paper in favor of a classic book. He pulls books from the shelves—*Oliver Twist, Treasure Island, Kidnapped, Alice in Wonderland*, even Shakespeare. All contain violence and mayhem. By the time the father has destroyed all the objectionable books in the house, all that remains is the phone book.

Outraged by Capp's comparing the violence in comics to that in great literature, and by Capp's assertion that Dickens might have written comics if he were alive today, Marya Mannes used much of her allotted rebuttal time to attack Capp personally. "I'd just like to say that Mr. Capp has plenty of humor but little humility," she told the audience. "Otherwise, he wouldn't speak of himself and Dickens in the same breath, because Dickens is a creative artist and Mr. Capp is a conveyor belt."

The debate touched off a furious reaction. ABC received more than six thousand letters—the most ever received by the program. It was covered in *Newsweek* and the *Saturday Review of Literature*, which also published an essay entitled "A Half-Century of Comic Art," a snarky piece that played into the argument that comics were inferior art for inferior minds. "As drawing comic art is of the same genre as the doodles or sketches schoolboys pencil on the margins of geography books, or ebullient sales men on restaurant menus," the essay's author wrote. As for those reading comic strips, "one is not required to be either a child or a dolt, although conceivably it helps. One is required, however, to relax for the fun of it, to turn off the intellect like a faucet so as not to dampen the comics' earthy vivacity."

Comments such as these annoyed Capp no end. Comics, he insisted, then and always, were fine art, whether critics wanted to acknowledge it or not. If young people enjoyed "Li'l Abner," that was fine, but the stories and commentary were aimed at older readers.

Capp was fired up, inspired enough to create a brief "Li'l Abner Fights for His Rights" strip, in which Li'l Abner, horrified to learn that the Dogpatch Mammys' Club had declared "Fearless Fosdick" "bad fo' chillen on account they is full o' crime," argues that fairy tales like "Jack and the Beanstalk" and the stories of Edgar Allan Poe are full of violence, mayhem, and crime. The Dogpatch Mammys' Club, after hearing Li'l Abner's argument, concludes that "those psy-cho-logists is jest trying to make a soft dollar by frighten' us pore mammys."

This was the kind of skirmish that Capp relished. Comics' opponents, who could be pompous, self-righteous, sanctimonious, paranoid, overly protective, and mean-spirited, were ideal targets for ridicule, Dogpatch style. Capp's following had bestowed upon him, by sheer numbers, a power that he was happy to wield.

The war, however, was only beginning.

When readers turned to their newspaper's August 29, 1948, comics section and saw the beginning of a new "Li'l Abner" story, they could not possibly have been prepared for the response that one little strip would face in the following months. Al Capp himself couldn't have predicted it.

The story began with Li'l Abner awakening from a dream in Ole Man Mose's cave. The sound of "strange moosic" brought him out of the cave and eventually to the Valley of the Shmoon, home to millions of creatures capable of making the sound Li'l Abner had heard. Ole Man Mose had attempted to describe the shmoo to Li'l Abner, cautioning that the creature was "th' greatest menace to hoomanity th' world has ever known," and explaining that it was dangerous because of its goodness. Abner, naturally, was too stupid to listen.

"Why did I call it a shmoo?" Capp wrote later. "You wouldn't call a moose anything but a moose, would you? I called the shmoo a shmoo because that's what it was. I didn't have any message—except that it's good to be alive."

The lovable shmoo, introduced in "Li'l Abner" on August 29, 1948, captured the public's heart in unprecedented fashion. This strip ran September 10 of that same year.

The story was one of the most convoluted Capp would ever tell, full of twists and turns, interrupted narratives, non sequiturs, and just plain nonsense, all serving to introduce the reader to a lovable creature that, in years to come, would earn Capp millions of dollars. The shmoo was a little animal that rose out of another one of Capp's "what if" ideas: what if humans never had to work again, if their needs for food, shelter, and clothing were guaranteed without their having to lift a finger to earn them?

Shaped like a bowling pin, with feet (but no hands), whiskers, big eyes, and an endearing smile, the shmoo was a creature designed to serve. It could lay eggs, bottled milk, cakes, sticks of butter, and any number of other foodstuffs with no effort. If a human looked at a shmoo as if he or she were hungry, the shmoo would die of joy and serve as the person's meal. If you broiled them, they tasted like steak; if you fried them, they tasted like chicken. They were boneless, so there was no waste. Their whiskers could be used as toothpicks, their eyes as buttons. Their hides could be made into cloth or leather, depending upon how you sliced them. They could also be cut into lumber. They didn't eat, so their upkeep was absolutely free. Best of all, they reproduced faster than they could be used.

Li'l Abner was thrilled when he saw their sheer numbers in the Valley of the Shmoon.

"Wif these around, nobody won't nevah hafta work no more!" he shouted, kicking up his heels. "All hoomanity kin now live off th' fat o' th' land—namely shmoos!!"

The joyful reception of the shmoo in Dogpatch was offset by the concern they caused businesses. What would become of Soft-Hearted John, whose general store had been ripping off Dogpatchers for as long as anyone could remember, or, more to the point, J. Roaringham Fatback, the pork tycoon? Meanwhile, in the larger world, the shmoo continuity was being debated almost as soon as it appeared in the papers. What was Capp really saying? Was he promoting socialism with these creatures? Capitalism? *Time*, *Life*, *Newsweek*, and other publications weighed in with their analysis.

The public reaction to the shmoo, sudden and combustible, was unprecedented in comic strip history. Fan mail overwhelmed the United Feature mailroom; members of the media fell over each other in a rush to find the next angle to the overnight sensation. It was an election year, and Thomas Dewey, the Republican hoping to unseat Harry S. Truman as president, accused the incumbent of promising "everything including the Shmoo" in exchange for the vote. Simon & Schuster offered Capp a bundle for the rights to reprint the story (selling over a million copies of a paperback collection); Capp Enterprises, a newly created family company, formed after Capp's successful battle with the syndicate, negotiated with manufacturers clamoring for the rights to market a wide range of shmoo-related merchandise. Within a year, Capp would be standing alongside Harry Truman as the newly elected president presented a special savings bond certificate decorated with the shmoo—an enterprise that Capp devoted an entire Sunday "Li'l Abner" strip to advertise. The "Capp-italist Revolution," as *Life* called the shmoo phenomenon, had begun.

The shmoo even became involved in international politics. The Cold War was just beginning, and in April 1948 the Soviet Union had blocked the roads leading into Berlin, in response to the Marshall Plan—a plan designed to help Europe recover from the ravages of World War II while holding Communism at bay. The Berlin blockade might have looked like a bold political move on the international chessboard, but it meant much more than that to the people in Berlin, trapped without food, medicine, clothing, and other provisions. Truman responded to the blockade with a massive airlift that parachuted tons of food and provisions into Berlin every day.

The Seventeenth Military Air Transport Squadron, responsible for the airlift operations, approached Capp in September. Besides its regular duties, the squadron privately sponsored the morale-boosting Operation Little Vittles, which involved dropping candy to the city's children. The bags of candy would float down on specially designed parachutes.

Operation Little Vittles hoped Capp would contribute plastic shmoos filled with chocolates to the cause—a proposal Capp gladly accepted—and a plane, bound for Frankfurt and carrying about one hundred candy-filled shmoos, left LaGuardia Airport on October 13.

Capp basked in the publicity that the shmoo brought "Li'l Abner," and Capp Enterprises, celebrating its first anniversary, pushed hard to accommodate the increasing demand for shmoo-related commercial products. Capp complained, tongue in cheek, that the shmoo was costing him his sanity: he was constantly badgered in public, by everyone from waiters in restaurants to people in the street, all wanting more shmoo stories than he could provide, all quick with jokes and puns about the little creatures.

"My first sensation was the joy of having made the shmoo," Capp told *Time*. "Then came the feeling of annoyance. I've been subjected to all the shmoo jokes in the world, like 'there's good shmoos tonight,' and I mustn't say go-to-hell to anybody. Now I'm delighted again, having read that the shmoo has all sorts of economic meanings."

The shmoo story continued until December 22, making it one of the longer-running "Li'l Abner" continuities yet—and there would be more to follow. The annual Sadie Hawkins festivities were absorbed into the first shmoo story, as was another item that attracted great reader attention.

Beginning on October 11, 1948, Capp hid the words "Nancy O" in almost every daily strip. He remained silent on what it meant, but the "Nancy O" mystery continued, unbelievably enough, until May 1951. Every day, readers would scan the rocks, trees, buildings, and even characters' clothing until the words appeared. In the past, Capp had demonstrated that he would go to almost any lengths to gain a reader's attention and fidelity to his strip; the "Nancy O" mystery continued the tradition.

Although he would feign annoyance over the overwhelming response to the shmoo, Capp couldn't wait to follow it up. The shmoo had been generous to death—literally—and this generosity had offered Capp countless ways to comment on human laziness, greed, avarice, and other foibles. What else was out there?

The answer was the kigmy, a short, squat, hunched-over creature whose biggest joy in life was a strong, swift kick in the hind end. The kigmy was the answer to human anger, frustration, aggression, disappointment, hostility, and sorrow. Rather than lash out at other human beings (or even inanimate objects), people could kick kigmies in the rump, relieving tension and pleasing their targets at the same time.

The kigmy was introduced in the last will and testament of Uncle Honeysuckle Yokum, before he was hanged for murder. The document offered what he called "mah Sure-Fire, It-never-Fails plan fo' peace."

There was a flaw in human thinking, Yokum claimed. People everywhere assumed that humans wanted to be nice to one another when, in fact, the opposite was true. People loved to kick each other around; it gave them a feeling of superiority. But therein was the rub: the kick demanded retaliation.

"And there yo' has the cause of all Trouble, and War," Honeysuckle Yokum concluded.

As a parting gesture, Yokum was leaving humanity fifty million kigmies, "a handy-sized li'l critter I have developed, who loves to be kicked. A kigmy is built for kicking—he yearns for it. The harder and more viciously you kick a kigmy, the happier the li'l varmint is."

But what would such a creature look like? Capp drew dozens of prototypes, rejecting his first idea almost immediately after he sketched it. The first kigmy was human, smaller than average, with a black face, large nose, and beard. It was guaranteed to offend just about anyone.

"Since the Kigmy was to be a kickable minority," Capp wrote in notes about the evolution of the kigmy, "it was only natural that the True Kigmy be a colored Jew."

After setting aside that idea, Capp developed other very human-looking models, some clothed and some not, some with targets on their butts, others not. Capp tossed these ideas aside because they looked too much like people, "and the whole idea of the Kigmy," as he saw it, "was that he was to be a substitute for people." It was imperative, he felt, "to get away from the human look and still retain the pitifulness and lovableness of little and kicked-around humanity."

He ruminated over how he would distinguish between male and female kigmies, and whether they would have children. Weeks turned into months.

"I doodled Kigmies on trains, at the phone, on table-cloths, and on menus," he'd remember. "None of 'em seemed to come out right. The IDEA was completely formed in my mind. I had known for a long time about the function of the Kigmy."

He finally settled on a small, rotund creature with such human features as a face capable of expression, and hands and feet, but it was also furry, except for a bald patch on its butt. Its gender was determined by its clothing. It might have been a distant cousin of the shmoo.

Readers did not respond to the kigmy the way they had to the shmoo. Capp and the United Feature Syndicate saw to it that this new creation received plenty of publicity, but the reception was, at best, lukewarm. Capp even brought the shmoo and the kigmy together in a holiday strip published at the end of the year, but the kigmy just didn't take off like its cousin.

One of Capp's greatest strengths had been his keen understanding of what amused his readers, but he must have known that it was unrealistic to expect the kigmy to be another marketing sensation like he one he'd enjoyed with the shmoo. He had no reason to complain. At a time when

In 1949, a year after the shmoo phenomenon, Al Capp created a new creature, the kigmy, who loved to be kicked. His initial concept drew on stereotypes of Jews and African Americans—two minorities frequently kicked around. From this starting point, the kigmy evolved into a much more generic creature.

comics had taken a dip in popularity, "Li'l Abner" was riding the crest of a wave of reader interest—and for good reason. "Li'l Abner" had reached creative maturity, in story and artwork alike.

Capp might have been disappointed by the kigmy's reception, but he had other things on his mind. He was in love again. For the first time since his prolonged affair with Nina Luce, Capp had found a woman who caught his attention in a way that made him consider, although only briefly, whether he should leave Catherine and his children for life with another woman.

The woman, Carol Saroyan, wife of the writer/playwright William

Saroyan, was vivacious, passionate, bright, and beautiful, and her New York City proximity made Capp's pursuit of the affair logistically much less troublesome than his previous long-distance relationship with Nina Luce. The Saroyans had a tempestuous marriage, and the two were separated in July, when Capp met Carol through Leila Hadley, a publicist who counted Capp Enterprises as a client.

Capp was in love, but there were complications. The Saroyans had two children, and the couple's relationship, although fractured to the extent of their filing for divorce, was mercurial. The two barely spoke to each other one day, and on the next they were considering reconciliation.

Capp ignored the potential pitfalls. He concealed the affair from Catherine, but it was hardly a secret elsewhere. William Saroyan, for one, was well aware that Capp was involved with his wife, and jealous of the man who might become his replacement once the divorce became final.

However, Capp was not to become Carol's next husband. Once again he couldn't bring himself to leave his family. He loved his children and, if he was being totally honest with himself, he still had strong feelings for Catherine. For all of his wandering ways, he still missed his family when he was away for any length of time, and he still sent Catherine letters expressing his love. Whenever he thought of leaving her, he knew it wasn't possible.

He also knew he couldn't carry on with Carol indefinitely. This was quite apparent when the holiday season rolled around, William Saroyan returned to New York, and Capp found himself jockeying for Carol's time. Saroyan wanted to spend time with his children during the season, and the scheduling of picking up and dropping off the kids conflicted with some of the time Capp allotted for Carol. As it was, he was trying to keep a low profile around Carol while Saroyan was around, but for all his efforts, the comings and goings were sloppy, leading to unpleasant scenes between Carol and her increasingly jealous and distraught husband. Carol had custody of the children, but she could ill afford to upset her husband in ways that would look bad if he decided to challenge the arrangement in court.

Capp had never been in such a volatile situation. Saroyan would write a letter to Capp, stating that he was willing to let Capp marry his wife for the sake of their children's welfare, but then he'd have second thoughts and refuse to send it. The Saroyans would go out together for an evening, conclude it with sex, and then consider traveling to Europe together the following summer. It was dizzying.

On January 24, 1950, Carol called her former husband from the hotel room where she and Capp were staying, and Capp wound up being dragged into a long, bizarre conversation with Saroyan. Capp told him that he loved Carol and intended to marry her after he divorced Catherine—a course of action he had no intention of taking. After considering the conversation, Saroyan wrote a letter to Carol, which he copied and sent to Capp, in which he protested the affair as being a negative influence on the children. He allowed that he expected Carol to move on with her social life after the divorce, but carrying on "an open and notorious affair with a married man" was an entirely different matter. The children, he maintained, were confused.

"With the immeasurable harm already inflicted on our children, I cannot stand by impassively and permit a continuation of these destructive conditions," Saroyan wrote, concluding that he wanted custody of the children and was reluctantly willing to take Carol to court.

Saroyan enclosed a brief cover letter with the copy he sent to Capp, in which he implored Capp to use his influence "to help her to make the important decision which confronts her."

Capp bowed out of the relationship shortly after receiving the letter.

Work, as always, stabilized his life. "Li'l Abner" and "Abbie an' Slats" kept him busy on a daily basis, and the surge in merchandizing demanded more attention than ever. Shmoo merchandise was still selling at a brisk pace, and new kigmy items were being developed. Capp would have preferred to let his brother Bence oversee the day-to-day operations of Capp Enterprises, but he never trusted him to make crucial decisions on contracts and new products.

Capp Enterprises presented a convincing case for the complaint Capp had voiced in his lawsuit against United Feature, that the syndicate had neglected to exploit the full marketing potential of "Li'l Abner." The early postsuit returns were modest, mostly the result of "Li'l Abner" comic book sales, which had previously been licensed to Harvey Comics, with a tiny net return to Capp. Elliott Caplin, a comics writer himself, with connections to *Parents* magazine, supervised the comic book production via the Capp-family-owned Toby Press, and while sales figures on these reconfigured and colorized reprints of the syndicated "Li'l Abner" strips were respectable, they were hardly earth-shattering. The shmoo marketing blitz reached a whole new level. According to figures published by *Editor & Publisher*, by July 1949, just under a year from the shmoo's initial appearance in "Li'l Abner," Capp Enterprises boasted of nearly one hundred different products made by seventy-five different manufacturers, with more on the way.

Bence Capp—or Jerry, as he was often called—Capp Enterprises' treasurer and general manager, sounded much like his older brother when joshing with reporters about the company's success. The shmoo items, he moaned, were "nothing but a menace . . . They're making us millionaires. And nobody likes millionaires."

The creativity in the marketing of the shmoo set a standard for comic strip merchandising. There were shmoo clocks, purses, wallets, dolls, salt and pepper shakers, air fresheners, key rings, nesting dolls, ashtrays, glasses, clothing items, and greeting cards; only Walt Disney could boast of a comparable marketing style. The shmoo balloons alone sold more than five million units. New products were constantly being developed. The shmoo, Al Capp noted, had taken on a life of its own—a positive development, undoubtedly, for Capp Enterprises but a bit of an albatross for the cartoonist, who was now dealing with a constant clamor for more shmoo adventures in the comic strip. As if to remind the Capp Enterprises staff of priorities, the walls and desks in the Capp Enterprises offices bore signs proclaiming, "The strip comes first."

There were bound to be glitches as the strip crossed over into commercial territory. United Feature Syndicate, recipient of a percentage of gross merchandise sales under its settlement with Capp, was not pleased when, during the celebration of the first anniversary of the shmoo's appearance in "Li'l Abner," Procter & Gamble and Al Capp announced a shmoo-naming contest, with $50,000 in prizes to be awarded to contestants turning in entries using only the letters present in "Ivory Snow," "Duz," and "Dreft"—all Procter & Gamble soap products. An ad for the contest, inserted in all but one newspaper subscribing to "Li'l Abner," as well as in 340 nonsubscribing papers, featured a "Li'l Abner" strip specially created for the ad, along with the promise from Capp that he would include hints on how to name the shmoo in his regular strip.

As Capp saw it, the contest was another reader participation event, not unlike the previous Lena the Hyena competition—in short, good publicity for the strip and the syndicate. United Feature disagreed. The syndicate had received what it described as "a flurry of letters" from subscribing newspaper editors protesting the crossover from comic strip to advertisement.

The protests began as an answer to an innocuous July 16, 1949, article, "'Li'l Abner' Sideline Is Shmoopendous," in *Editor & Publisher*. The reporter had gushed about the steamrolling success of Capp Enterprises and Toby Press, the Capp-run publisher set up in March to handle the publication and sales of "Abner"-related comic books. The article, appearing before the shmoo-naming contest was announced, drew the ire of A. H. Kirchhofer, the managing editor of the *Buffalo Evening News*. In separate letters to United Feature and Capp, Kirchhofer strenuously objected to Capp Enterprises' profiting from comic strip characters appearing in newspapers. The subscribing papers were already paying for the strips; they felt that their exclusivity to "Li'l Abner" as a feature had been diluted and compromised, and now they were acting as advertisers for other highly profitable endeavors.

"We think this is commercialism gone hog wild, and cashing in on the popularity of a strip which is brought to the attention of the public through newspaper publication," Kirchhofer complained.

He was just as pointed in his letter to Capp: "We think that an editorial feature should not be mixed with an advertising scheme. It is a matter of very great regret to us to see that this has been done in the case of 'Li'l Abner.'"

The announcement of the contest set off angry letters from others. *Editor & Publisher* covered the flap with four lengthy articles. Capp Enterprises waited until the third had appeared before responding. Bence Capp, writing the rebuttal, defended the contest as a benefit to newspapers. The publicity, he argued, was good for everyone.

"If through the use of a campaign instrument such as the Procter & Gamble contest through a period of five slow circulation months we can excite, humor and interest millions of people in Li'l Abner and consequently in the newspaper that carries Li'l Abner, then we think we are assisting the newspaper which is the home of the Li'l Abner strip," he wrote.

Ironically, although caught in the middle of the dispute, United Feature received no remuneration in connection with the contest, and prior to the objections from the newspapers, the syndicate had prohibited Capp from making any mention of the contest in the daily and Sunday strips. United Feature was in no position to prohibit Capp Enterprises from pursuing income tied into "Li'l Abner," but there had to be a line drawn between editorial and commercial content.

The contest showed just how fine that line could be.

Turbulent waters figured heavily in the future of Capp Enterprises. For all his creativity in cartooning and genius in marketing, Al Capp was, at his best, a mediocre boss. He had strong business acumen, but with employees he could be demanding, unreasonable, impatient, and, on occasion, cruel. On the creative side, he and his studio assistants were extraordinary in generating ideas and following them through to production; day-to-day operations ran smoothly, and the studio was a happy place.

Capp Enterprises, based in New York City, in an entirely different atmosphere than Capp's Boston studio, did not operate as smoothly as Capp hoped, and at least a portion of the problem could be placed on his brother Bence's shoulders. Bence was very bright—perhaps the most intelligent of the three brothers, according to Louis Gardner, Madeline's husband, who had observed all three brothers over many years—but Bence, like Al, could be very strong-willed. Besides holding significant stock and officer positions in four family corporations—treasurer of Capp Enterprises, president of Dogpatch Styles, treasurer of Toby Press, and director of Pictorial Advertising—Bence served as Al's personal manager, an amazing list of positions and responsibilities, given the fact that Tillie Caplin had to badger Al into hiring Bence in the first place, after his discharge from the service. Bence and Al had been close since childhood, when Bence would cart his brother around in a wagon after Al had lost his leg, and as adults, they shared many views, including their liberal political leanings. Bence even followed suit and formally changed his name from Caplin to Capp when Al legally changed his name in 1949.

This closeness might have been the main reason for their incompatibility in business. Al would ask Bence to perform a task, and Bence would carry it out in his own way and at his own leisure—if, that is, he deemed it worth his time and effort. Sometimes he would delegate the responsibility to another Capp Enterprises employee; other times he would ignore the request entirely. Al would repeat his request, politely on occasion, forcefully as often as not, and it burned him when Bence didn't seem to recognize him as his employer, as well as a brother. The grumblings began almost as soon as Capp Enterprises was founded, coinciding with the favorable settlement of Capp's lawsuit against United Feature Syndicate in the late 1940s, and they increased as the company took on more and more work. By 1949 and the Procter & Gamble shmoo promotion mess, Capp was becoming downright testy when dealing with Bence.

It had been an eventful year, packed with business propositions. Capp had been pressing the *New York Daily Mirror* for a renewal of "Li'l Abner," not only at a higher price but also with front-page placement in the color Sunday section. Bence was caught in the middle. Angered by Ham Fisher's relentless attempts to damage his and "Li'l Abner's" standing in the comics community, Capp sought revenge by demanding that his strip replace "Joe Palooka" on the front page of the Sunday *Mirror*, a prestigious placement that Fisher had enjoyed with his flagship paper for years. Bence did not share his brother's deep hatred of Fisher, and he was reluctant to pressure the *Mirror* editors when they dragged their feet in caving to Capp's demands. Capp, fuming from the back-and-forth between the editors at the *Mirror* and his office, blamed Bence for the lack of movement.

"These matters are of immense importance to me. Why must I nag you to get action on them?" he scolded Bence, demanding that he find out whether a poll had been conducted to determine if "Li'l Abner" had taken over as the *Mirror's* most popular strip. At the beginning of the year, the *Mirror* had promised Capp the front page of the Sunday comics section if "Li'l Abner" proved to be more popular than "Joe Palooka," and Capp was incredulous that his brother had not forced the issue. "Have these things no interest to you?" he asked Bence.

If Bence ever doubted the enormity of his brother's ego, he was now receiving confirmation on a regular basis. Capp had never been content to be merely a famous cartoonist. He saw the rapid rise of television as another opportunity to show off his myriad talents, as well as to publicize his strip. Capp admonished Bence for failing to nail down a television or radio program he was generically calling *Who and Why*, a quiz show designed to play into Capp's quick wit and outrageous sense of humor. Capp could not understand why Bence couldn't close a deal on such a project. Then, in an unrelated matter, when Capp accepted an invitation to a state dinner in Washington, D.C., where he believed he was to give a speech, accept an award, and pose for pictures with President Truman, only to learn later that none of this was going to occur, Capp found himself in an awkward position. He'd set up a deal with the *Boston Globe*, which planned to run, on the paper's front page, the text of his speech and a photo of Capp posing with the president. When none of it happened, Capp was, by his own admission, humiliated, and he lit into Bence. Capp was similarly chastened when Bence submitted a piece about the kigmy to such magazines as the *New Yorker* and *Collier's*, only to be rejected, not because the work was subpar, but because this was not the kind of material these magazines published. All three fiascos had been bruising to his ego.

"This is not what I hoped Capp Enterprises would be," Capp informed his brother.

Capp suspected, with some justification, that Bence viewed Capp Enterprises as an entity totally separate from "Li'l Abner" and the opportunities the strip presented for Al Capp's other companies. Capp angrily reminded Bence that, without the strip, there would be no Capp Enterprises, no Dogpatch Styles, no Toby Press, and therefore none of the generous salaries being earned by members of the family. Capp relied heavily on Bence's carrying out his orders, from keeping his contacts abreast of upcoming "Abner" events to sending along statements about earnings from "Abner"-related advertising, from checking into why some of the Sunday "Li'l Abner" entries were poorly rendered in some newspapers to executing new commercial tie-ins to "Li'l Abner" strips.

The shmoo had proven just how successful the tie-ins could be; Capp developed new ideas and continuities to promote them, such as a clever campaign tied into a story about the "nogoodnik," an evil, green shmoo lookalike hailing from Lower Slobbovia. The nogoodnik, whose name touched on the growing Cold War, McCarthyism, and the United States' distrust of the Soviet Union, wreaked havoc everywhere it went and could not be destroyed. Blow it to bits and every piece became an individual nogoodnik.

From this creative concept rose another Capp promotional idea. The story would continue through a half-dozen Sunday installments, and it would be revealed that the nogoodniks could be destroyed only if they were exposed to the sound of George Jessel's singing. Capp urged Bence to move into action. He was to contact Jessel or at least buy the rights to one of his songs. Capp had little doubt that the aging vaudevillian, who made fun of his own limited singing skills, would go along with the idea or, going one step further, would consent to recording a song that could be made into an inexpensive record that could be inserted in an eventual comic book reprint of the nogoodnik sequence.

"In the Sunday page of July 3rd, Arthur Dogflea"—the disk jockey of radio station SLOP—"announces that on the following Monday nite, on his talent show, he will have Jessel himself sing the song that killed the nogoodniks," Capp told Bence. Dogflea was to be a send-up of radio and TV star Arthur Godfrey, a friend of Capp's, and after giving it some thought, Capp decided to use Godfrey in the strip. It all worked as planned: Jessel appeared on Godfrey's popular radio show and sang "Wagon Wheels." The following Sunday, Capp devoted a panel of "Li'l Abner" to Jessel's singing the same song. The nogoodniks keeled over from the sound of Jessel's singing, and "Abner" had its happy ending. But too many of Bence and Al's interactions did not.

12 DEMISE OF THE MONSTER

Al Capp's feud with Ham Fisher reached a boiling point when the *Atlantic Monthly* published his autobiographical piece "I Remember Monster" in its April 1950 issue. In recollecting some of his unhappy days as Fisher's assistant, Capp pulled no punches.

> When fans ask me, "How does a normal-looking fella like you think up all those—b-r-r!!!—creatures?" I always evade a straightforward answer. Because the truth is I don't think 'em up. I was lucky enough to know them—all of them—and what was luckier, all in the person of one man. One veritable gold mine of human swinishness.
>
> It was my privilege, as a boy, to be associated with a certain treasure-trove of lousiness, who, in the normal course of each day of his life, managed to be, in dazzling succession, every conceivable kind of a heel. It was an advantage few young cartoonists have enjoyed—or could survive.

Capp avoided mentioning Fisher by name, but for everyone in the comics business and much of the public (*Newsweek* had covered the feud just over a year earlier), there could be no question as to whom Capp was targeting. That same year Capp's strip featured a swinish cartoonist named Happy Vermin, an unquestionable caricature of Fisher. Capp's and Fisher's fighting had been so public, for so long, that it had taken on the dimensions of a soap opera. Their intense dislike for each other was becoming a burden to cartoonists who had to listen to them loudly ramble on about their grievances.

Fisher had never been much of a match for his opponent. He complained bitterly about Capp's stealing his hillbilly characters—he even had a note, supposedly written by Capp, in which Capp admitted that Fisher had created Big Leviticus for "Joe Palooka"—but no one cared to know about it. With the possible exception of the evil Scragg family, Li'l Abner and his Dogpatch neighbors bore no resemblance to Fisher's characters, and copyright laws did not grant Fisher exclusive rights to all things hillbilly. Fisher took his campaign to the public whenever his strip revisited the hills. These were the original hillbillies, he'd state in a message to his readers, and anything else was just a cheap imitation.

The behind-the-scenes shenanigans were cruel and occasionally childish. Things boiled over when Capp and his family traveled by ship to France for a European vacation. Capp's fame had made him a most welcome passenger, and he and his family were treated well—until, that is, the ship's captain received a telegram from an "H. C. Anderson." The telegram advised the captain that the police would board the ship and arrest Capp on "grave charges" as soon as they docked in Le Havre. Capp investigated the telegram and was at last able to prove that it was a fake. But the trip had already gone sour. The Capps suddenly went from dining regularly with the captain and his officers to being persona non grata.

"I knew [that] when I returned, I must fight Fisher," Capp wrote in his autobiography, "or let the tormented, addled soul destroy me."

Capp exacted his revenge by toying with Fisher in a variety of ways, always by phone. He called the supervisor of Fisher's apartment building and, after identifying himself as the father of a fat boy living in the building, complained that a famous bachelor tenant was "constantly feeling my child up on the elevator." Fisher was never confronted by the building's super, but he couldn't help but notice that the doorman was always on the elevator with the boy.

There were other forms of retaliation. Whenever Fisher set him off, Capp found a way of exacting revenge. He paid people to watch Fisher. Once he called Fisher's residence and, after presenting himself as Fisher's psychiatrist, managed to convince Fisher's Filipino valet that Fisher desperately needed help. The valet could do him a great service if he noted and reported to him all of Fisher's phone calls; knowing the people Fisher was talking to, Capp said, would give him clues as to how to help him. Armed with the names and number of Fisher's callers, Capp would call individuals,

particularly Fisher's dates, and rearrange appointments and meetings, causing an unsuspecting Fisher embarrassment and distress.

Capp's biggest victory, however, had been on the professional front.
Fisher had always taken great pride in seeing "Joe Palooka" on the front page
of the comics section of the Sunday *Mirror*, his flagship paper. When Capp
convinced the *Mirror* to instead give the prized placement to "Li'l Abner,"
proving its greater popularity, Fisher was apoplectic.

Capp also worked his feud with Fisher into "Li'l Abner" episodes.
When Fisher, whose vanity was legend in comics circles, had plastic surgery
on his nose, Capp created a racehorse named "Ham's Nose-bob." In another
"Li'l Abner" sequence, Li'l Abner found work as an assistant to a cheapskate
comic strip artist who, rather than offer him a raise for his contributions to
the strip's success, rewards him with a new lamp after his strip becomes
nationally renowned.

One of Fisher's few victories over Capp occurred when he managed to
lure away Capp's first assistant, Moe Leff. Capp heavily depended on Leff
in the early days of the strip, and though he was able to hire new assistants
after losing Leff to him, Capp never forgave Fisher.

Fisher also made ongoing efforts to prove that Capp had hidden suggestive or pornographic images in "Li'l Abner." With the cultural controversy
surrounding comics, these were dangerous accusations, and they struck
closer to the truth than Capp dared to admit. He would hear of Fisher's ex-
pounding about the pornographic images at some of New York's high-
visibility watering holes, or bending fellow cartoonists' ears about the topic
at National Cartoonists Society meetings.

"I Remember Monster" became Capp's lengthiest public statement
about Fisher. Rather than reveal the name of the man who, Capp explained,
had become a model for so many "Li'l Abner" villains, Capp merely referred
to Fisher as his "Benefactor," the moniker put forth with all the derision
Capp could muster. In Capp's account, Fisher was miserly, insensitive, lech-
erous, and evil. At the end of the memoir, Capp sneered at the popular no-
tion that Good would overcome Evil in a person's lifetime. His Benefactor
was living proof that this was not necessarily the case. He had gone
unpunished.

"He grew richer and healthier, more famous and honored," Capp wrote.

"He kept no old friends, but he made lots of shiny new friends. Nothing happened. He just grew older and eviler."

"I Remember Monster" created quite a stir, not because Capp had successfully nailed Fisher with some clever, well-placed zingers, but because the portrait was so spot-on accurate. By 1950, Fisher had alienated most of his fellow comic strip artists with his relentless complaining about almost everything in his life. Capp was engaging where Fisher was off-putting; people laughed at Capp's jokes but laughed at Fisher behind his back. By some accounts, they enjoyed watching him wallow in his misery. His comic strip had risen to the top; it had made him a wealthy man, brought him fame, and set him up so that he could choose the life he wanted to lead. Why was he so unhappy?

Capp would publish scores of newspaper and magazine pieces over the years, including other work for the *Atlantic Monthly*, but "I Remember Monster" would remain his best-known work of prose. His relentless attack had bruised and beaten Fisher; it offered concrete examples of Fisher's nasty, parsimonious, self-centered disposition.

For Fisher, "I Remember Monster" represented his most degrading humiliation at the hands of Al Capp. His obsession with Capp, unhealthy to begin with, rose to ridiculous heights, blinding him from the truth that, try as he might, he would never defeat his enemy. He had nothing ahead but loss.

The campaign against comics had not disappeared. The brouhaha of the late 1940s, led by Fredric Wertham, had mobilized local civic and church groups, nudging them into meetings, protests, letter-writing campaigns, occasional book burnings, and a general dialogue about comics' effects on their young readers. Comic books, particularly the more violent crime and horror titles, were still far greater targets for criticism than newspaper comic strips, but the unabated attempts to connect comics to juvenile delinquency kept the newspaper syndicates and subscribing newspaper editors on alert for any material that might be deemed objectionable. For Al Capp, McCarthyism, new in the political consciousness but gaining momentum with each passing month, was affecting his ability to satirize anything connected with the government. The last thing he needed was additional opposition to the content of comics.

In May 1950, the U.S. Senate's Special Committee to Investigate Crime in Interstate Commerce, aimed at organized crime, began still another investigation into the relationship between comic books and juvenile delinquency. Estes Kefauver, a Democratic senator from Tennessee, chaired the committee composed of two other Democrats and two Republicans. Kefauver had served five terms in the House of Representatives before winning his first Senate race in 1948, but his sights were set much higher—on a wide-open presidential race in 1952—when he led a committee guaranteed to garner a lot of publicity. His trademark, used in political campaigns, was a coonskin cap, making Kefauver look more like a Dogpatch resident than a U.S. senator to many. Serving as a consultant to the committee was one Dr. Fredric Wertham.

Kefauver put together a seven-question survey, which was sent to a wide variety of professionals with knowledge and experience in comics and juvenile crime, from judges, probation officers, social workers, and psychologists to comics artists and publishers. The first four questions on the survey were designed to determine whether there had been an increase in juvenile crime since 1945 and, if so, whether the crimes had become more violent in nature. The final three questions on the survey focused on the possible correlation between comics and juvenile delinquency:

Do you believe that there is any relationship between reading crime comic books and juvenile delinquency?

Please specifically give statistics and, if possible, state specific cases of juvenile crime which you believe can be traced to reading crime comic books.

Do you believe that juvenile delinquency would decrease if crime comic books were not readily available to children?

The focus on crime comic books was misleading and certainly subject to problems with definition and interpretation. With the exception of comics aimed specifically at young children, such as those issued by Walt Disney, almost any comic could technically be tied in with crime, from the super-hero comic books to such newspaper strips as "Dick Tracy" or even "Li'l Abner," with its "Fearless Fosdick" entries.

Fortunately for the comics industry, those filling out the surveys, as well as those testifying before the committee, reached a much different conclusion from the one expected and perhaps hoped for. Almost six out of ten survey respondents found no connection between comic books and juvenile delinquency, and nearly 70 percent believed that banning comic books would have no effect on preventing delinquency. Some of those testifying before the committee believed in a cause-and-effect relationship between comics and juvenile crime, but the majority, including FBI director J. Edgar Hoover, found nothing of substance to be worried about.

Milton Caniff, one of the comics industry's representatives offering his thoughts to the committee, scoffed at the belief that professionals could draw an accurate connection between comics and criminal behavior. "Practitioners of the inexact science of psychiatry," Caniff said, "have long served as apologists for the present parental generation by attributing every childhood ill from the measles to shyness to the reading of comic books."

Capp applauded his friend's observations. When reflecting on the days of attempted censorship and legislation against comic books, Capp offered a word of caution to those with short memories who might have seen Fredric Wertham as a minor player in the history of censorship. Wertham and his cronies, Capp said, had caused a hysteria that destroyed an art form before it had the chance to fully develop.

"The doctor," Capp said of Wertham, "was no creation of pen and ink; he was as real as any old Salem judge who ever ordered any granny burned alive as a witch."

Kefauver filed his committee's report, and, for the time being, the formal government scrutiny of comics died down. But the issue would be revisited in three years, with some of the same participants, heavy media coverage, and Capp more involved than at any time in the past.

Of all the certainties in life, "Li'l Abner" readers knew they could count on Li'l Abner's escaping the matrimonial clutches of Daisy Mae Scragg. The one-sided romance had sparked many a story over the strip's eighteen years, and the only real question was how Li'l Abner would escape the increasingly complicated and devious snares that Capp designed for any given story cycle. On one occasion, Abner was spared by an explosion; on another, by the moving of a mountain; on still another, by the sudden expiration of Marryin' Sam's license. The annual Sadie Hawkins Day stories had readers wondering whether Daisy Mae would finally run Li'l Abner down and present him to Marryin' Sam for the obligatory nuptials.

"The fact that Li'l Abner always managed somehow to escape Daisy Mae's warm, eager arms provided me with a story that I could tell whenever I couldn't think of anything better," Capp explained. "I never intended to have Li'l Abner marry Daisy Mae."

Over the years, Capp was inundated with letters from readers wondering when Li'l Abner and Daisy Mae would finally tie the knot. Students formed clubs to lobby Capp with petitions. Women, Capp noted, were almost without exception the ones disappointed by Li'l Abner's latest close shave; men, he joked, were so confident in the stories' outcomes that they would promise their girlfriends that they'd get married the day Daisy Mae and Li'l Abner stood willingly before Marryin' Sam.

All this changed on March 28–29, 1952, when Li'l Abner awoke to the sight of Daisy Mae standing at his bedside, with Marryin' Sam standing at the foot of the bed and Mammy and Pappy Yokum off to the side. Before he realized what was happening, he and Daisy Mae had been declared man and wife.

Capp's lead-in to the wedding was an episode of "Fearless Fosdick." Li'l Abner had joined a Fearless Fosdick fan club, in which members vowed to follow the hapless detective's example. What Li'l Abner didn't realize was that Fosdick's creator, Lester Gooch, while driving near Dogpatch, had nearly hit Daisy Mae with his car, and after Daisy Mae told him that Fosdick, by not getting married, was setting a bad example for American youth, Gooch decided the time had come to marry him off to his longtime fiancée, Prudence Pimpleton. He dreamed up an episode in which Fosdick's police chief announced that, due to tough times, only married officers would be retained on the force.

Li'l Abner was horrified to read about all this in his favorite comic

After stretching the central tension of his comic strip for nearly twenty years, Al Capp did the unthinkable in 1952: he married Li'l Abner and Daisy Mae.

strip. He remained confident that Fosdick would escape matrimony at the last minute, but he didn't, and soon Li'l Abner, after all those years, was forced to keep his word and follow his example.

The wedding story was greeted with great fanfare. *Time* magazine gave it the full treatment, complete with two panels from the story and an explanation from Capp. *Life* went much further. The wedding was its cover story, and Capp wrote a lengthy essay, "It's Hideously True: Creator of Li'l Abner Tells Why His Hero Is (Sob!) Wed."

Capp blamed a national climate of fear for forcing his decision. "Li'l Abner" had, by that point, evolved from a suspense strip to a no-holds-barred satire unlike anything the funny papers had ever seen. He'd been free to lampoon anyone and anything, from politicians to the movies. "I was exhilarated by the privilege this gave me to kid hell out of everything," he wrote.

But times had changed. Criticism of the government was frowned upon. Communism was found lurking in the most innocuous places. Even something as seemingly innocent as the shmoo or the kigmy was under attack in some quarters, where critics saw them as negative criticism of the American way of life. In Capp's opinion, the fifth freedom—"the freedom to laugh at each other"—was under siege.

"That was when I decided to go back to fairy tales until the atmosphere is gone," Capp told *Life* readers. "That is the real reason why Li'l Abner married Daisy Mae."

Capp hoped this would open new creative possibilities for the strip. Li'l Abner had never held a job; now, as head of the household, he'd have to find a way of supporting Daisy Mae and, God forbid, any children they might have. Would Daisy Mae's attitudes about Li'l Abner change, now that she had finally won him over? And what would become of Pappy and Mammy Yokum, now that their only child had moved away and left them alone together? Capp looked forward to exploring these new storylines.

Not everyone felt the move was a good creative choice. Charles Schulz, creator of "Peanuts" and one of the comics industry's rapidly rising stars, thought the marriage was "probably the biggest mistake ever made in comic-strip history." Comics readers, he said, weren't open to such drastic change; they were comfortable with the characters that initially attracted them to the strip and could only take change a little at a time. With the marriage of Li'l Abner and Daisy Mae, "the premise of the strip collapsed."

These were not thoughts that Capp wanted to hear, especially since he felt he was pushed in that direction by circumstances beyond his control. It didn't help, either, that "Peanuts" was on its way to pushing past "Li'l Abner" in readership.

Capp Enterprises, under Bence Capp's guidance, was constantly searching for new ways to expand its operations. It continued to profit from the strip's international popularity, but aside from the disastrous feature-length motion picture in 1940 and a series of insipid animated cartoons a few years later, "Li'l Abner" failed to crack the potentially lucrative film and television markets. When Bence was approached with a proposal to put "Li'l Abner" on television, he was initially skeptical. The group approaching him wanted to use marionettes, rather than produce it as a live-action show with actors and actresses, and he feared this aimed squarely at the children's audience, while "Li'l Abner' had never been just for kids. Bence took the idea to his brother, and Al had reservations of his own. The comic strip had its own distinct look, and he would not agree to the project unless the program's creators were able to make the puppets look like the characters in the strip.

Fortunately, he wasn't dealing with amateurs. Mary Chase, the designer of the marionettes, had been pulling the strings professionally on her creations for a decade, beginning with small productions in her native Chicago and, in time, progressing to bigger commercial projects in New York. She was quite capable of designing marionettes that looked like Capp's characters. Her prototypes for Li'l Abner, Daisy Mae, and Mammy Yokum impressed the Capp brothers, but Al was still hesitant to sign over the rights to "Li'l Abner" to what he felt was "a novelty like a TV puppet show." He had higher plans for "Abner." He countered with a suggestion of his own: why not make the show about Fearless Fosdick?

This would be no easy task if the program was to be aimed at children. "Fosdick," in "Li'l Abner," was anything but kiddie fare. It was violent, and its satirical content was too advanced for young minds. Further, it was a parody of "Dick Tracy," and while Capp had been able to get away with mimicking Chester Gould's character for the sake of comic strip satire, a television production might present copyright problems. Finally, there were questions about how marionettes would hold up in action sequences. Still, both parties agreed to produce a pilot.

For the pilot, the puppet designer changed Fosdick's facial features just enough to distinguish him from Dick Tracy and had him wearing a bowler rather than Tracy's trademark fedora. To temper the violence and adult content of the strip, Fosdick was recast as more of a slapstick character, more apt to step into an open manhole than get shot full of holes—the kind of character Peter Sellers would perfect two decades later as Inspector Clouseau in the Pink Panther movies. Experienced professional actors and actresses were brought in to dub the characters' voices. The Capps approved the pilot, and the project was given the green light.

The first installment of the series aired on June 15, 1952, on NBC, and the network ordered thirteen episodes for what would be a summer replacement program. But *Fosdick* was telecast on Sunday afternoons, at a time

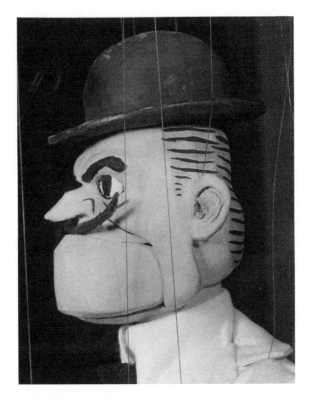

In the summer of 1952, Fearless Fosdick, *a puppet show, debuted on NBC on Sunday afternoons. The summer replacement show found no sponsor for renewal and ended after thirteen episodes.*

when kids were rarely sitting in front of a television, and, for all its silliness, it was still too adult in content and tone for children. Not a single sponsor signed on for either the trial run or a projected fall season. Other than *TV Guide,* major newspapers and magazines pretended the program didn't exist. NBC pulled the plug.

For Al Capp, it stood as further proof that, for all its popularity, "Li'l Abner" was still a disappointing distance from being accepted as anything but a comic strip.

Some good did come out of the experience, however. As a tie-in to the TV show, Capp published *The World of Li'l Abner,* a selection of his best strips. He'd asked John Steinbeck to write an introduction. The novelist had known Capp socially for years, and he admired Capp's satires and parodies, even when the cartoonist was sending up his classic *The Grapes of Wrath.*

In his introduction, Steinbeck claimed that he had not seen the contents of the book, that Capp had merely told him that "it was going to have hard covers and dignity," This, as far as Steinbeck was concerned, was sufficient. Capp, he suggested, was more than a mere cartoonist; he was a literary practitioner.

"I think Capp may very possibly be the best writer in the world today," he wrote, comparing Capp to Cervantes and Rabelais in his ability to make the butts of his satire "accept and enjoy the criticism.

"In my claim that Capp is probably the greatest contemporary writer, and in my suggestion that if the Nobel prize committee is at all alert they should seriously consider him, I run into people who seem to feel that literature is all words and that those words should preferably be a little stuffy. Who knows what literature is?"

Of course, Steinbeck himself would later win the Nobel Prize for Literature. His endorsement would stay with Capp for the rest of his life.

Capp's objections to the way his brother handled Capp Enterprises had simmered down over the past two years, but they reached an explosive point in late 1952, when Capp took out his frustrations over contractual and business matters on Bence and their attorneys. This was anything but new. In the early months of 1950, when Al and Bence seemed to have reached an impasse over Bence's work with Capp Enterprises, Bence had tendered his resignation as Capp's personal manager. The tension and fighting, Bence said, were causing him more grief than the job was worth. Al's attorney, alarmed at the confusion that might result from Bence's walking away from the job, had intervened, and the two brothers had come up with a working arrangement amenable to both. There had been problems over the ensuing two years, but they had been resolved with minimal bickering.

Still, by the first week of December 1952, Al was dissatisfied enough with Bence to demand that he leave Capp Enterprises. Capp's initial feeling, put in writing in a letter to Bence, lacked the bile of his letters in the past. He was disappointed more than angry. He could not fathom why Bence habitually ignored his orders and went about business as he saw fit, even if he did so with the best of intentions.

"No one on earth would have gone along so long with your practices of setting your own hours, your own policies in handling work, your own handling of finances that do not belong to you," Capp said, stating that he believed that Bence was too set in his ways to change. "Let's make this pleasant and quiet," he concluded. "I will help you all I can—you need only name what. This time it's final."

Capp asked that Bence complete a few tasks, set the Capp Enterprises financial books in order, and otherwise turn everything else over to him or Elliott. Capp's patience disappeared when Bence moved more slowly than he thought necessary, but he still kept an even, if more formal, tone in his correspondence.

The politeness came to a halt when Capp received a chippie call from an editor at *Life* magazine. Capp had set up an arrangement with *Life* granting the publication the right of first refusal of his essays. The high-circulation magazine had treated Capp very well over the years, including the cover story on the marriage of Li'l Abner and Daisy Mae just a short time earlier, and Capp valued the association. The relationship, however, was now in jeopardy. Bence, it turned out, had not only marketed an Al Capp piece to another magazine; he had sold the same piece to two competing magazines—*Pageant* and *Coronet*—and it was running concurrently in the magazines' issues cover-dated March 1953. *Life* had approved of Capp's selling the brief essay to *Pageant*, but the same piece to two magazines was way over the mark.

Capp attempted to explain that he knew nothing of the *Coronet* sale, but the *Life* editor found it difficult to believe that he wouldn't know where his work was being submitted.

Capp was apoplectic. He'd been trying unsuccessfully to remove Bence from his professional life for months, and this latest mishap was one of Bence's worst transgressions yet. If Bence wouldn't leave Capp Enterprises quietly and voluntarily, as Capp had hoped, drastic measures would be required. Capp contacted Elliott and Madeline, explained the situation, and looked for some kind of support. Bence, he told them, meant well, but he was useless. Further, since Capp had received no payment for the two magazine articles, Bence must have pocketed the money.

"There must be some way I can rid myself of the thieving, crazy son-ofabitch," he railed in a letter to Madeline and Elliott. "There must be some way I can disinfect my life and work of his lunatic influences."

In a separate letter to Elliott, he went back over the details of the *Life* magazine fiasco and proposed that Elliott declare bankruptcy for Toby Press. They could re-form the publishing house later, with Bence written out of the company. In any event, Al wanted out.

"Every prediction I made about Bense [*sic*] has come luridly true, truer than I expected," Capp complained. "He is a cancer."

The real fighting, as one might expect, involved Al and Bence. Al flung insult after insult at his brother, accusing him of everything from incompetency to thievery, but Bence had heard it all before. This time, however, he was not going to sit back and silently take it.

"You are and have been to me a malicious, vindictive monster," Bence told Al. "I've stored seven years of such accusation—'indigent, unemployable, crook, chiseler, back stabber, slothful,' and the rest of it." Bence challenged Al to call a meeting of Capp Enterprises' board of directors, at which time both he and Al could present their sides of the dispute, once and for all. At that meeting, Bence would formally request the establishment of a mediation commission to gather evidence and testimony and decide what would happen to Bence and Capp Enterprises.

Capp responded with a relentless attack, first by letter, followed up by a phone call. Capp was vicious, even by his standards, and it's possible that he hoped that, in taking this approach, he would finally persuade Bence to walk away from the dispute. In his letter, Capp repeated the familiar charge that Bence would be destitute without him—or, at least, a "charity" for Elliott and others. He reiterated his threat of pulling out of Toby Press and bankrupting it, leaving Bence with nothing from that company. Further, he was withdrawing all support from other family members on the Capp dole because he could no longer be certain that Bence wouldn't turn to them for financial assistance. In the end, Capp had no one to blame for Bence's dependency but himself.

"The last six years have been the most hideous of my career, the most expensive in my emotions and my savings," he said. "You can lie and fake and trip me up as much as you like, you pig, and I deserve it for ever having permitted you to infect my hard working life."

The phone call was even more vituperative. Bence listened for a half hour as his brother unloaded on him, telling him that he hoped Bence would be run over and killed by a truck, that his violent death would be a blessing to Capp's children, who would otherwise have to grow up and "suffer the mortification that [Bence's] stubborn continuance of breathing would bring to them."

Bence held his ground. He again demanded a hearing to vindicate himself, and he counterpunched his way through his brother's assault.

"Are you so swept by anti-human hatred that you have to vilify your friends' integrity, your associates' principles, and your family's honor?" he wondered, admitting that he was now prepared to fight him to the end, though it gave him no pleasure or satisfaction.

"I understand that the genius that you have and the unhappy background makes a number of these flights in dastardy an almost automatic reaction," he said, "but in this thing you are injuring yourself almost mortally."

Bence was weary of the slugfest, though. He ultimately relented and agreed to leave his positions in the miscellaneous Capp family businesses and sell off his stock, which—one of the few things he and Al could agree on—was virtually without monetary value. In exchange, Bence wanted a buyout of his interests in the companies. The Capp lawyers stayed busy, especially when Bence, convinced that Al was not honoring his end of the agreement, repudiated his earlier arrangement. The battle had become so intensely personal that it spread to include anyone daring to take a side—or even to show a shred of understanding or sympathy for one of the combatants.

Lawsuits were threatened, company assets and accounts frozen. What had begun as a strong disagreement had degenerated into a territorial dispute, with each brother defending a turf of indeterminate value; it threatened to devolve even further, into a warped form of blood sport.

The quarreling was bound to distract Capp from his work, though "Li'l Abner" continued without any apparent evidence of the strain. After nearly two decades of turning in strips and honoring other commitments under deadline pressures and personal issues of every type imaginable, Capp and his assistants could handle anything that came their way. Still, the troubles with Bence pushed Capp to the limit.

"It is tragic that my energies must be eaten up by these machinations of yours," Capp wrote Bence. He went on to include a list of crushing obligations threatened by the time he spent dealing with fighting with his brother. "Your actions," he continued, "have greatly disturbed my mind and my peace, and have endangered and will continue to endanger my ability to carry on my many public and private responsibilities."

Al Foster, who, as a bank official with the Merchants National Bank of Boston, worked with both Capp brothers, was exasperated.

"I certainly wish personalities on all sides could be postponed at least long enough to have a businessman's final settlement," he told Bence. "You may give me hell and say that I just do not understand. Well, maybe I do not. Therefore I am taking no sides, but what we do know and understand, Jerry, is that both sides always lose in such a case."

Foster echoed Al's concerns about how the fighting might affect Capp's work and, by extension, his responsibilities.

"I can well imagine that this has been quite a strain on you and I know from personal observation what a terrific strain it has been on Al," he said. "I just don't know how he continues with the work. It is going to be just too bad for a lot of people if anything happens to Al or his work starts to slip because he cannot give it his undivided attention."

Capp knew he had no choice but to carry on while lawyers and bankers and accountants sorted through the broken pieces of all that had, not so long ago, started out as a dream.

* * *

By late 1953, Capp and his three primary assistants were scrambling to shoulder the studio's workload. "Li'l Abner" and Al Capp had become a cottage industry, a brand name roaring along at breakneck pace, and though Capp and his artists had little to do with the production of the constantly growing number of merchandising items—an Honest Abe doll, initially marketed as Mysterious Yokum before Abner and Daisy's son was finally named, was among the new offerings on the market in 1954—their print media obligations kept them busy. Capp, Andy Amato, Walter Johnston, and Harvey Curtis had been working as a team since the late thirties, long enough to crank out the daily and Sunday strips like a General Motors assembly line turning out cars. The advertising commitments, however, cut into their time. "Li'l Abner" characters graced the pages of magazines, boxes of cereal, newspapers, posters, and signs, whether it was Fearless Fosdick hawking Wildroot Cream-Oil for hair or Li'l Abner starring in Cream of Wheat ads. There were ads for Grape-Nuts, Kraft caramels, Ivory soap products, Fruit of the Loom underwear, and General Electric lightbulbs. Keeping up with all the work was demanding. A steady stream of assistants and freelancers passed through the studio as the varying workload required. Milt Story was a particularly valuable fourth hand in the late forties and early fifties, while Stu Hample was integrally involved in the Fosdick ads.

When Capp decided to hire another assistant in 1954, he had one particular artist in mind. Some years earlier, Frank Frazetta was doing his own hillbilly comic, "Looie Lazybones," which owed much to "Li'l Abner," and from his work on other features, including his short-lived "Johnny Comet" strip, Capp concluded that Frazetta was not only very talented; he was also capable of mimicking a wide range of styles.

Later in his life, after achieving international fame as a fantasy and science fiction artist, Frazetta would say that he probably stunted his artistic growth by working for Capp, but he would also confess that he was naturally lazy and tempted by big-bucks-for-little-work offers. Capp was offering $500 a week, a large enough sum to convince a young artist to put his own interests on hold for a while. Jobs in the business were hard to find, especially with anticomics crusaders making enough of an inroad to eliminate many of the regularly produced comic books. Frazetta was especially pleased to learn that Capp had no problem with his freelancing elsewhere, as long as

*Daisy Mae, drawn here by Frank Frazetta, an assistant added to Al Capp's staff
in 1954. Frazetta penciled the Sunday "Li'l Abner" strips for the better part of a
decade. After leaving Capp's employ, he went on to fame as a fantasy painter and
illustrator.*

"Li'l Abner" remained his first priority. He agreed to the job, in spite of the
fact that it involved commuting to Boston from his Brooklyn home.

Throughout 1954, Frazetta did much of the penciling on the daily "Li'l
Abner" strips; he inked many of the strips as well. He could mimic Capp's
style so sharply that, aside from the heads, which Capp always inked, no
one could positively say who was doing what. Before the end of the year,
Capp trusted Frazetta enough to let him pencil the Sunday entries, a primary role that he soon settled into.

His most memorable work during that first year came about as the result of Capp's assigning him a continuity in which he would inject his own
distinct style into the strip. Capp wanted to do another movie parody, this
one sending up producer Stanley Kramer's *The Wild One*, the Marlon

Brando–driven film about a motorcycle gang that menaces a small town. For the parody, Capp needed two distinct styles: the style he'd been using for years, plus a more sophisticated, detailed style for the biker antagonist, a Frazetta creation named, not coincidentally, Frankie. Frazetta, who would gain his reputation for his mastery of the disproportionate female form, would also be turned loose on Wolf Gal, a character who, some might have argued, needed no improvement. In Frazetta's hands, the feral character became even sexier and more menacing.

The sequence was much more ambitious than the typical "Li'l Abner" parody. A new, continuing character—Li'l Abner's fifteen-and-a-half-year-old brother, Tiny, who appeared out of nowhere in Dogpatch—was an integral part of the continuity. Tiny Yokum was drawn like a Dogpatcher, and his interactions with Frankie, a Frazetta self-portrait drawn more realistically, produced an effect not unlike plopping Felix the Cat down into a Milton Caniff strip.

The syndicate hated it. This was not the "Li'l Abner" that readers picked through the papers to see. Capp listened to the complaints and agreed to return to the time-tested style.

Frazetta lasted the year before requesting that he be allowed to work out of his home in Brooklyn. Capp agreed, and a new process was put in motion. Capp would mail four weeks' worth of Sunday strip roughs to Frazetta, who would tightly pencil the strips and send them back. This method took full advantage of Frazetta's undeniable skills on the highest-circulation "Li'l Abner" strips, yet largely sublimated Frazetta's distinctive style to the house brand. Frazetta loved the arrangement.

"The pay was wonderful and it took me only a day to pencil his Sunday page and I had the rest of the week off!" he remembered. "What more could I ask for? On a couple of occasions, I went up to his Boston studio and he paid me $100 a day, which was really big money back then."

The long-distance working relationship would last into 1962, with less than optimal results. Frazetta had early on been an integral part of the story meetings that developed and refined the continuities in "Li'l Abner," but with him away in New York, there was such a disconnect that Capp, in later years, couldn't remember how long Frazetta had actually worked for him.

"This claim that he worked for me for several years—it may have seemed like several years, but in reality it was for under a year," Capp would say. "Oh, he may have come back for two months at one point, that kind of thing." Capp's limited recollection of Frazetta's tenure was probably disingenuous, out of resentment that a former assistant was eclipsing his own fame.

Frazetta was too talented to stay in Capp's employ indefinitely. He wanted to paint, and he was good enough to work in the highly competitive field of commercial illustration. When Frazetta approached Capp for a raise in the early sixties, Capp was ready to sever ties. Times were tough, he told Frazetta; he was losing newspapers and, as a result, he was making less from the syndicate.

"Instead of getting a raise," Capp told Frazetta, "you should take a pay cut, like me."

As Capp himself had left Ham Fisher, the assistant left his mentor largely over issues of money. Capp had gone on to make his name on his own. Frazetta would do the same.

Comics opponents never relented in their efforts to eliminate, or at the very least regulate the content of, comics they deemed to be too violent or sexually suggestive for young readers. The horror and crime genres were especially vulnerable to attack. Protective parents cringed when their children passed newsstands or drugstore racks displaying such titles as *Crime Does Not Pay* or *Shock SuspenStories*. Even less openly objectionable titles, such as *Batman* or *Wonder Woman*, had hidden messages, the former suggestive of homosexuality, the latter of lesbianism and sadomasochistic sexuality.

Newspaper comic strips generally escaped close scrutiny, but an artist like Al Capp, with his buxom women and adult plotlines, had to be careful. There could be only so much cleavage in the funny papers. Over the first two decades of "Li'l Abner," Capp's syndicate editors, citing client newspaper editors' complaints, had regularly asked Capp to tone down the sex and violence in the strip. He would comply for a short period of time, but he'd soon be presenting a new continuity steaming with scantily dressed women and charged with sexual energy barely hidden beneath the surface of a story.

The bombshell hit in the spring of 1954, in what Capp might have labeled a double whammy: Just days before Fredric Wertham's *Seduction of the Innocent* arrived in bookstores, yet another Senate subcommittee on juvenile delinquency convened to examine the possible relationship of comics to youthful misbehavior and crime. Not surprisingly, Wertham was invited to testify at the hearings.

Wertham was a natural storyteller, and *Seduction of the Innocent* was a magnum opus of pop psychology. Wertham wasn't willing to say that comics led to juvenile delinquency, but he was prepared to detail his position that comics filled young readers' heads with all the wrong messages; in the wrong heads, comics could encourage antisocial or criminal behavior.

Wertham became a star witness at the Senate subcommittee hearing in New York, held in the same courtroom where the Kefauver Committee had convened four years earlier. Kefauver was present for these hearings, which promised to be every bit as spirited and controversial. Wertham, who used his appearance as a platform for hawking *Seduction of the Innocent*, testified that the comic book industry made Hitler look like a novice when it came to teaching children racial hatred. As an example, he pointed to a seven-page story, "The Whipping," published by EC Comics, in which a racist murders his daughter because she is attracted to a Mexican—a story more readily interpreted as a lesson on racial tolerance.

Al Capp was neither present at the hearings nor invited to testify, but his work was once again under scrutiny. As in the 1950 hearings, the committee members had received photostats of "Li'l Abner" strips that the anonymous donor deemed to be pornographic. Nothing had changed. These were the same examples, with similar notations in the margins, that Ham Fisher had submitted to the earlier subcommittee.

Nothing came of Fisher's latest attempt to discredit his rival, other than its riling up Capp for another round of battles. Infuriated, Capp decided to take action.

In 1955, seven years after he had created the shmoo, and six years after the kigmy, Al Capp tried again to create a cuddly creature that might capture the public's imagination and simultaneously reinvigorate Capp Enterprises' lagging merchandise revenues. The bald iggle, an import smuggled from Lower Slobbovia, was a small round character with birdlike feet and a bald spot on top of its otherwise furry body. Its key characteristic was its large, brown, and irresistible eyes. Any human looking into the bald iggle's eyes was compelled to tell the truth. Like the shmoo, a creature so good for humanity that it proved bad for humanity, the bald iggle as a truth machine threatened the underpinnings of relationships, politics, and business, and like its earlier strip counterpart, it ultimately had to be exterminated.

The bald iggle story was collected as a book by Simon & Schuster in 1956, no small accomplishment, but it did not inspire merchandise like its predecessors and was to be Capp's last serious effort at inventing a character than might rival the overnight popularity of the shmoo. In retrospect, what is perhaps most significant about the bald iggle episode is the satirist's prophetic observation about himself a decade ahead. A journalist interviews "a leading critic of the younger generation," asking him what's wrong with students today. The growling curmudgeon begins to answer, "All they're interested in is FUN, FUN!! Now when I was young . . ." Then a bald iggle suddenly looks into the critic's eyes, forcing him to blurt out, "Really, the only thing I have against the younger generation is that I'm too old to be one of 'em!! (sob!! sob!!)."

The Al Capp–Ham Fisher feud, two decades running, came to an abrupt ending on December 27, 1955, when Fisher was found dead in his New York office, a sleeping pill bottle and suicide note nearby. He was fifty-five.

To Capp, Fisher's death was a personal victory, and he'd go as far as to state that driving Fisher to suicide was his greatest accomplishment.

Once again, Capp exaggerated. It was true that the feud weighed heavily in Fisher's demise, but when Fisher was discovered on his office couch, he had died a lonely man, all but friendless, an outcast in the comics world, blaming everyone but himself for his troubles, lost in a haze of paranoia from which he could not escape. Capp's role in all this was significant, but it was not the sole reason.

Fisher's final year had been extremely difficult. A storm destroyed his

Wisconsin summer home. His health began to slide. Most significantly, early in the year, in February, he had been banned from the National Cartoonists Society (NCS), an organization he'd cofounded. He had brought his dismissal upon himself when he anonymously sent photocopies of "Li'l Abner" strips to the Senate subcommittee and, more recently, to the Federal Communications Commission (FCC), which was considering Al Capp's application for a permit for part ownership of a Boston television station. It was the same approach Fisher had taken with the New York State Joint Legislative Committee to Study the Publication of Comics. These earlier attempts to ruin Capp had been messy affairs, widely reported in the media. Embarrassed, the NCS admonished Fisher, and for a while he had avoided further public conflict—until the spring of 1954. The fact that he'd anonymously submitted the "Li'l Abner" strips fooled nobody: it was Ham Fisher's modus operandi.

Capp seethed. Fisher had gone too far when he submitted the photostats to the FCC. Not only could his actions have a grave effect on Capp's hopes of securing a permit for a small share of the television station; it also affected the lives of other investors. Capp's group, the Massachusetts Bay Telecasters, was competing with a second group for the franchise. When attorneys from that second group suggested at the FCC hearings that Capp, as a pornographer, might not be a suitable buyer, Capp decided to take action. He instructed his attorney to find a handwriting authority to prove that it was Fisher who had written comments in the margins of the photostats.

The FCC hearings, which received nearly a full page of coverage in *Time* magazine, went poorly for Capp. His tongue-in-cheek remarks about his youthful drawing in Miss Mandelbaum's class, published in his *New Yorker* profile—"I became an expert in pornography"—had come back to haunt him. When Capp attempted to inform the FCC that the *New Yorker* writer was a humorist, and that his statements were supposed to be exaggerations, he found no sympathizers. When confronted with Fisher's photostats, Capp lost his composure.

"These are forgeries," he insisted. "We conducted our investigation of the source of the forgeries. We are in the last stage of finding the forger."

This 1948 daily supports critics' claims that the shmoo was intentionally phallic. Further supporting such a reading, Abner calls the suggestively positioned shmoo a "Benedick" Arnold. Verbal and visual double entendres were common in the strip.

The FCC didn't have time to wait.

Capp had no choice but to withdraw from the buying group. He did not let the issue go. He approached the National Cartoonists Society and demanded that it examine what one of its members was doing to another cartoonist.

Another blatant example of sexual innuendo in a 1951 daily, with another phallic form, the "Dogpatch ham."

The NCS had reached the end of its patience with the public bickering between Ham Fisher and Al Capp. It brought the wrong kind of attention to the group at a time when comics artists and writers were under intense scrutiny. While Capp and his lawyers set out to positively identify the source of the most recently submitted batch of "offensive" strips, the NCS looked for a way to squelch the fighting, once and for all.

Walt Kelly, creator of "Pogo," a satirical strip owing much to "Li'l Abner," sent a letter to Capp detailing the NCS's difficulties.

"To be quite blunt, I feel, as President of the National Cartoonists Society, that the continued brawl between you and one of our members is not only hurting the 'good name' of cartooning but has become a distinct pain in the derriere to me in particular," Kelly wrote. He was outraged that anyone might alter another cartoonist's artwork in an effort to discredit him, and felt that anyone doing such a thing should be forced to leave the NCS. Yet Kelly also pointedly reminded Capp that Fisher was a current member of the NCS and Capp, who had left the organization, was not. Kelly had little doubt that Capp's work had been altered in some way or another, but until a name could be attached to the misdeed, the public squabbling had to cease.

"We cannot entertain any foggy accusations and we will not listen to vituperation," Kelly scolded. "In the name of all we hold dear, I feel this damned foolish harmful affair should come to an end. I am hopeful that you, with restraint, will bend every effort, including making a full report to us, toward making an end to this nonsense. As cartoonists, and especially as syndicate men, we absolutely cannot afford to have it go on."

Capp's own attorney urged him to exercise restraint while an expert in handwriting matched the writing in the margins of the photostats with samples of Ham Fisher's writing.

"Be careful that you do not stoop for even a second to the level of your maligner," he warned. "If it were not for the potential harm he might do you, he should be treated with pity as a pathological case."

Fisher would have been hard-pressed to come up with a list of allies. NCS members tried to avoid him at their meetings. At best, he was the proverbial wet blanket capable of dampening anyone's mood in very short order; at his worst, he was nasty and spiteful, a man who had no friends for good reason. Moe Leff, his longtime assistant, could barely tolerate a workday with him. Marilyn Fisher, Ham's wife, had hinted that she was growing tired of his tirades at home.

Cartoonist Morris Weiss, the artist on "Mickey Finn" and other strips, might have been Fisher's only true friend during the ordeal of his final months. Fisher would frequently drop by Weiss's apartment, and the two men would play checkers. Weiss, in his own words, became Fisher's "father confessor." Fisher would air his gripes, and Weiss would push his checkers across the board and listen.

"He was very unhappy," Weiss remembered. "It bothered him very much that he wasn't getting appreciation from his fellow cartoonists. And Capp engineered his being expelled from the Society. Ham had photostats blown up of suggestive things in 'Li'l Abner.' He sent them out to the newspapers. When it came to the Cartoonists Society ethics committee, Ham denied that he had done it. Capp was able to prove that it was [Fisher's] signature on the borders."

In the end, it was proved that the writing on the borders belonged to Fisher, but there was never conclusive proof that Fisher had altered the images, as Capp asserted. For discerning readers, including Fisher, Capp's frequent visual and verbal double entendres were indisputable, but they were always clever enough to be ambiguous and thus fly below the radar of the vast majority of unassuming readers. Fisher wasn't the only one seeing blue and thinking Capp's naughty inserts were self-evident. In 1953 the popular scandal magazine *Confidential* had run a cover story, "Al Capp Exposed: The Secret Sex Life of Li'l Abner," discussing and picturing some of the same things Fisher was asserting.

Two sworn affidavits, submitted by William H. Mauldin, who had examined the photostats of the "Li'l Abner" strips prior to the 1950 New York State Joint Legislative Committee's investigation, and Charles A. Appel Jr., a Washington, D.C., document examiner hired to look into the current set, testified that some tampering was present, but neither was prepared to say that Fisher had created or added new images to the strips. In all likelihood, Fisher had enhanced or edited the existing images to prove his point. Mauldin was especially direct in his conclusion: "I think this stuff has been deliberately presented in a way to suggest dirt where no dirt existed in the original." Appel's conclusion—"that the questioned notations were written by . . . Ham Fisher"—sealed Fisher's fate. He was formally expelled from the National Cartoonists Society on February 9, 1955.

For Fisher, this was the final defeat and humiliation at the hands of Al

Capp. He would never understand that the NCS was more interested in ending an embarrassing public feud than in exposing Capp for his suggestive art in "Li'l Abner."

In the months that passed between his expulsion from the NCS and his death, Fisher raged about the inequities of his life, most often to Morris Weiss.

"He came to our apartment one day and he went off on a tirade," Weiss's wife, Blanche, would recall. "He just kept spewing and spewing. I never heard such hatred come out of a person in my life."

Morris Weiss listened to it for as long as he could, but as the year drew to an end, he'd finally heard enough.

"I did sincerely want to help him," he insisted, adding that he had approached members of the Cartoonists Society on Fisher's behalf, to no avail. But Fisher's daily visits were taking Weiss away from his own work and creating friction between him and his wife. Fisher asked Weiss to come work for him; Weiss politely declined. When Fisher continued with his black rages, showing no indication that he was willing to do anything to improve his life, Weiss finally stood up to him.

"I don't want you to come to me with any more of your problems unless you do something concrete to help yourself," he told Fisher. "Moe Leff is driving you crazy? Fire Moe Leff. You'll get another. Believe me, I'll have no trouble getting you an assistant who will do just as good. You're tired of the strip? Go to England—London. You have enough money to travel. Do things. You're unhappy with Marilyn? Get a divorce. I don't want to hear from you until you're doing something concrete to help yourself."

Fisher considered what Weiss was saying. "I'm going to do something tomorrow," he promised.

The following afternoon, Weiss received a call from a very worried Marilyn Fisher. Her husband hadn't called, and no one answered when she called Moe Leff's studio, where Fisher was working. Ham Fisher always called for his messages—he never failed. Weiss reassured her that there had to be a good reason for her husband's silence, but Marilyn continued to worry. She called Weiss several more times, each call increasingly desperate. Eventually, around six o'clock that evening, Weiss dressed and drove first to Marilyn's, where he attempted to calm her in person, and then to

Leff's Manhattan studio. With Leff gone, vacationing in Florida, Weiss had to talk the building superintendent into using his passkey to let him into the studio.

Fisher had been dead for some time when Weiss discovered his body. The suicide letter, written in pencil, was brief:

> My sight has gone to a great extent, is getting progressively worse, and my health has gone with it. May God and my beloved ones forgive me. I have provided for them amply.

Weiss picked up the phone and called the *New York Daily Mirror*, the flagship paper for "Joe Palooka" since 1930. Weiss figured they deserved the scoop on the story. Then he called the police.

While waiting for the police to arrive, Weiss returned to the couch. "I stood over him and called him a miserable son of a bitch for doing it," he recalled.

Fisher's suicide brought an ending to the Capp-Fisher feud, but Capp still couldn't let it rest. Within days of Fisher's funeral, he was entertaining listeners in Sardi's, the high-visibility bar and restaurant in Manhattan's theater district. An article in the *New York Daily News* reported on Capp's meeting there with Lee Falk, writer for "Mandrake the Magician" and "The Phantom."

"He has ennobled our feud," Capp told Falk. Not satisfied to share what he considered to be a brilliant observation with just one man, Capp turned to everyone in the room.

"He ennobled it," he proclaimed, in his big, booming voice. "It is a noble thing he did."

Falk stared down into his glass. "My God," he thought. "The man thinks this is *Tristan and Isolde*."

This was not enough. About nine months after Fisher's demise, Capp wrote Milton Caniff and asked that he use his position in the Cartoonists Society to put into writing the society's findings on Fisher and his complaints about the sexual content in "Li'l Abner."

"With the FCC business ended and Fisher gone," Capp wrote, "the final act of the Society—to say plainly what its findings were and to say plainly that the stigma attached to my work by one of its members was a crime against the Society and against me—has one value, and that is that my kids and my grandchildren will know that I was an honorable man and no discredit to my profession."

13 BRIGHT LIGHTS

Al Capp had been disappointed by earlier attempts to move "Li'l Abner" off the newspaper pages and into other forms of entertainment. The 1940 movie adaptation had been a bomb, and the animated cartoon version was even worse. The *Fearless Fosdick* kids' show had gone nowhere. "Li'l Abner" possessed all the qualities, from characters to storylines, found in successes on the big screen, onstage, and in early television, yet no one seemed to be up to making the adaptation. Nevertheless, Capp was hopeful when it looked as if a "Li'l Abner" play might actually take a bow on Broadway.

The Broadway adaptation had been in the works for four years, dating back to 1952, when lyricist Alan Jay Lerner (*Brigadoon, My Fair Lady, Camelot*) purchased the rights. Capp was elated, but as the months gave way without any sign of the play moving forward, he grew skeptical of its ever being produced. Lerner let the option expire in 1955. Capp attempted a script on his own, but he discovered that there was an enormous difference between producing a comic strip and tackling the logistics of a Broadway play.

Fortunately, other film and theater producers were now lining up for a shot at bringing "Li'l Abner" to life. Paramount Pictures made the most attractive offer: the company would purchase the stage and film rights for "Li'l Abner," reportedly for an amount in excess of $300,000. As a bonus, Capp would be awarded a small role—playing himself—in *That Certain Feeling*, a Paramount film starring Bob Hope.

"They asked me who I might suggest to play the role of Al Capp," he quipped, adding that his first choice would have been Tyrone Power. "We finally compromised on me because I would be cheapest, and so I came out and did play myself with only forty-six years of rehearsal."

The team involved in the Broadway production was as fine as could be assembled. Norman Panama and Melvin Frank, the brain trust behind the films *White Christmas*, *Knock on Wood*, and others, produced, directed, and wrote *Li'l Abner*. Choreographer Michael Kidd, whose work included *Finian's Rainbow*, the stage and screen versions of *Guys and Dolls*, and the film *Seven Brides for Seven Brothers*, was enlisted to choreograph the dancing through Dogpatch and would also direct. The team responsible for the Oscar-winning score for *Seven Brides for Seven Brothers* was brought in to do the same with Li'l Abner. The songs would be written by Gene de Paul, a veteran of countless film scores, with lyricist Johnny Mercer ("You Must Have Been a Beautiful Baby," "Blues in the Night," "That Old Black Magic," "Autumn Leaves").

Casting for the leading roles of Li'l Abner and Daisy Mae wound up yielding two relative newcomers. After an extensive search that included Andy Griffith and even inquiries about the availability of Elvis Presley, comedic actor Dick Shawn was selected for the role of Li'l Abner. Panama and Frank, however, weren't totally satisfied with the selection. Li'l Abner was taller and more muscular than Shawn. He'd have to develop a physique for the role. While Shawn worked with a trainer to add bulk to his frame, casting continued for other parts. Then, one Sunday evening, while watching *The Ed Sullivan Show*, Panama, Frank, and Kidd saw a young man dressed in a military uniform, singing "Granada." He was blond, but at 6'4" and 220 pounds, sporting the muscular build of the offensive tackle he'd been at the University of Illinois, and possessing a singing voice much better than Shawn's, Peter Palmer was the Li'l Abner they were looking for. After delivering the bad news to Shawn, the producers placed a few calls to Washington, D.C., and secured an early discharge for Palmer.

Finding someone to play Daisy Mae was much easier—and, ironically, came as the result of another *Ed Sullivan* appearance. Singer/actress Edie Adams had loved "Li'l Abner" since she was a teenager and, dressed as Daisy Mae, had won a Sadie Hawkins competition. When she learned that a "Li'l Abner" Broadway musical was in development, she had her agent send out the word that she was interested in the part of Daisy Mae. The sultry blonde with Marilyn Monroe looks was married to popular comedian Ernie Kovacs and had gained national exposure on his television programs. She was slated for an appearance on *The Ed Sullivan Show*, and she made a

Sunday panels from Ham Fisher's "Joe Palooka" dated October 29, 1933, ghosted by his assistant Alfred Caplin. The question of which man created Big Leviticus, the hillbilly in the red shirt, was at the heart of a bitter lifelong feud between the two cartoonists.

Al Capp created hundreds of colorful characters over four and a half decades to supplement Dogpatch's Yokum clan, the cornerstone of the epic comic strip. Two dozen recurring cast members are pictured here.

When crusading psychiatrist Dr. Fredric Wertham (*Seduction of the Innocent*) and others lobbied against the perceived evils of comic books during the late forties and early fifties, Al Capp responded with this satiric 1948 Sunday strip. To underscore the message, he had the page reprinted multiple times in "Li'l Abner" comic books.

In 1937, the ever-ambitious Capp created and wrote a second syndicated comic strip, "Abbie an' Slats," but he struggled to maintain script deadlines for artist Raeburn Van Buren. Finally, in 1945, Capp's brother Elliot took over the writing of the series. Pictured here is a comic book edition.

From the late 1930s to the early 1950s, comic books were hugely popular in America. "Li'l Abner" newspaper strips were routinely recycled into this inexpensive format, first by other publishers, and eventually by Capp Enterprises' own Toby Press.

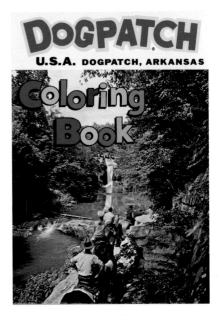

Bumbling detective Fearless Fosdick—Li'l Abner's "ideel" and the star of Capp's periodic strip-within-a-strip was popular enough to sometimes take over the cover of "Li'l Abner" comic books.

Dogpatch USA opened its doors in Arkansas in 1968, making Al Capp the only cartoonist besides Walt Disney with his own theme park.

CONTINUED ON OTHER SIDE

Al Capp conveniently settled his lawsuit against United Feature Syndicate and wrested control of "Li'l Abner" merchandising rights just as the nation's phenomenal love affair with the shmoo began in 1948. He and his brothers (Capp Enterprises, Inc.) were very successful in marketing the property, but one license, for Proctor & Gamble's "Name the Shmoo" ad campaign, backfired. Some subscribing newspapers loudly complained that such exploitation diluted the value of the strip they were buying.

Al Capp's prominence in the culture during his lifetime cannot be overstated. During one five-year period, he and his characters were featured as cover stories in three of America's most popular magazines. He was a longtime regular guest on *The Tonight Show* and other TV talk venues, and, in addition to his enormously popular comic strip, the tireless Capp was for a while both a syndicated radio commentator and a newspaper columnist.

The appearance of the shmoo in "Li'l Abner," starting in August 1948, generated an overwhelming demand for merchandise, only a small fraction of which is pictured here. Over one hundred shmoo products from seventy-five different manufacturers were produced within a year of the character's inception, all of it licensed through Capp's family-run corporation.

In 1959, Milton Caniff (l) and Al Capp posed nose-to-nose in a mock confrontation on the twenty-fifth anniversary of their respective creations "Terry and the Pirates" and "Li'l Abner." The close lifelong friends met in 1932 as lowly staff artists at the Associated Press in New York. Each briefly drew the AP strip "Mr. Gilfeather" before going on to fame and fortune.

The musical adaptation *Li'l Abner* opened on Broadway in 1955, running nearly seven hundred performances. Actress Edie Adams, as Daisy Mae, and choreographer Michael Kidd won Tony Awards, while newcomer Peter Palmer won a Theatre World Award in the title role. Though the context may be lost to modern audiences, the musical continues to be reprised in numerous high school, college, and repertory theaters.

Paramount released its big screen version of the *Li'l Abner* musical in 1959. With the exceptions of Edie Adams and Tina Louise (Appassionata von Climax), the core Broadway cast remained intact for the Hollywood version. Jerry Lewis made an uncredited cameo performance.

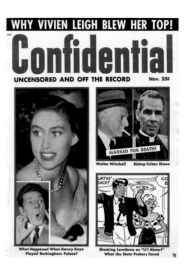

In October 1952, *TV Guide* devoted a cover story to the *Al Capp Show*, one of several Capp forays into television in its early days. Capp worked with all four networks at varying times to develop a starring platform, but each effort, whether involving a game show or satire and commentary, was short-lived.

The notorious muckraking magazine *Confidential* targeted Capp in a November 1953 partial cover story. The article, "Al Capp Exposed: The Secret Sex Life of Li'l Abner," reported that the strip often contained sexual innuendo and suggestive visuals intended for "special readers," mirroring accusations spouted for years by Capp's arch enemy Ham Fisher.

In 1995, the U.S. Postal Service honored Al Capp's creation with a postage stamp depicting Daisy Mae and Li'l Abner.

Sadie Hawkins Day, invented by Al Capp in 1937, was celebrated every November at hundreds of college events for decades. Its wide appeal was based on the temporary social license it gave young women to be aggressors during an era when only men customarily initiated dates. This drawing of Sadie, who inspired the tradition, is by Capp's most famous assistant, Frank Frazetta.

point of seeing that certain people knew about it. She called Milton Caniff and asked him to be sure Al Capp was watching.

It wouldn't have been the first time Al Capp saw Adams, though he may not have remembered the prior occasion. Six years earlier he was a judge on the DuMont Network's 1950 Miss U.S. Television beauty contest, and the fresh-faced New York entry, one Edith Adams, had been the winner.

As Adams recalled, she never had to audition for the role. The *Ed Sullivan* appearance convinced the Broadway production's powers-that-be of her qualifications to play Daisy Mae.

She wasn't pleased, however, by the play's script. She had counted on its capturing some of the snappy satire she so admired in the comic strip, but by her thinking, the script wound up being more of a formulaic, predictable comedy that even a stellar cast couldn't save. Her role had little substance—"in a possible acting range of ten, poor Daisy seemed no more than a three," she complained—and because she was barefoot throughout the performance, the dance numbers were more physically demanding than usual. Adams hoped that some of the play's shortcomings might improve when Al Capp eventually visited the rehearsals and made script alterations, but it didn't happen.

"Not only did he not fix the show," she recalled, "[but] he made passes at all the gorgeous girls in the cast and at me, a very publicly married woman. He took me to dinner and made some adolescent and amateurish passes at me. I wasn't even upset, just disappointed."

It would come as no surprise that the womanizing Capp found much to admire in the cast. The women were featured in a pictorial in *Playboy* and in a cover story—with a large photo spread—in *Life*. Julie Newmar, as Stupefyin' Jones, didn't have a line in the play, but she would make enough of an impression to push her career forward. Tina Louise, who would later star in the role of Ginger on television's *Gilligan's Island*, won the role of Appassionata von Climax.

Capp was satisfied with the way his strip had been adapted to the stage. All the major characters were accounted for, the hillbilly language was preserved, Sadie Hawkins Day figured prominently in the script, the song and dance numbers were snappy, and the costumes were colorfully trashy. The story, centered around the government's intention of making Dogpatch a nuclear testing ground, might have been strictly formula, as Adams had asserted, but it was complex enough that songs had to be rewritten or eliminated in order to bring the show in at a reasonable performance time.

Li'l Abner opened on November 15, 1956, at the St. James Theater and would run for 693 performances—the most successful run of a play based on a comic strip until *Annie* opened in 1977. When the 1957 Tony Award nominations were announced, Michael Kidd was nominated for (and won) the Outstanding Choreographer award, while Edie Adams was nominated for Distinguished Supporting or Featured Musical Actress.

She had to be coaxed into attending the awards ceremony. She had disliked the Daisy Mae role from the beginning, and when her one-year contract expired, she'd dropped out of the production and been replaced. (Charlotte Rae, who played Mammy Yokum, and Tina Louise also left the play when their contracts were up.) Adams was flabbergasted when she was nominated for the Tony. As far as she was concerned, there had been very little to the part—certainly not enough to compete with much bigger roles—and she couldn't imagine that she had any chance of winning. Talked into attending the ceremony at the last minute, she accepted the Tony when she won. She would never win another.

Capp was on a roll. "Li'l Abner" had hit a new peak. The comic strip was now appearing in seven hundred newspapers, with a circulation of forty million. The Broadway musical had garnered national attention, with articles and pictorials running in major magazines and newspapers across the country. Capp was earning more than a quarter of a million a year.

He was now working on a second strip, "Long Sam," for which he was the writer, similar to his earlier role with "Abbie an' Slats." "Long Sam" was a sort of "Li'l Abner" from the female perspective. The title character was a mountain girl who had been hidden away from civilization by her mother, a woman distrustful of all men. She, like the Strange Gal characater in "Li'l Abner," was eventually exposed to the modern, "civilized" world, which gave Capp the opportunity to present the contrasts in a humorous way. The strip opened in 1954.

Bob Lubbers, the artist on the strip, had earned his reputation after taking over "Tarzan" from Burne Hogarth in 1950. He was recommended for the job by Raeburn Van Buren, Capp's artist for "Abbie an' Slats." He met Capp at just the right moment.

"One day in November 1953, as my 'Tarzan' contract was nearing renewal, he called me, inviting me to his Waldorf suite for a chat about a new project he thought might interest me. He had seen my pretty girl stuff and thought his scripts and my art would be a happy combo. That was the start of our 25-year alliance."

Capp would eventually turn the writing over to his brother Elliott, as he'd done with "Abbie an' Slats," but Lubbers would reunite with Capp to work on "Li'l Abner" during its last years. "Long Sam," while entertaining, never matched "Li'l Abner" in either popularity or content, and it would become a footnote in Capp's career.

Capp began 1957 with a take-no-prisoners "Li'l Abner" commentary on the youth culture, as powered by a new phenomenon called rock 'n' roll. Where he once roasted Frank Sinatra and his horde of swooning female fans, he now gave the treatment to the effects that Elvis Presley and his swiveling hips had on American youth. Presley had scored heavily on the music charts the previous year with "Heartbreak Hotel," "Hound Dog," and "Love Me Tender" among five hits reaching No. 1 status on the Billboard charts; Capp, who preferred the time-honored sagas of opera over the amplified energy of rock 'n' roll, took notice. His "Li'l Abner" story, featuring an Elvis-like character named Hawg McCall, lambasted the youthful hero-worship of his fans while attacking the adult world striving to cash in on the fad.

This would be a year of parodies. Capp trained his sights on two popular comic strips: the soap opera strip "Mary Worth" and his friend Milton Caniff's action strip, "Steve Canyon." In the case of "Mary Worth," Capp added a wrinkle by manufacturing another public feud, this one with "Mary Worth" writer Allen Saunders. The idea for the feud had been hatched the previous year in Washington, D.C., at a meeting of the cartoonists committee of President Dwight Eisenhower's People to People program—a committee that Capp chaired.

"We cartoonists decided that ours was the dullest possible profession, since we all liked each other," Capp cracked. "We decided it might add some interest to the entire profession if a couple of us murdered each other."

"Mary Worth" was natural fodder for a satirist. Capp had included overheated elements of the soap opera genre in "Li'l Abner" dating back to the strip's earliest days, always with a cynical slant that made it utterly clear that Capp held a very low opinion of accepted dating habits, the idealized marriage, and, in general, any starry-eyed dynamics in human relation-ships. The public debate over the wedding of Li'l Abner and Daisy Mae showed that readers had indeed been more interested in Daisy Mae's pur-suits and frustrations than in an idealized happy ending.

Capp held back nothing in his parody of "Mary Worth," which ran on Sundays. The title character of Allen Saunders's strip was a kindly, aging woman helping the lovelorn solve their romantic problems. Capp depicted her as a huge, imposing, ill-tempered shrew whose advice was nothing but stomach-churning clichés. The victim of her endless bloviating was her long-suffering son-in-law, Allen Flounder, a wonderfully rendered carica-ture of Saunders, right down to his receding hairline and ever-present pipe. Flounder produced a comic strip, "Mary Worm, America's Most Beloved Old Busybody," which happened to be Daisy Mae's favorite strip. Li'l Abner, noting that his wife's reading of the strip came at the expense of her taking care of his happy home, demanded that Daisy Mae choose between her husband and "Mary Worm." After tossing him out of the house, Daisy Mae wrote Mary Worm, imploring her to come to Dogpatch and save her mar-riage. Flounder's mother-in-law, the model for his comic strip, took off to investigate, and rather than help, the old meddler compounded Daisy Mae's marital problems by dispensing such wisdom as "Make him suffer!! One of my sweetest wise sayings is—'A husband that suffers is a husband that ap-preciates.'" Mammy Yokum, as usual, wound up saving the day.

Allen Saunders proved more than capable of holding up his end of the feud. His response began in "Mary Worth" a few days after Capp's opening salvo. In Saunders's retaliation, Mary Worth, who volunteered at the box office of a local theater group, was dispatched to deliver tickets to the sum-mer home of Hal Rapp, the famous cartoonist. Rapp turned out to be an intolerable, self-centered boor; he did virtually no work while a group of

In 1957, Al Capp and friendly rival Allen Saunders, creator of "Mary Worth,"
concocted feuding parodies for publicity. Capp's "Mary Worm" was portrayed as
an insufferable busybody.

artists, working in a space more sweatshop than studio, produced his strip,
"Big Abe." Saunders knew Capp was a teetotaler but slyly depicted him as a
drunk. Artist Ken Ernst's caricature of Al Capp, like Capp's of Allen Saunders, was dead-on.

Capp used his connections to see that his feud with Saunders was well
publicized. Both combatants took public swipes at each other, all written
up by an increasingly amused press.

"Mary Worth is a nasty, blackhearted, nosey old hag," Capp said in mock disgust, referring to the Hal Rapp sequence as "unpardonable slander, something disgraceful, humiliating." Responded Saunders, "Al Capp is surrounded by phonies—he doesn't know any real, true, honest people. It is impossible for him to understand a fine character like Mary Worth." Saunders was equally disdainful of Capp's caricature of him: "Obviously the real reason he drew such a poor likeness is because he's such a lousy artist."

At least one newspaper took the feud to heart. Calling Saunders's "Mary Worth" story a "thinly disguised attack on the creator of another comic strip," the *Des Moines Tribune* suspended publication of "Mary Worth" until the Hal Rapp story had run its course. "The editors of the *Tribune* believe that readers want to be entertained by comic strips and are not interested in the jealousies and rivalries that exist between comic strip creators," the paper explained.

Capp moved straight from his "Mary Worm" parody to a send-up of Milton Caniff's "Steve Canyon." This sequence also ran in the Sunday papers. The comic strip within a comic strip "Steve Cantor" written by one Milton Goniff, found Li'l Abner and Steve Cantor teaming up against the evil Jewel Brynner, "the most dangerous bald girl spy in the Orient." Capp's uncanny imitation of Caniff's style harked back to the day when young Al Caplin, desperate for a job in cartooning, lugged a portfolio of imitations from job interview to job interview, with no success. Nobody wanted imitations. Now here he was, being paid top dollar for his parodies. It was an irony he could appreciate.

After ending its successful run on Broadway, *Li'l Abner* hit the road, beginning at the Riviera Hotel in Las Vegas. Most of the Broadway cast members traveled with the road show. Audiences responded enthusiastically.

The musical had still been in full swing on Broadway when officials at Paramount Pictures began their preliminary talks about converting it into a movie, as had been their intention all along. Musicals were still very popular in movie houses, and *Li'l Abner* offered something appealing to audiences of all ages. Executives at Paramount hoped to have the movie ready for a Christmas 1959 release, which meant that preproduction, filming and postproduction had to go quickly and efficiently.

Luckily, two thirds of the musical's Broadway brain trust stayed aboard. Norman Panama and Melvin Frank would again be heavily involved, with Panama producing, Frank directing, and the two teaming up on the screenplay. Michael Kidd, however, was out. The play's award-winning choreographer fought with Paramount over his contract, and an agreement was never reached. Dee Dee Wood, his assistant in choreographing the dance numbers on Broadway, was brought on board to see that nothing would be lost in the film adaptation. Given the tight production schedule, there was no time for drawn-out rehearsals.

To facilitate a smooth transition, Panama and Frank cast as many of the Broadway actors and dancers as possible in the film, but three of the important players had to be replaced. Edie Adams and Charlotte Rae were pregnant; neither had cared much for her Broadway role, anyway. Tina Louise wasn't interested, either. Peter Palmer, Billie Hayes (who took over the role of Mammy Yokum on Broadway after Charlotte Rae dropped out), Stubby Kaye (Marryin' Sam), Julie Newmar, and Howard St. John (General Bullmoose) reprised their Broadway roles in the film.

Panama and Frank conducted dozens of screen tests before settling on Leslie Parrish as the movie's Daisy Mae—a surprise selection since Parrish was a relative newcomer. Working under the name of Marjorie Hellen, Parrish had appeared in minor roles in other movies, but this would be her first starring role. Stella Stevens, who would be the January 1960 *Playboy* Playmate centerfold, was cast as Appassionata von Climax. Theater posters and ads would say that *Li'l Abner* was the "most girl-stacked musical ever made," a double entendre that proved to be truth in advertising.

As comics writer and historian Mark Evanier pointed out in a detailed article on the making of *Li'l Abner*, Paramount bigwigs were not happy that the film didn't have a box office heavyweight to entice moviegoers into theaters. Jerry Lewis was Paramount's biggest draw at the time, and to appease Paramount, Melvin Frank talked him into dropping by to shoot a cameo appearance during one of his breaks from filming *Don't Give Up the Ship* on a nearby soundstage.

"He also insisted that his name not be used in advertising," Evanier reported, "to which Panama and Frank agreed, apparently hoping that Paramount brass could later persuade Lewis to waive his 'no billing' condition."

Li'l Abner hit the movie screens on schedule. Capp provided nine images of the "Li'l Abner" characters in the movie, to accompany the cast photos in publicity materials. A private screening of the film was arranged for Capp and his family in Boston.

The movie was well received by critics, praised as enjoyable, if lowbrow, entertainment. For Capp, the film was a satisfying conclusion to another strong year. The strip, celebrating its twenty-fifth anniversary, had offered two time-proven audience pleasers—a reappearance of the shmoo and an especially inspired "Fearless Fosdick," a commentary on the persistent complaints about comic book violence, in which Fosdick is forced to fight crime without the use of a weapon.

After twenty-five years, Al Capp was still delivering.

The "Abner" silver anniversary fell during the same year as Capp's fiftieth birthday, and Bence Capp pulled out all the stops to guarantee that it would be an unforgettable year for his brother. By working closely with Capp family members, United Feature, and others, Bence coordinated a series of events in Washington, D.C., that commemorated the twenty-fifth anniversary of "Li'l Abner," honored cartoonists in general, kicked off the publicity for another Capp book, and celebrated Al Capp's accomplishments over his first fifty years.

That Bence was still involved in Capp Enterprises was nothing short of remarkable. He and Al had worked out a solution to their hostilities of six years earlier, most likely because both realized that they needed each other much more than either was willing to admit during their heated exchanges and threats of courtroom battles. There had been renewed flare-ups over the ensuing years, usually when Bence failed to follow Al's directives, but Bence had brokered deals that proved to be beneficial to both brothers—and, when all was said and done, the bottom line was all that really mattered.

Despite the occasional glitch, 1959 had been Bence's finest year in representing Al's best interests. When Al decided to run an extended shmoo story as a lead-in to another book-length shmoo collection for Simon & Schuster, Bence worked the phones and wrote numerous letters to newspaper and magazine editors, seeing that everyone was aware of the book's publication date, as well as trying to find possibilities for excerpts in periodicals. He applied creative touches to the publicity for the release of Paramount's *Li'l Abner* movie. He tried to push new merchandising proposals. Al was enjoying another banner year for creative ideas, and he relied on Bence to implement them.

The events in Washington coincided with the planning of the year-end releases of the shmoo book and the movie, making the last quarter of 1959 as frenetic as any Bence had experienced during his tenure at Capp Enterprises. September 28 alone was packed with activities demanding stringent planning. An invitation-only luncheon included an A-list of politicians and government officials (including Vice President Richard Nixon, Chief Justice Earl Warren, and Senator John F. Kennedy), cartoonists (Milton Caniff, Mort Walker, Rube Goldberg, Raeburn Van Buren), newspaper, magazine, and publishing executives, television bigwigs, and Eisenhower cabinet members. After the luncheon, the cartoonists met with U.S. Post Office officials to discuss the creation of a stamp commemorating the American cartoon. (It would take another thirty-six years for the post office to issue a set of stamps commemorating comic strips, but when they did in 1995 "Li'l Abner" was one of them.)

Immediately following that meeting, Capp was spirited away to another government building, where he accepted a key to the city. Capp walked away from the day's events with an armload of gifts, awards, and plaques, including a Waldo Peirce oil painting of "Li'l Abner" characters, presented by Paramount Pictures; a statue of "Li'l Abner" from the Sister Kenny Foundation, in recognition of his years of charitable work with the organization; a series of medallions from the Treasury Department, each featuring one of the secretaries of the treasury serving when Capp was contributing to the U.S. Savings Bond effort; and plaques from the Ad Council and United Feature Syndicate, honoring the "Li'l Abner" anniversary.

Bence Capp saw that the festivities were announced to the media prior to September 28 and that thank-you letters were sent to key contacts and contributors afterward. The publicity, as Bence hoped, was invaluable, especially as an introduction to the release of the movie and book. Al was having the time of his life, and "Li'l Abner" received a boost in public attention that, had Capp been forced to pay advertising rates for it, would have cost a fortune.

This would be the last time the two brothers would be close and working well together. Shortly afterward, Bence asked for a $50-a-week raise—a 12 percent increase over the $400 weekly salary he was currently earning. Capp turned him down. Between salary and commissions, Al maintained, Bence was earning "an excellent living from me and my work, and a very easy one."

Bence could not legitimately dispute the claim. Four hundred dollars a week was a substantial salary in 1959, especially when combined with commissions and extras (not to mention that Bence had other businesses on the side). Over the years, Capp had supplied Bence with a company car, paid for his lavish lifestyle (including an apartment for his girlfriend), and provided other amenities, all written off as expenses. Al was correct when he reminded Bence that his commission percentages—usually 50 percent, but often 100 percent—vastly exceeded the 10 percent industry standard. He might have sold Bence short when he spoke of how little effort the job required, but it was also true that there were long stretches of time when Bence had very little to do around the office.

Nor is there any doubt about the justification of Al's long-standing complaints about the way Bence conducted business at Capp Enterprises. Al acknowledged Bence's considerable skills in establishing valuable connections with differing businesses, yet he hated the way Bence would make unilateral decisions, often in conflict with Al's orders. Since the beginning of Capp Enterprises, Al had shouted at Bence (literally and through the mail), kicked him out of the business, threatened him with lawsuits, and otherwise made his life miserable, only to relent, take him back, and start over.

Two business propositions led to a final split. In both cases, Bence stepped outside his authority at Capp Enterprises, misrepresented business points to the companies he was dealing with, as well as to his brother, and, in general, created an unholy mess that wound up involving attorneys, costing Al money and causing considerable embarrassment.

The first transaction, in early 1960, concerned the development of another *Fearless Fosdick* television show, this time a half-hour animated series, and involved powerful forces in entertainment and advertising. The original idea, enthusiastically endorsed by Al, had been a good one. The show would have involved some of the most highly regarded behind-the-scenes names in television, and all Al Capp had to do was sign off on the copyrights and provide scripts, which he could write himself or assign to others. The compensation was substantial, leading Bence to tell Al that it was one of the best deals in the business. Procter & Gamble, a giant in television advertising, would be underwriting the production. Unfortunately, Bence, seeing an opportunity for a huge payday, insisted on being listed as an executive producer (with a salary of $1,000 per episode), and his interference in the planning of the program nearly sank the deal. Al was furious. Bence had acted without conferring with him, and in cutting himself in on the profits—above and beyond his usual commission—Bence had misrepresented the way the money was being distributed.

The second transaction was even more outrageous. In December 1960, Al Capp's attorney, Al Hochberg, formally notified Bence that he no longer represented Capp Enterprises or any of his brother's other interests, but in early 1961 Bence had set up an agreement with U.S. Tire's Royal Tire brand to create a series of magazine ads. Royal Tire wanted the distinctive Al Capp look for their ads. Bence, knowing that door had been slammed, hired Al's longtime off-site assistant, Frank Frazetta, to do the artwork—with no notification to Al. Though not using trademark "Li'l Abner" characters, the ads featured characters that looked like they were drawn by Capp and could have appeared in the strip.

When Al Capp and United Feature Syndicate saw the ads in print, all hell broke loose. First, there was the question of copyright violation and plagiarism. Second, there was the possibility that Capp had violated his contractual agreement with United Feature by not informing the syndicate of the deal. Finally, there was the issue of Bence's keeping the profits from the advertising campaign for himself and deceiving Royal Tire.

Once again, Al had to talk to the aggrieved parties and do damage control, causing him some embarrassment and loss of income. Al again instructed Hochberg to see that Bence was completely removed from his duties at Capp Enterprises, right down to disconnecting the company phone and informing Bence that he could no longer use company letterhead.

"Maybe you're a blind spot with me, or vice-versa," he told Bence. "At

NOW U.S. ROYAL SOLVES
THE HEAT PROBLEM

Lower, wider *"Low Profile"* tire <u>flexes less so it runs cooler.</u>
And grade for grade, its sidewalls are stronger, its tread gives
more mileage by far. *It's the tire that doesn't get tired!*

FLEX BUILDS UP HEAT. Heat murders tires—actually wears 'em out. Old-fashioned tires flex too much, get hot, give out. But the new U.S. Royal "Low Profile" tire is *lower* and *wider* in shape, flexes less, runs cooler, *lasts longer.* Because it puts more rubber on the road, it performs more efficiently. Traction is improved. *Stops are faster and safer.*

"Low Profile" was pioneered by U.S. Royal, and its superior construction is protected by 234 different quality controls. It costs no more than ordinary tires, and it's available for every make and model car, including compacts. Your U.S. Royal Dealer has the right "Low Profile" tire for *your* car right now. Give it a try. *You'll find it doesn't get tired.*

U.S.ROYAL
LOW PROFILE* TIRES

"Low Profile" is United States Rubber Company's trademark for its lower, wider shape tire.

UNITED   STATES   RUBBER

By 1961, relations between Al and Bence Capp were strained, but a series of Royal Tire ads destroyed their personal and professional relationship. Bence hired Frank Frazetta to ape Capp's style for the ads, resulting in prolonged litigation.

any rate, we ought to know now that we cannot get along in business, as many people can't."

This time, there was no turning back. Al worked diligently through Hochberg to ensure that Bence had no legal recourse, and he made certain that Bence understood there could be severe legal repercussions if his indiscretions were brought out in court. Al avoided the name-calling that had peppered his previous exchanges with Bence, and, for his part, Bence knew that he had been defeated.

The two would never work together again. Nor were they able to resolve the hostilities between them. They rarely attended family gatherings and functions at the same time. Bence's son, Todd, said his father preferred not to be in Al's presence at such events, but that didn't prevent him from causing mischief. When Madeline and Louis hosted holiday events at their New York City apartment, Bence would send Todd to represent his family. Todd recalled that his father, on two occasions, after a few drinks following dinner, "would call the apartment and in a loud voice say he was showing up and would toss Al down the steps. He never followed up, but Al would inevitably beat a hasty retreat." On those occasions when they were forced to be together, such as posing for a family photograph taken on Otto Caplin's eightieth birthday, the best they could muster toward one another was a strained civility.

In the waning days of the 1950s, *Esquire* magazine asked Capp what changes he saw coming in comics in the forthcoming decade. Capp predicted that the people running the newspaper comic strip pages would finally come to their senses and realize that diminishing the size of the strip to fit more strips per page was destroying the art—and, by extension, lowering circulation figures.

"When the editors once again publish comic strips large enough for those with normal eyesight to see them," he predicted, "this will bring an enormous surge of added readership to the comic page and added circulation to the newspaper with readable comics."

The shrinking conic strip had been on Capp's mind for a long time. When he was initially designing "Li'l Abner," he'd tried to find a little edge, here or there, on the competition. As a draftsman, he couldn't compete with the cartoon realism of the likes of Alex Raymond, Milton Caniff, or any number of others, and since it was the art that caught the eye and drew readers into the strip, Capp sought ways to underplay his artistic shortcomings and still make "Li'l Abner" visually striking. While his natural style leaned toward the humorous and even grotesque, Capp's long hours attending art and anatomy classes paid off: as his drawing technique matured in the strip, he came to draw what many regarded as the sexiest females in comics and typically draped them in the most minimal attire that family newspapers could tolerate.

Capp also found his answer in being creatively loud. He used a lot of black in the strip, often showing characters in silhouette; he perfected the employment of different styles and sizes of lettering, incorporating as much boldface as possible. Emotional exclamations—SOB!!!, GASP!!!, EEK!!!, almost always presented in bold type—burst out of dialogue bubbles, punctuation marks running amok.

Those not-so-subtle touches set "Li'l Abner" apart from the competition. The strip screamed off the page. It promised something bold, maybe even aggressive, something no other strip was going to deliver, and readers noticed.

Reducing the size of the strip robbed "Li'l Abner" of its advantage. The letters shrank; the panels seemed top-heavy with dialogue. "Li'l Abner' had always featured more dialogue than the typical strip, but in a smaller format, the dialogue overwhelmed the art. It was not a good idea to make a reader strain to see the finer details. But this was a fight Capp was destined to lose. He would have to adjust to the new reality.

When Capp offered his observations about how the 1960s might affect his profession, he had no idea how history itself would change it. The 1950s had been all about Ike, the New York Yankees, finding a piece of real estate in the newly created suburbs, Elvis Presley, a young midwestern actor named Marlon Brando replacing the rebellious persona of James Dean, the Beat Generation, the spread of Communism, and the usual variety of hostilities between nations, including, for the United States, a Korean conflict in the early years of the decade. A space race was just starting up, and televisions glowed in more households than ever. The *Brown v. Board of Education of*

Topeka Supreme Court decision had begun a long-overdue movement toward racial equality.

Capp had seen fit to comment on much of it in "Li'l Abner," though he had avoided being too overtly political. He could savage pop culture, but McCarthyism had ruined careers, and Capp, despite his bluster, had been frightened.

Capp Enterprises continued to steadily move ahead. There seemed to be "Li'l Abner" tie-ins at every turn. By the mid-1960s, there would even be a Kickapoo Joy Juice soft drink, capitalizing on the mysterious, potent drink cooked up by Hairless Joe and Lonesome Polecat and used to stir up all kinds of mayhem in Dogpatch. Mammy Yokum and friends would be serving fried chicken in new restaurant franchises. The endorsement and merchandizing deals, coupled with the nine-hundred-plus newspapers subscribing to "Li'l Abner," were almost enough to make Capp forget that Charles Schulz and the kids in his strip, "Peanuts," were now capturing the public's fancy in a new way, as the Yokums had at the start. When Capp celebrated his strip's twenty-fifth anniversary in 1959, he could rest assured that he was still a major force in the world of comic strips.

What lay ahead was a wealth of material too vast even for Capp, a massive shift in culture that left Capp—who'd always had his finger on the pulse—suddenly at odds with a large portion of his readership. The sixties would rank among the most turbulent decades in American history, with social and political movements so divisive that one could not switch on the television without seeing disturbing reports about death, destruction, and violence on the American streets or in the battlefields of Vietnam. Capp abhorred violence, especially when it upset what he felt was a comfortable status quo. He supported equality for African Americans but preferred the tactics of Martin Luther King Jr.—about whom his studio produced an educational comic book—and demonized those of Stokely Carmichael, Eldridge Cleaver, Malcolm X, and the Black Panthers. He did, however, support the war and detested those who undermined the effort. He would never cotton to the demonstrations, protests, and theatrics of the antiwar movement. Folksingers made his flesh crawl; hippies, descendants of the beats, were examples of bad hygiene and disobedience. The Beatles offended his musical sensibilities.

His attitudes about all this and more would make their way into "Li'l Abner" continuities, but he also found other outlets for his opinions, of which there had never been a shortage. He had been seen regularly on television during the 1950s, but his appearances in the 1960s would signal a steady shift from being a cartoonist in the public eye to being a strong-willed, outspoken commentator on anything striking his fancy.

Capp joked that his opinions were strictly limited to "life, death, love, economics, the arts, man's inhumanity to man, metaphysics, cybernetics, and atomic fission." He was an authority on everything and nothing. Fortunately, he found different mass media sources receptive to his thoughts and audiences hooked on his opinions. When a strike affected New York's newspapers in 1963, Capp stepped in as a theater critic for the *New York Standard*, one of the alternate papers springing up to fill the void. His life-long love of plays might have made him an ideal replacement critic, but his reviews were impossibly mean-spirited. His magazine pieces, published more frequently than ever, were entertaining at the beginning of the decade and infuriating by its end. The same could be said about his guest spots on television. He'd been on *The Tonight Show* back when Steve Allen and Jack Paar were hosting it; Johnny Carson made him one of his most frequent guests on the show but soured on him as the decade wore on. According to legend, Carson gave up on him after Capp announced that he loved *Easy Rider* because of its happy ending.

Capp seemed to be everywhere at once. He had radio commentaries on both sides of the ocean—on *This Week* in England and on NBC's weekend *Monitor* program. A TV series adaptation of "Li'l Abner" and an Al Capp television show, were in development.

As the mayhem of the 1960s bothered him more and more, Capp slid further toward conservatism, and the shift would only become more noticeable when Capp discovered the ultimate target for his commentary: the college campus and the students he'd bait until his own missteps brought him down.

As late as the fall of 1964, Al Capp was still a bona fide liberal, publicly campaigning on behalf of Lyndon Johnson in the presidential election, lam-

Illustrated by Wallace Wood

Wally Wood, a cartoonist famous for his work in early MAD and EC science fiction comic books, parodied Al Capp's multiplatform career (and close friendship with Milton Caniff) in his 1964 Pageant strip.

pooning Barry Goldwater's propensity for pushing nuclear buttons, and mocking Goldwater's running mate William Miller for his advocacy of morality in government. But Capp's shift toward conservatism crystallized during the following year and was on full display in a lengthy, freewheeling interview published in *Playboy* in December 1965. The interview, conducted by Alvin Toffler over eleven hours of questioning, covered a wide range of topics, from politics to "Li'l Abner," from college campuses to his fellow comic strip artists.

As engaging as he could be, Capp only showed flashes of it in the interview. In his *New Yorker* profile of eighteen years earlier, he had been occasionally edgy but funny; in the *Playboy* interview, he came across like a humorless grump—the type you might find sitting on a porch and shaking his fists at kids stepping on his lawn.

"Under today's corruption of welfare," he groused, "any slut capable of impregnation is encouraged to produce bastards without end." In discussing youth and parenthood, he was even nastier. "Nobody cares enough to take the trouble to point out to kids how revolting they are to us. That's why they grow into savages. The only reason we don't murder them in their teens is that we're willing to wait for a crueler revenge—the day when the little bastards become parents themselves."

The idea was not a new one for Capp. Seven years earlier, newspaper columnist Art Buchwald had quoted Capp on teenagers in a similar way: "Teen-agers are repulsive to everybody except each other. We all know that children pass through various stages of insanity, so why try to understand them."

Capp, who described himself to Toffler as "cheerfully angry," was less contentious when discussing his career, and there were moments when the old humor beamed through. However, more often than not Capp's remarks reflected the expanding gulf between two generations, one that had fought in World War II and one that was beginning to protest the Vietnam War, a gulf that would become known as the Generation Gap. Capp's opinions reflected a polarization that would ultimately erupt in violence on college campuses across the country.

14 IN THE HALLS OF THE ENEMY

Capp rang in 1967 with a parody that expressed his contempt for the protests and student demonstrations he was seeing on college campuses throughout the United States. Folk and agitprop music had enjoyed an explosion of popularity over the past four or five years, acting as a lightning rod for the civil rights movement and protests against the war in Vietnam. Guitar-strumming songwriters, much to Capp's disgust, had become spokespeople for America's youth, wielding great influence in generational battles. Songs such as "Blowin' in the Wind," "We Shall Overcome," "The Times They Are A-Changin'" and "If I Had a Hammer" had become anthems in the push for change.

Capp weighed in with a "Li'l Abner" sequence featuring Joanie Phoanie, an obnoxious self-centered folksinger, whose songs "Let's Riot Tonight on the Old Campus Ground," "Let's Conga with the Viet Cong," and "On a Hammer and Sickle Built for Two" had made her a major attraction on college campuses and lined her pockets with a ton of cash. The story began with Joanie visiting an orphanage, promising neither money nor food for the orphans but "something to fill their starved little minds": protest songs. When the kids complain that they hate protest songs, the headmistress shuts them up by saying, "You'll take her protest songs and like 'em, you ungrateful li'l brats!!—she gets $10,000 a concert."

Joanie Phoanie was the epitome of the limousine liberal, espousing the cause while being chauffeured around town, bemoaning the starving children while feasting on roast beef and caviar in the back of the limo. Over the course of a six-week story, Joanie runs into Li'l Abner, falls madly in love with him, and vows to win him in an upcoming Sadie Hawkins race, though he is, of course, already married. She winds up trying to adopt Abner's son, Honest Abe Yokum, and hires Li'l Abner and Daisy Mae as servants.

Capp left little doubt about the real-life identity of the model for Joanie Phoanie. Joan Baez had begun her career playing the coffeehouses and clubs in Boston and Cambridge and had risen to the top of the folksinging ranks by the early sixties, when she was very young and singing traditional folk songs. By the mid-sixties, she had become a vocal antiwar activist and a powerful voice in the quest for social change.

Although she bore no physical resemblance to Joanie Phoanie, Baez was clearly the person Capp had in mind when he created the character. Not surprisingly, she reacted angrily when she saw her depiction in the "Li'l Abner" strip.

"The whole thing is disgusting," she said. "He can say anything about me—that is his right and privilege—but he takes a jab at the whole protest movement, students and everyone he can get his hands on . . . Either out of ignorance or malice, he has made being against the war and for peace equal to being for communism, the Viet Cong and narcotics."

Like Margaret Mitchell before her, Baez considered her legal options in dealing with the strip.

Asked for his response, Capp shrugged off Baez's statements. He had never listened to her records, he claimed, and he had no idea what she looked like. Joanie Phoanie was grotesque—six feet tall and large-boned, with long, straight blond hair; she wore a perpetually dazed expression, as if she were lost in the corridors of her own ego. If Baez remotely resembled Joanie Phoanie, Capp said, he felt sorry for her.

"I've never seen Joan Baez but I understand that she's a rather slight brunette, and Joanie Phoanie is a big, virile blonde," Capp told *Newsweek* magazine. "If Joanie Phoanie looks like any singer, she looks like Nelson Eddy."

In its coverage, *Time* magazine ridiculed Baez's sensitivity, quoting Capp's counterpunch to her objections to the strip—"She should remember that protest singers don't own protest. When she protests about others' rights to protest, she is killing the whole racket"—and noting that, like Joanie Phoanie, Baez was earning a bundle of money plying her trade. *Time* claimed she was earning $8,500 at each of her stops on her current tour of Japan; Baez countered that it was $5,000 an appearance.

Like most satire, Capp's was fueled by anger, resentment, and even sorrow. Behind his savage commentary lay contempt for antiwar activists that grew with the escalation of the war itself. Capp supported the war effort, and he was damned if he was going to remain silent while young Americans lost their lives in defense of the very rights the protesters were demanding.

His own son was of draft age. Kim, much more liberal than his father, had no enthusiasm for joining the fighting but, as he would later remember, Capp "told me he wouldn't do a damn thing to get me out of it." He had no objection, he said, to Kim's staying out of Vietnam, as long as he did so legally.

Capp's ridicule of Baez was consistent with his scorn for all young people who demanded the benefits of a free country as if it were their birthright.

"Joan Baez refuses to pay her taxes because of the war effort," he pointed out, "but she travels all over the world guarded by a passport which means something because the armed might of this country is behind it. A helluva lot of kids are in uniform so Joan Baez can travel on that passport."

The Joanie Phoanie story ran to its conclusion, without retraction, though the syndicate did convince Capp to soften his originals in five of the daily strips, taking a slight edge off his commentary.

Baez, who would say that she never really intended to sue Al Capp, dropped the issue. Capp moved on as well, though he continued to take occasional potshots at her long after the Joanie Phoanie continuity had faded from readers' memories. She was, he quipped, "the greatest war-time singer since Tokyo Rose" and "in the same Olympic league as such thinkers as Jane Fonda." The war in Vietnam was escalating to such an extent that it would cost Lyndon Johnson the presidency in 1968, the student protesters were now strong voices influencing the country's policies, and more bloodshed lay ahead. Capp found it intolerable that those demanding to be heard thought nothing of trying to silence those who did not share their opinions.

"Nobody is going to tell me who and what I can satirize," he said.

For more than three decades, Capp had been a master at overseeing the way his "Li'l Abner" characters were used for commercial gain. There had been comic books, toys, clothing, watches, board games, drinking glasses, candy, and Sadie Hawkins marriage certificates. The shmoo products alone were a small industry.

For years, however, he had resisted all offers to use his "Li'l Abner" characters in theme parks. Park proprietors, he said, just didn't understand what he was trying to do with his comic strip.

This stance ended on October 3, 1967, when he and Catherine traveled to the Deep South and attended a formal groundbreaking ceremony for a Dogpatch theme park in Marble Falls, a small Arkansas town located between Jasper and Harrison and, more significantly, a short drive to the entertainment vacation spot of Branson, Missouri. Marble Falls was so excited by the new influx of tourists and capital into its impoverished town that the city renamed itself Dogpatch—a name it would keep until 1997.

The idea for the theme park had been the brainchild of Oscar J. Snow, a real estate broker. Snow, along with nine other investors, bought a thousand acres of undeveloped land in 1967. With its rolling topography, complete with plenty of trees and water, it offered a lot of possibilities. At first, Snow considered a pioneer-village theme. The Dogpatch idea came while he was sitting on a rock and looking down at the waterfall in the valley below.

"It suddenly occurred to me that this was Bottomless Gorge," he explained, referring to the Bottomless Canyon in "Li'l Abner." "I could see Dogpatch and its people and I knew I had to call Mr. Capp."

Capp liked what he heard. The ambitious plans for the park involved two distinct phases. Landscapers and construction workers would initially convert the wild, rustic property into a natural setting for Dogpatch, complete with nine small lakes, streams, and even a hollow. A Swiss tram would wind through the property, taking visitors from the parking area into the theme park below. An existing old mill would grind corn for use in the Dogpatch restaurant. The center of the village would feature a series of shops, including Soft-Hearted John's General Store. A statue of Jubilation T. Cornpone, Dogpatch's dubious war hero, would stand in the square. An assortment of amusement park rides would be stationed around the grounds. The second phase involved the construction of a ski chalet and skating rink near the parking lot. Log cabin lodging would give visitors the option of staying overnight.

At the groundbreaking, Capp spoke enthusiastically of the park's potential and his enthusiasm about seeing his characters used to create a new kind of Disneyland.

"Of all the by-products of the strip, this is the one I'm most proud of," he announced. "This is the one which will finally gain me some respect from my grandchildren, who until now have always thought of me as a silly man who just draws pictures."

Capp held a tiny percentage of ownership in the park, though he had little to do with day-to-day operations. His son, Kim, however, was hired to

Dogpatch USA opened for business in 1968 in northern Arkansas. The park's designers did their best to translate the ramshackle hillbilly town from "Li'l Abner" into actual buildings, such as this ticket office.

handle sales of the Dogpatch branch of Capp Enterprises. Kim was living in Miami when he received a call from his father: "You have forty-eight hours to be in Harrison, Arkansas."

The first phase of the park cost $1,332,000 to complete. Capp was on hand, enjoying the festivities, when Dogpatch USA opened in May 1968, and before the park's inaugural season was over, 300,000 visitors, paying $1.50 (half price for children) would see the 823-acre facility.

"It is every kid's dream to own his own amusement park, and here it is," Capp said at the grand opening, calling the park "the greatest Urban Renewal project I've ever seen."

Capp never forgot Charles Schulz's opinion that marrying off Li'l Abner to Daisy Mae constituted the biggest mistake in comics history. Schulz had been a young upstart, only two years into comic strip syndication, when Li'l Abner had taken the plunge. If Schulz's comment bothered Capp as a violation of the unwritten rule that comics artists didn't criticize one another in public (unless, of course, it was Capp doing the criticizing), it must have grated on him even more over the ensuing years, when it became evident that there was a fair amount of truth in Schulz's observation. The strip hadn't been the same after the wedding.

The press, aware of Capp's competitive nature, made a point of occasionally asking him for his opinions of other cartoonists' work, including Schulz and "Peanuts." Capp would offer a generic response ("I find 'Peanuts' not as exciting as some people do. It's a trick that's wearing thin—having kids speak like adults. It is damn well drawn, however"), but he would also state, as if there had ever been any doubt, that he and Schulz were very different and he wasn't really interested in what Schulz was doing.

You could not have found two cartoonists less alike. Capp, a loud, brash, aggressive East Coast Jew with an almost desperate need for attention, produced, in "Li'l Abner," a heavily detailed, extremely talkative satire that thundered off the page like its creator in person. Schulz, a quiet midwestern Methodist who tended to stay away from the spotlight, produced minimalist panels, with very little background and sparse (in comparison to Capp, certainly) dialogue, the action on the page as reserved as its creator.

"Li'l Abner" was set in a world almost devoid of children; "Peanuts" was set in a world almost devoid of adults.

Although there was no open animosity between the two cartoonists, they were never going to be good friends, either. They'd met at a National Cartoonists Society function in the 1950s and maintained a professional civility, but, as Capp learned in October 1968, when he published "Peewee Unlimited," a parody of "Peanuts," Schulz could be touchy about criticism of his strip. He was not amused by some of the spoof's nastiness, especially when Capp implied that Schulz couldn't draw, or that the musings of the "Peanuts" gang were cheap pop psychology drummed up for financial gain.

Schulz contacted Capp and asked him to stop.

"I told him I was flattered by the attention," Schulz told a reporter, "but I didn't think it was very funny."

Capp pulled the plug on the parody, but he still walked away with favorable publicity when he stated that he dropped the sequence out of respect for Schulz and cartoonists everywhere.

"I wouldn't do that for Joan Baez or Lyndon Johnson," he said, "or for any other group in the world but cartoonists."

Whether he intended to or not, Capp reinvented himself through his numerous college appearances, directing a barrage of insults at students. He could still be very funny and deadly as a satirist, as he proved in a "Li'l Abner" continuity in which a student activist group, Students Wildly Indignant about Nearly Everything (S.W.I.N.E.) finds itself in charge when a chemical gas accident paralyzes anyone who has recently bathed. The students have been so busy protesting that they cannot perform the simplest tasks, and they're helpless when enemy troops arrive and threaten to take over Dogpatch. Fortunately for all, the effects of the chemical wear off and the unparalyzed adults fight off the intruders, freeing S.W.I.N.E. members to do what they do best: protest.

Defending his satire of students, he said, "It is the duty of those who know better to give them the sort of indulgent contempt they deserve, and keep them from doing anything either harmful to the world or themselves until they simmer down."

As the Vietnam War dragged on in the 1960s and protest grew on college campuses, Al Capp responded with his creation of the unkempt and clueless protestors of S.W.I.N.E. (Students Wildly Indignant about Nearly Everything).

By the late 1960s, Capp had worked his campus appearances into a routine he could sleepwalk his way through. He would address his audience in a brief speech focusing on the particular issues of the day and then take questions from the audience. He met with students before his appearances, and he would survey their opinions on the issues that those attending the school might favor; he would distribute cards for students to use in questioning him. By the time he took the stage, he was ready for battle, and by the time he left it, he knew he had been in one. He joked that he charged Ivy League schools an additional thousand dollars for combat pay.

Capp's speaking fee of $3,500 to $5,000 was among the highest of the period. Millie Maffei, his personal assistant in the late sixties and early seventies, who answered his fan mail, paid the bills, and made his travel arrangements, was pulled into the vortex of Capp's college engagements. Capp, who disliked paying for something when he could avoid it, decided that Millie could also arrange his speaking engagements, so he fired his speaking bureau and she added the colleges to her list of duties. But as Capp eventually grew tired of the campus grind, he hinted to Millie that he wanted to slow down the pace. "I took his cue," she said. "When the next college inquired, I said that Mr. Capp's rate was $10,000. To my shock they said 'OK!'"

A May 24, 1969, appearance at Penn State University symbolized the antagonistic relationship between Capp and students. Capp had agreed to participate, along with Ralph Nader and Muhammad Ali, in an event sponsored by the student organization Colloquy. The committee planning the event intended it to be an open exchange of ideas between the students and the guests of honor, but any thoughts of an orderly exchange evaporated when Capp, the last of the three to speak, addressed the estimated audience of five thousand packed into the university's Rec Hall.

He had prepared for his customary jousting with his audience. He was ready to unleash his bon mots, one-liners, and personal darts. Capp roasted the student activists by ridiculing them as inmates running the asylum. He attacked the Students for a Democratic Society by calling the membership a leper colony, drew laughter when he approved of premarital sex "as long as it's only practice," and elicited boos of derision when he refused to allow students the opportunity to finish their remarks when they addressed him. It was the typical Capp performance, drawing mixed responses, the usual parade of walkouts, and enough controversy to give the local press something to report.

The Colloquy Committee traditionally gave its guest speakers a small statue of a Nittany Lion, the Penn State mascot and symbol, but on this occasion, the master of ceremonies, Don Shall, announced that Capp would not be awarded his statue because his presentation "was not in the spirit of the Colloquy program." Shall left the stage to a chorus of boos; a student rushed up to the stage and presented the statue to Capp, to the general approval of the audience; and Capp found himself answering unanticipated questions from the media.

The event's aftermath demonstrated how polarizing Capp's provocative university appearances had become. Shall and the Colloquy Committee offered formal apologies to Capp—which he accepted—and he was formally presented with his statue. Students argued over the event in the *Daily Collegian,* the student newspaper. Although it was generally agreed that Capp was out of line—letter-writers called him disgusting, rude, and pompous—there was debate over whether he had been treated fairly. An editorial noted, "He did not come here under false pretenses. His manners may have been despicable by our standards, but our manners were worse."

In its official statement, the Colloquy Committee accepted blame for "errors in judgment." Capp had been invited for his conservative viewpoints, they said. The committee's mistake was that they had accidentally "hired a performer to entertain, and not a speaker to interact."

Capp fully expected to be treated as a guest, regardless of how deeply he insulted his hosts.

"Any concerted booing, any rhythmic chanting that is an attempt to silence me is an attempt of animals," he declared, perhaps forgetting that he made a habit of interrupting or shouting down these same people. "They cease to be humans at that point and I treat them as animals."

Capp's theatrics did not go unnoticed or unremarked upon by his friends and peers. Friends such as John Kenneth Galbraith and Arthur Schlesinger Jr. became former friends. William F. Buckley Jr., the conservative columnist and host of the television program *Firing Line,* invited Capp to be a guest on his show, but after his appearance, which largely featured Capp rehashing earlier campus remarks, Buckley wondered if Capp might be more effective if he toned down his act.

"I think Mr. Capp, as undeniably hilarious as he is, might be a more effective advocate if he varied his technique a bit and eased the doses of ridicule he administers," Buckley said. "His is a cause that needs persuasive advocates, and it is unfortunate that he dissipates the moral cogency of his position by overkill which at times borders on vulgarity."

Columnist Garry Wills was more pointed in his criticism of Capp. Writing a year after Capp's Penn State appearance, Wills compared Capp to a clown clapping at a funeral. Capp, he noted, had set high standards for himself, and now he had to be judged by them.

"Now we must pity him," Wills concluded, "as he becomes ever more despicably ludicrous."

No one could accuse Al Capp of aiming his darts at low-level targets. He'd sparred with Ham Fisher; mercilessly lampooned Chester Gould and "Dick Tracy"; parodied Frank Sinatra, Orson Welles, Liberace, Elvis Presley, the Beatles, Joan Baez, and a host of others when they were at the peak of their success; and carved up countercultural leaders during his television appearances and college campus visits. He never quit searching for targets, and as the sixties drew to a close, he set his sights on two of the biggest cultural icons of all: John Lennon and Yoko Ono.

Lennon represented a target too good to ignore. The Beatles were reaching the end of their long and winding road, and Lennon, more than any of the band's three other members, was using his celebrity status to advance a social and political agenda. He sought a peaceful resolution to war and violent times, and he was willing to wager that he had the audience necessary to push his vision forward. In cynical times, Lennon stood as a symbol of hope.

Capp felt nothing but contempt for Lennon and his pronouncements. In Capp's mind, Lennon was as phony as any figure to rise out of the sixties. The songs, the protests, the press conferences—all they represented, Capp averred, was a cheesy, poorly disguised way to earn more money.

Capp decided to go to Montreal, where Lennon and Ono were engaged in their very public "Bed-In for Peace." As a publicity stunt, it offered everything Capp could have yearned for: an internationally revered figure, fattened for the slaughter; a substantial group of starstruck hangers-on, all leaning forward to hear Lennon's next utterance; and a hungry press, eager to record the confrontation for televised news reports and the next day's papers.

Capp arrived on June 1, and the game was on from the moment he made his way through the group standing in the doorway to room 1742 of the Queen Elizabeth Hotel. The group spilled into the room and gathered around the bed, where John and Yoko were holding court.

"I'm that dreadful Neanderthal fascist," Capp began, extending a hand to Lennon and Ono. "How do you do?"

Lennon shot an inquisitive look at the famous cartoonist, dressed smartly in a dark business suit contrasting wildly with the white pajamas he and Yoko were wearing.

"We're those famous freaks," Lennon said in response to Capp's self-deprecatory introduction.

Someone brought Capp a chair, and he sat down at the foot of the bed. Lennon and Ono sat cross-legged at the headboard.

"So far, you've been confronted mainly with admirers," Capp said, "and I may wind up to be one, you never can tell."

"We've had all sorts in here, believe me," Lennon said.

"I'm sure you have," Capp shot back.

Capp opened the debate by questioning Lennon and Ono's theatrical methods for publicizing their agenda for world peace. Perhaps, he proposed, the two could do more than just sit in bed; perhaps they could shower together. What would happen, Capp wondered, if Hitler and Churchill had crawled into bed together. Lennon proposed that lives might have been saved. The three sparred about Lennon and Ono's being in Montreal, rather than in Peking or Hanoi, and Lennon grew annoyed when he perceived that Capp was ridiculing their hopes to defusing tense situations by dialogue, such as Lennon's daily radio contacts with dissidents in Berkeley.

Capp did not take the bait. He reminded Lennon that dissidents had been throwing rocks at the police. Lennon shrugged it off by saying that at least nobody had been shot.

"What are you doing about it?" he challenged Capp.

"I'm cheering the police," Capp replied, returning to his consistent stance that he detested violence and bad behavior by activists.

Suddenly, everybody was talking at once. When Ono tried to turn the conversation to Joan Baez, Capp tossed out the first personal insult.

"Good God, you've got to live with that?" he asked Lennon. "I can see why you want peace. God knows you can't have much, from my own observation."

Talking over Ono, Capp moved on.

"I read something that—you said that you were very shy people," Capp said.

"Yes. We are, sir," Ono answered.

"And yet, these are . . ." Capp, with a slight smirk, held up a copy of *Two Virgins*, the controversial Lennon/Ono album featuring a cover of the couple posing nude.

"Does that prove that you're not shy?" Lennon wondered.

"Certainly not. Only the shyest people in the world would take pictures like this," Capp shot back sarcastically.

The two traded verbal punches until Capp suggested that the photograph was "filth."

Lennon held his temper. "Do you think that's filth?" he asked Capp.

"Certainly not," Capp said again. This was going to be his moment, and you could sense that he might have rehearsed the lines that followed. "I think that everybody owes it to the world to prove they have pubic hair," he continued, "and you've done it. You've done it and I tell you that I applaud you for it."

The audience in the hotel room became more animated. Some laughed at Capp's remark; others muttered. These were people who subscribed to John and Yoko's vision for world peace, and the tranquility of the "bed-in" was suddenly being interrupted by a visitor on the attack.

Capp remained on the offensive. He brushed off the couple's challenge to take off his clothes and "prove it" (that he had pubic hair) in front of all those gathered in the room, then concluded this portion of the exchange by proposing that Lennon and Ono's posing in full frontal nudity was "one of the greatest contributions to enlightenment and culture of our time."

"I'm glad you noticed," Lennon replied.

Capp moved on to another source of irritation to him: the lyrics to "The Ballad of John and Yoko." He began by misquoting the song's chorus, with Lennon correcting him, and moved on immediately to dispute Lennon's assertion that the lyrics about the trials of being a public figure could apply to Capp as well.

"We are all together in this world," Ono interjected, "married together in this world." Capp retorted that the thought of being married to her would possibly produce nightmares that would awaken him screaming in the night.

When Lennon attempted to bring the conversation back to the original topic, saying he was speaking for the human race, Capp refused to concede that he could write a song that represented the feelings of everyone.

"Whatever race you're the representative of," Capp continued, "I ain't part of it."

Lennon asked Capp who he created his cartoons for.

"I write my cartoons for money," Capp declared, "just as you sing your songs—exactly the same reason. And exactly the same reason much of this is happening, too, if the truth be told."

"You think I couldn't earn money by some other way than by sitting in bed for seven days, taking shit from people like you?" Lennon was clearly angry. "I could write a song in an hour and earn more money."

This was the payoff for Capp. He had Lennon frustrated and defensive. Capp feigned to be hurt. After all, he was Lennon's guest and Lennon was showing no manners.

The meeting, however, was over. It had not gone as well as planned, and neither Capp nor Lennon acquitted himself well in the confrontation. As he prepared to leave, Capp turned to Yoko Ono and delivered a blow that crystallized all the venom she'd been hearing since she and Lennon had become a public couple three years earlier.

"I'm delighted to have met you, Madame Nhu," he said, referring to the controversial sister-in-law of South Vietnam's slain president, Ngo Dinh Diem, who blamed the United States for the military coup and the assassination. Madame Nhu had become one of the most polarizing figures in the debate over the war.

"It was great meeting you, Barabbas," Lennon said in return.

Derek Taylor, the Beatles' press secretary, ordered Capp from the room, but Lennon stopped him.

"Leave it," Lennon said. "We asked him here. He's right."

As Capp worked his way out of the room, Timothy Leary approached him and shook his hand. Lennon sang an impromptu revision of his song:

Christ, you know it ain't easy,
You know how hard it can be,
The way things are going,
They're gonna crucify Capp.

Later that day, in that same room, John and Yoko recorded "Give Peace a Chance."

Capp's campus dialogues kept him under the observation of at least one group that he openly endorsed and praised: the Federal Bureau of Investigation. He was alerted to the FBI's most recent interest in his coming and goings, first, when he was contacted by an official from the Boston branch, and then, a short time later, when he received a July 3, 1969, letter from J. Edgar Hoover. The FBI director wrote to thank him for a letter Capp had written, published in the *Boston Globe*, responding to remarks by John Kenneth Galbraith in a commencement speech at the Massachusetts Institute of Technology.

This was not the first time Capp had drawn the attention of the FBI. Nine years earlier, in August 1960, he'd received a letter from an overzealous agent in Arkansas. The letter, written in response to the July 31 "Li'l Abner," chastised Capp for ridiculing senators investigating un-American activities.

"That surreptitious attack is a disservice to your country," the agent wrote, "since the F.B.I., American Legion, American Bar Association and other American groups who have seriously and objectively studied communist infiltration warn that the House Committee on Un-American Activities and the Senate Internal Subcommittee constitute the very heart of our defense against communist takeover from within by revealing their inroads specifically."

The letter-writer went on to suggest that Capp issue a statement or publish a comic strip stating that his satire "in no manner seriously implies that these committees actually perform as you depicted." To better inform Capp of the Communist Party's methods of infiltration, he enclosed several articles, including the FBI handout "Communists' New Look: A Study in Duplicity."

Capp responded with a letter that he copied and forwarded to J. Edgar Hoover.

"My studies of the Communist system," Capp began, "have convinced me that its greatest evil lies in its rigid policing of the mind, its frenzy and fear of the slightest deviation from approved thinking.

"I am sure your typically Communist reaction to the mildly critical tone used in my strip," he continued, ". . . was an unfortunate and unintentional resemblance to Communist response to the slightest criticism of Communist orthodoxy. I am also sure that investigation of your political affiliations would reveal no tie-up with subversive elements."

Capp's sarcasm might have been wasted on a man who missed the point in the "Li'l Abner" strip, but the episode ended without further action. No one in Washington, D.C., responded to Capp's letter, and the FBI sent the Arkansas agent a letter that commended his concern and reassured him that Capp was being watched.

No one, of course, would ever find Hoover anything but diligent. The bureau kept files on everyone. In Capp's case, they had at least some reason to suspect that he might be connected with the Communist Party: Capp's brother Bence had been a member of the party and had worked to recruit new members and given lectures in several of the country's large cities. He had even testified at Senate hearings investigating Communism in the United States.

Bence had become involved with the party in the summer of 1932, while studying at Commonwealth College in Mena, Arkansas. He had taken classes in labor history and politics, as well as Communist theory, and he'd spent time talking to students who were open Communists. He returned to New York, found a job in a drugstore, and reconnected with a high school friend who had originally recommended that he attend Commonwealth College. They attended Communist meetings together, but it wasn't until 1938 that Bence became interested in formally joining the party. Once he was a member, he was shipped down to New Orleans, where he held the title of district organizer, which involved little more than sitting in a bookstore stocked with Communist literature, handing out *Daily Worker* newspapers, and meeting with occasional individuals, usually merchant seamen, interested in learning more about the party. He worked under the alias of Jerry Benton and eventually advanced to the position of secretary of the Communist Party in Louisiana.

He told no one in his family about his work, and brother Al would know nothing of his affiliation until long after Bence had left the party. While in New Orleans, Bence met his first wife, Ruth, and she, too, became a party member.

Bence worked in other capacities for the party in New York and Pennsylvania. He organized meetings and lectured; he handed out leaflets and *Daily Worker*s in front of factories. He served as a delegate to the 11th Convention of the Communist Party of Western Pennsylvania. He met some of the party's influential leaders. Eventually he grew tired of the activism. His wife dropped out of the party, and his involvement officially ended shortly before he enlisted in the army during World War II.

Bence was called to testify before the U.S. Senate subcommittee hearings in 1958. He'd been working for Capp Enterprises, and Al Capp knew of his party involvement at that point. Bence, testifying under the name of Jerome Caplin, cooperated fully and agreed to offer further assistance if needed. Oddly enough, no one at the hearing connected him to the famous cartoonist, even when he offered the name of the company employing him, and Al escaped the embarrassment of having to explain his brother's past. Al never uttered a word about his brother's Communist background to anyone.

Capp was back in the FBI's sights three years later, in September 1961, when Frank J. Becker, a New York Republican congressman, took exception to Capp's skewering corrupt policemen in a "Li'l Abner" story.

"One of the primary causes of juvenile delinquency is the loss of respect and confidence in authority," Becker scolded. "If the youngsters read this kind of garbage in the funny papers, what respect are they going to have for police officers?"

Becker also contacted the FBI. In his letter to the organization, he enclosed a letter of protest that he'd submitted to the United Feature Syndicate. The syndicate had informed the congressman that Capp was an independent contractor and not an employee. The FBI responded with a letter commending Becker's "forthright statement in defense of the loyal and dedicated members of the law enforcement profession," but as before, the bureau did not bother to contact Capp. However, the FBI continued to monitor Capp's activities and add to his growing file, which now included letters, news clippings, and FBI interoffice communications.

Capp's conservative turn seemed to mollify the FBI in the mid- to late 1960s. He was regarded as a type of convert; his contentious speeches on college campuses were useful, particularly his statements critical of student agitation. In the wake of the violence at the 1968 Democratic National Convention—violence, as history would show, largely due to the actions of FBI agent provocateurs—the bureau appreciated any attempts to maintain peace on the campuses.

The campus unrest struck close to home for Capp when students at Harvard, "a stone's throw" from his Cambridge home, as he complained, staged a series of demonstrations. He lashed out about the recent events at Harvard in an April 27, 1969, commencement address at Franklin Pierce College. Rather than speak directly about the issues relevant to the Rindge,

New Hampshire, school, Capp ranted on in one of the most blistering speeches he would ever deliver. Harvard, he declared, had become "an ivy-covered Fagin" unwilling or unable to control its student body.

Feeling that the Franklin Pierce students might be in need of a history lesson, Capp took his audience back to the events of a couple of years earlier, when Lyndon Johnson's secretary of defense Robert McNamara had appeared at Harvard and protesters had shouted him down during his speech; afterward, a band of demonstrators from the Students for a Democratic Society had stopped McNamara's car and menaced him as he was trying to leave the campus. But this was only the beginning. The fomentation at Harvard had continued, culminating in the recent events that, in Capp's words, had turned the Ivy League institution "into the pigpen and playpen it is today."

The address demonstrated the morbid shift in Capp's professional life—a shift that left his comic strip a mess, his writing a polemical disaster, and his appearances so edgy that he risked losing influence every time he stepped up to a podium. The speech was pure venom, lacking the sharp humor that he'd used to score points earlier in his career. The assaults had become personal. At Franklin Pierce, Capp singled out a number of Harvard professors and administrators, including John Kenneth Galbraith, for what he considered to be woefully inadequate responses to the campus problems.

"Harvard," he said, wrapping up, "which educated the President who brought America into the war that defeated fascism, today honors and encourages and rewards its fascists. Harvard, which once turned out scholars and gentlemen, now turns out thugs and thieves." Here at the end, he brought Franklin Pierce back into his talk in the same manner he'd included the school in the beginning: Franklin Pierce College was fortunate that it wasn't Harvard.

John Kenneth Galbraith had to wait until June 12 to publicly rebuke Capp's remarks, and he did so in a commencement address. Galbraith's speech at the Massachusetts Institute of Technology also addressed the student unrest on the nation's college campuses. Galbraith deplored that some of the loudest voices responding to it were not "men with a record of long and intimate concern with the war in Vietnam, the military-industrial complex, the draft, race, [and] educational administration." He listed a hand-ful of the voices against campus disorder, including Vice President Spiro Agnew, J. Edgar Hoover, and, of course, Al Capp, whom he ridiculed as "the Fearless Fosdick of the youth-baiting right."

Capp struck back in his letter to the editor of the *Boston Globe*.

"Instead of being the 'youth baiter' he called me," Capp wrote, "it's youth which offers me bait, namely the highest fees paid to any campus speaker, even knowing that for it they will get the roughest treatment."

Capp devoted nearly half of his letter to a defense of Hoover, whom Galbraith had characterized as "a poor old man" trying to make "the un-happy transition from the good old-fashioned Communists he knows and cherishes to the incomprehensible S.D.S."

"It is true that Mr. Hoover has grown old in the service of his country," Capp said in Hoover's defense, "and that, of course, makes him a legitimate object of Galbraith's contempt." It was not true, Capp argued, that Hoover lacked the credentials of an educational man. He possessed bachelor's and master's degrees; he'd founded his own learning institution, the FBI Na-tional Academy, in 1935.

"No student of Hoover's ever burned his country's flag, beat up his in-structors, or screeched obscenities at his school the day he graduated," Capp concluded.

Capp's remarks pleased the FBI.

"Despite Capp's previous background," a July 2, 1969, memorandum read, "inasmuch as he has in recent years shown a tendency toward a more conservative point of view and since his letter to the Globe does contain favorable comments regarding the Director and the Bureau, it would seem appropriate to write him a letter expressing appreciation for these kinds of comments."

J. Edgar Hoover's letter, written on July 3, thanked Capp for his remarks. "I trust that our future endeavors will continue to merit your approval," he said.

Less than two years later, the FBI would again be tracking Capp's actions, for reasons that Capp would have preferred to avoid.

* * *

As influential as he'd become as a social commentator, moralist, and public figure, and as well connected as he was in political, media, and entertainment circles, Capp had never considered running for public office.

But late in the spring of 1970, word began to circulate that he was tossing around the idea of running for senator against incumbent Edward M. Kennedy. When pressed about these rumors, Capp offered vague, coy explanations about his intentions. He said he'd been approached by someone high in the Nixon administration—he declined to supply a name—and by what he described as "hordes of people" urging him to challenge Kennedy for his seat. He wasn't sure that he wanted to run. He'd been assured by the Republican Party in Massachusetts that it was willing to match Kennedy "dollar for dollar in campaign financing" in what would undoubtedly be an expensive, spirited contest. Capp amped up the talk when he told the Boston press that he'd also been approached about running for office in New York, where he still maintained a residence and office. He admitted that he'd visited the White House twice during the month of May.

Capp might have been using the media attention as a means of gauging his general popularity, or he might have been using it as the first building block in a serious campaign, but there were other major reasons for his reluctance to formally announce his candidacy: he wasn't a registered Republican in Massachusetts, and, perhaps most important, Catherine was dead-set against it. Capp could drudge up all the support he needed, including an endorsement from Nixon himself, but either of these two factors would have sunk his campaign before he filed his papers.

Massachusetts state election laws required that a candidate be a registered member of his chosen party for at least one year prior to running as a member of that party. Capp was not just unregistered as a Republican; he was, in fact, still a registered Democrat. Capp learned of the election law when he met with Cambridge election commissioner Francis P. Burns on June 24. Capp made noises about checking further into the law and exploring possible options, but he didn't sound confident about his chances.

Still, this stumbling block to his candidacy, he said, was bad for the people of the state. Josiah Spaulding, already campaigning as a Republican candidate, was too far to the left, Capp thought, for those expecting conservatism in the GOP, and was unelectable.

Al Capp, encouraged by the Nixon White House, entertained a Republican challenge to Ted Kennedy's Massachusetts Senate seat in 1970. The two appeared together at a public event in Boston's Statler Hotel in June 1970.

"I think it's fine to be Teddy Kennedy," Capp told the press. "But I think Teddy Kennedy deserves an opponent who is as vigorous a champion of the other side as he is of his side."

He went on to quip that his feelings about Spaulding and Kennedy didn't matter anyway, since Catherine had threatened to divorce him if he ran. This was more than just a throwaway line. Catherine, who enjoyed entertaining at home but was not the extrovert that her husband was, was very emphatic about wanting nothing to do with being a senator's wife.

Capp milked the publicity for all it was worth before issuing a formal statement about his candidacy on July 2. He announced that, after consulting with several experts on Massachusetts election laws, he had reached the conclusion that he could not run against Kennedy in the current election.

"I will remain, as always, interested in Massachusetts politics," he stated, before delivering his parting shot. "A state which doesn't object to a visit from Jerry Rubin or Abbie Hoffman but does object to a visit from the Vice President is not a healthy state."

In the upcoming months, Capp registered to become a Republican. He made a special appearance at a fund-raiser for another Republican running against Kennedy; the fund-raiser became as much a bait-Kennedy event as an evening devoted to bolstering his opponent. By now, Capp could all but sleepwalk through these events. He'd mix heavy doses of cynicism, hard-core criticism, humor, and sarcasm into provocative speeches that usually outshined the candidates. An editor from the *Worcester Telegram*, after seeing Capp in action, wrote an editorial praising his endorsement of Kennedy's opponent, calling Capp's shift from Roosevelt Democrat to Nixon Republican "one of the most amazing political transformations of our era."

Despite all evidence to the contrary, Capp repeatedly insisted that he was not a conservative.

"I was always astonished when anyone called me a conservative," he declared. "I said that I had once been a champion of liberalism, until it had gotten drunk with sanctimoniousness and that if it ever sobered up, I'd champion it again."

In his early days, he explained, the far right had been the butt of most humorists' and satirists' jokes—and rightfully so. The Depression and its recovery period demanded progressive thinking. Conservatives looked foolish and pompous favoring big business when the average American was struggling to get by. Joe McCarthy and his supporters made it easy to dislike the paranoia of right-wingers suspicious of everyone. Conservatives invited derision.

But no more.

"Believe me, it was a wrenching experience for me suddenly to realize that the main source of lunacy in our society had moved over to the left," he stated.

Television was a godsend for someone as gregarious, opinionated, and egotistical as Capp. He'd been around at the advent of the medium, and he'd seen its potential. He was as comfortable sitting in the guest seat of *The Merv Griffin Show* as he was at his drawing board, bantering with his assistants and inking the heads of his "Li'l Abner" characters. He could be charming or churlish, often on the same program.

When he was approached by two producers offering him his own television slot, he eagerly accepted. To Capp, the program represented a regular venue for the voice of opposition in an otherwise liberal medium. He would contribute five five-minute televised commentaries per week, and the show's producers, John Thayer and Don Bruce, hoped he would attract the kind of audiences already listening to his daily radio commentaries, now running three times a day in 120 cities.

"The TV show is a logical extension of Mr. Capp's phenomenally successful endeavors," Thayer stated in an October news release announcing the show. "Mr. Capp's success communicating in person, in print, and on radio has already evoked much interest in all parts of the country."

On November 12, Capp made one of his most highly visible public appearances when he emceed a $150-per-plate "Salute to the Vice President" fund-raiser at the Sheraton Park Hotel in Washington, D.C., sponsored by the District of Columbia Republican Committee and the Republican National Committee and attended by 1,100 guests. Vice President Spiro Agnew and Martha Mitchell, the outspoken, controversial wife of Attorney General John Mitchell, were featured speakers.

Capp was at the top of his game for the occasion, schmoozing with attendees and Republican bigwigs, posing for pictures, and drawing some of the evening's biggest laughs during his speech. He had become a kind of Nixon administration insider. Nixon and Agnew had been behind the idea of Capp running against Kennedy, and Nixon valued Capp's opinion—so much so that he would call after a televised address and ask Capp for his take on the speech. When, on one occasion, Capp missed a speech, Nixon expressed his disappointment and Capp made a point of never missing another.

Capp's speech at the fund-raiser lauded Agnew's efforts in helping elect James Buckley, brother of conservative columnist William F. Buckley Jr.

"Whoever thought a conservative could win in New York?" he wondered. "I remember when you only confessed your conservatism to your rabbi, your priest or your doctor. But now it's legal between consenting adults."

It was a fitting exclamation point to a politically active year. With his public appearances, newspaper columns, and radio and television shows, Capp had reached the apex of his public career. "Li'l Abner" boasted a circulation of nine hundred million, its highest numbers yet. Capp's lecture fee, he liked to say, ranked at the top of the circuit. His move to the right had cost him a share of his liberal fans, but those losses had been replaced by those who, like Capp, had grown weary of the pyrotechnics of the 1960s and were aiming at a quieter, more controlled way of daily life. There was still plenty of dissent on college campuses, and a core of liberal leadership pushing for change and an ending to the Vietnam War, but as the elections of the past two years seemed to indicate, the conservatives were making inroads in taking back the night.

15 SCANDALS

Despite his growing public profile, Capp had always kept his private life out of the spotlight. He was perhaps known to the public as a curmudgeon, but also as a solid family man, married to the same woman for nearly four decades, the father of three, a patriotic American and hardworking artist.

All this changed in April 1971, when nationally syndicated newspaper columnist Jack Anderson published a piece addressing serious sexual improprieties that Capp undoubtedly hoped would stay buried in his past. Anderson's muckraking credentials had long been established. He'd gone after some of the most powerful figures on the political spectrum; his tenacity as a researcher was equaled only by his determination to publish what he discovered.

In Capp's case, what he discovered was shocking. Based on interviews and sworn affidavits with four of Capp's victims, Anderson's column painted a grim picture of events three years earlier, in early February 1968, in Tuscaloosa, Alabama, where Capp made an appearance at an annual arts festival sponsored by the University of Alabama. According to Anderson, Capp checked into the Stafford Hotel and arranged to meet four coeds, each at a separate time, each under what seemed to be innocent auspices. One of them was to deliver a yearbook that Capp requested; another worked for the university and acted as an official greeter to guest speakers, and Capp was supposedly going to examine his schedule with her. Once in Capp's room, each found herself face-to-face with what, in charitable terms, could be described as a dirty old man who, according to Anderson, made "suggestive comments" leading to his "exposing himself" and making "forceful advances" toward the young woman. All four fled before the situation progressed any further, and all reported the incidents to university officials.

The officials found themselves in an extremely awkward position: Capp's celebrity status all but guaranteed a glut of negative publicity that might further embarrass the young women involved and cast a bad light on the university. Since the coeds were reluctant to press charges, university president Frank Rose met with Capp, confronted him with the reports, and banished him from the campus. Campus security escorted Capp out of town, following his car to the city limits.

Nothing further came out of these incidents. Sarah Healey, the dean of women at the university, defended the school's course of action by telling Anderson that "the young women were not physically harmed and we felt that the publicity and notoriety should be avoided."

Years later, nationally respected television journalist Brit Hume, who worked as Anderson's top assistant on the story, expressed dismay at the way Capp's actions were covered up.

"We found out . . . that it had happened elsewhere," he said in a 2008 television interview broadcast on C-SPAN, "and that the colleges, doing everything they could to avoid scandal, would not make a fuss about it, would not see that he was charged or anything like that. And they would also not warn the next stop on the tour. So, he was in the clear."

The story was nearly tossed out before it was written. Anderson, as it turned out, had little stomach for it. A short time earlier, he had written a column, loaded with innuendo, about Randy Agnew, son of the vice president. Randy Agnew had split up with his wife and moved into an apartment with a male hairdresser, and though there was no proof that the two were anything but roommates, Anderson pushed Brit Hume into investigating the story. The vice president, Anderson argued, was setting himself up as a critic of the way parents were raising their children, and the public had the right to know what his son was up to.

Hume argued against pursuing the story but wound up looking into it. When the Anderson piece appeared, it was poorly received by readers, who felt the columnist had crossed the line in presenting what was little more than sleazy gossip.

So when Hume received an unsigned letter about Al Capp's behavior at the University of Alabama, he didn't immediately follow up on the letter-writer's accusations. He wasn't about to be burned again. He put the letter aside and moved on. Capp, in the meantime, continued to assail the coun-

Jack Anderson

CAPP ON CAMPUS

WASHINGTON.

Al Capp, the famed cartoonist and caustic critic of college students, was shown out of town by University of Alabama police a few years ago after he allegedly made indecent advances toward several coeds.

The incident, hushed up for three years by the university administration, is both ironic and significant. For Capp's scathing denunciations of college students and their morals have made him one of the most controversial commentators of the day.

He now has a syndicated newspaper column and his broadcast commentaries are heard on some 200 radio stations. He was even approached to run for the Senate. But his principal forum has been the campus, where some of his biting remarks have become famous.

*　　*　　*

In a widely quoted speech at Princeton, for example, Capp said: "Princeton has sunk to a moral level that a chimpanzee can live with, but only a chimpanzee. It has become a combination playpen and pigpen because it disregards the inferiority of the college student to every other class."

"President Nixon," Capp has said, "showed angelic restraint when he called students bums." On another occasion, he said: "Colleges today are filled with Fagin professors who don't teach. . . . They just corrupt."

Although Capp denies any misconduct and says he cannot remember being asked to leave Tuscaloosa, we have confirmed the Alabama incident with a number of high-level university officials.

They include dean of women Sarah Healy and university security director Col. Beverly Lee. On instructions from then university president Dr. Frank Rose, Lee went to Capp's hotel, asked him to leave and followed his car to the town limit.

In addition, we have established the details of Capp's alleged encounters with the four young women involved. Two of them have given us notarized affidavits recounting their experiences.

Based on our interviews and affidavits, here is what occurred: Capp arrived in Tuscaloosa Sunday, Feb. 11, 1968, to make a speech as part of the university's annual arts festival.

Late that afternoon, a coed, active in the arts program, went to his room at the Stafford Hotel to deliver a university yearbook and other materials he had requested for his speech the next night.

Capp told the young woman he was impressed with her and discussed the possibility of hiring her to help produce the "Capp on Campus" radio series, then in progress. Then, according to the girl, he began making forceful advances toward her and exposing himself to her. She tried to leave but found she could not get the door open. She said she finally broke free and locked herself in the bathroom until he agreed to let her go.

Although she was not injured, she was sufficiently upset by the experience to be admitted a few days later to the university infirmary where she remained under sedation for several days.

That evening, another coed, whose job it was to greet visiting speakers, went to see Capp at his hotel. She said that he exposed himself to her and made suggestive comments. She, too, found she could not open the door, but she said Capp let her go when she threatened to open a window and scream.

The next afternoon Capp was introduced in his room to another woman student who had just completed a taped interview with his staff for a planned broadcast, called the "Now"

Morality." She said that Capp exposed himself to her and made suggestive comments. She immediately left.

Late that night, he brought another coed to his room where he said a party was planned. There was no party, however, and the girl said Capp made an unsuccessful pass at her.

By the next morning, reports of the four incidents had reached the university administration and Dr. Rose sent Col. Lee to Capp's room. "He was asked to get out and he did get out and went to Birmingham," Lee told us.

Asked why no charges were preferred against Capp, Dean Healy explained: "The young women were not physically harmed and we felt that the publicity and notoriety should be avoided."

*　　*　　*

Reached at his studio in Cambridge, Mass., Capp told my associate Brit Hume that the Alabama allegations made him sick and he would neither confirm nor deny them. Instead, he immediately boarded a plane and flew to Washington to discuss the matter with us.

In our office, he repeatedly declined to discuss the episode, claiming it made him ill. All he would say was: "I have never become involved with any student." Pressed, he finally listened to a review of the allegations and, when questioned about them specifically, denied them.

It gives us no pleasure to make these revelations about a man whose legendary "Li'l Abner" cartoon creations have amused millions of Americans for generations.

But Al Capp today is much more than a gifted cartoonist and brilliant humorist. He is a major public figure, whose views reach and influence millions. He is even seriously considered running against Sen. Edward Kennedy (D-Mass.).

Therefore, we believe the public has a right to any information which may bear on his qualifications to speak, particularly when the incident involved is so obviously relevant to the selfsame subjects on which he has been holding forth.

Jack Anderson's 1971 syndicated column brought the first national attention to allegations of Al Capp's sexual misconduct. The report was researched and written by Anderson's assistant Brit Hume, who later became a well-known TV journalist and commentator.

try's youths as being morally bankrupt, eventually giving Hume reason to reconsider his position. After a few preliminary calls convinced him that there was merit to the story, Hume approached Jack Anderson with the idea of investigating it.

Hume's first call had been to a former university official in Alabama, who confirmed that Capp had been involved in a series of sexual incidents on the campus. One of the victims, the former official said, had been chased around Capp's hotel room, unable to escape, while a naked Al Capp, his prosthetic leg removed, pursued her. Hume's source provided him with the names of others familiar with the assault, including the university's police chief and the dean of women; he also supplied Hume with the information about how he might contact one of the victims. The former official, however, did not want his name included in the published article.

It wasn't necessary. The dean and security chief corroborated the official's account. Hume located the first victim, and her account was jaw-dropping, indicating that Capp's actions had been carefully planned and even involved an assistant to help pull off the ruse. On February 10, 1968, the day before he arrived at the university, Capp had called and informed the coed that he hoped to tape interviews with students for an NBC program called *Al Capp on Campus*. Most of his previous interviews for the program had been with men, he told her, so he hoped to speak to women while at the University of Alabama. When the young woman and several other students picked him up at the airport the following day, Cap introduced his assistant as an NBC employee and asked the young woman to deliver copies of the university's yearbook and directory, supposedly so he could look at photos of and contact interviewees for the program.

The student returned to the university, picked up the requested materials, and met Capp in his hotel room. Capp began by complimenting his intended target, telling her that she was talented and efficient enough to work as an assistant on *Al Capp on Campus*. Capp's assistant left, and once the two were alone, Capp grabbed the young woman and attempted to kiss her. She struggled to get away, but Capp blocked the door and undressed. When he had removed his artificial leg, the coed broke free and locked herself in the bathroom. She screamed from behind the locked door, threatening to turn Capp in to campus officials. He finally let her go. She wound up spending a few days in the university's infirmary and, later, consulting a psychiatrist to address the aftereffects of Capp's actions.

Hume was shocked and sympathetic.

"What had been described to me was a sex crime, an attempted rape,' he wrote in his memoir, *Inside Story*. "Any doubts I might have had about the story were gone now. I was outraged."

This first victim gave Hume two other names, and Hume interviewed them, hearing of similar, if less aggressive, attacks. Hume eventually located the fourth victim, now living on the West Coast, who initially resisted talking about her experiences; she relented after Hume repeated what he'd learned from the others and convinced her that a published account might result in some justice and closure to the cases.

There was, of course, one other person to contact, but before alerting Al Capp to his investigation, Hume sent affidavits to three of the women he'd interviewed. (The woman on the West Coast wanted nothing to do with legal proceedings.) This was one of the biggest stories of Hume's early career, and before taking on someone of Capp's reputation and popularity, he wanted to be certain that he was standing on solid legal ground.

When Hume called Capp on April 12, 1971, and told him what he'd heard, Capp served up a few denials, calling Hume's listing of transgressions "sickening," but Hume could hear apprehension in his voice. Capp eventually asked Hume for an hour to compose himself and place calls to his attorney and his former assistant—time Hume readily granted—but within fifteen minutes of breaking off the conversation, Capp was back on the phone, telling Hume that they couldn't be reached. Would it be possible for him to catch the next flight to Washington, D.C., and meet face-to-face with Hume and Jack Anderson? Hume consented.

The meeting, held in Anderson's office, opened poorly, with Capp making a direct if desperate appeal for understanding.

"You speak on college campuses, don't you?" he asked Anderson.

Anderson replied that he visited university campuses nearly every week.

"Well," Capp went on, "you know how these young babes come up to you and . . ."

Anderson cut him off with what Hume described as "an icy, indignant stare." A devout Mormon, Anderson had nine children. One, a daughter, was a college student.

Capp knew that he was defeated. He repeated his earlier assertion that the details of the encounters sickened him; he categorically denied any involvement with the students. Then, contradicting his own denials, he appealed to Anderson for mercy. He would survive the bad publicity, he stated, but he worried about the effects the revelations might have on his grandchildren.

"I couldn't bear to have something come out that would be an embarrassment to them," he said.

Improbably, Anderson was moved. After Capp left, Anderson suggested that it might be best to drop the story. Capp, he told Hume, was "sick."

The suggestion upset Hume, who had not only done considerable legwork on the story but remembered, all too well, Anderson's insistence on publishing the Randy Agnew column. He found Capp's invocation of his grandchildren transparently manipulative.

"This guy's a goddamn sex criminal," Hume insisted, and as reporters, he and Anderson had a duty to publish what they had learned. Anderson, who had used this very argument to defend his decisions to print controversial columns in the past, agreed.

Hume consulted with Anderson's attorney and, assured that they were on safe legal ground, spent the better part of a week drafting the story. He chose his words judiciously. There was only so much detail one could publish in a family newspaper, and caution had to be used in aiming accusations at a popular public figure, but he stated firmly that the public had a right to know about the actions of a man who, as a speaker, offered opinions that influenced millions of people.

Hume submitted the draft to Jack Anderson, who read and approved it, affixed his name to the column, and sent it out for syndication. Neither Anderson nor Hume was prepared for the feedback they would receive.

Anderson was accustomed to seeing his column occasionally censored or edited. The Agnew column had been heavily edited by some newspapers and cut by others. Such was a muckraker's lot. The Capp piece, however, drew vitriolic responses from readers and editors alike. The *Washington Post*, Anderson's flagship newspaper, declined to publish, claiming that it had a policy of refusing to publish sex stories unless arrests or legal actions had been taken. The *Boston Globe*, the paper of record in Capp's backyard, also passed, as did virtually every major newspaper in the country's big cities. The *New York Post* ran the column; the *Atlanta Constitution*, *Chicago Daily News*, and *Baltimore News-American* did not. According to Hume, New York, Miami, and San Francisco were the only major cities where the column appeared. Curiously, someone in Boston had visited a newsstand in the city and bought out the stand's entire shipment of *New York Post*s.

Even so, letters from angry readers across the country poured into Anderson's office, accusing him of going too far. Two letters, though, hinted at a larger problem than Anderson and Hume were aware of: both were from California women who had been similarly victimized by Capp.

Capp, in an interview with the *News and Observer* in Raleigh, North Carolina, brushed off the accusations as the workings of the radical left. These kinds of allegations—"wholly and ludicrously faked and untrue"— sprang from the minds of those trying to discredit him, or worse. He said he'd been physically threatened and lived in fear of someone, or some group, bombing his home or car. Furthermore, one had only to know of his physical situation to realize that the charges were false. He'd lost one leg and had a bad ankle on the other. How would he stalk these young ladies, as they claimed he had?

It was Capp's word against the accusations of four young women, and since no complaints had been filed at the time of the offenses, no follow-up actions were taken.

The publicity died down, but Capp's escape would prove to be very short-lived.

On April 1, three weeks to the day before the publication of the Jack Anderson column, Al Capp had made an appearance at the University of Wisconsin– Eau Claire, a quiet campus near the state's western border. At approximately five thirty that afternoon, he received a married twenty-year-old student named Patricia Harry in his Holiday Inn suite, supposedly to interview her in preparation for his lecture later that evening. The university had set Capp up with a female assistant, who was present when Mrs. Harry arrived, but Capp dispatched her on an errand.

What was supposed to be a twenty-minute interview stretched out to more than an hour. Capp grilled Harry, a liberal, on a number of topics, including the forthcoming presidential election, before steering the conversation to what he called "the new morality." Capp's questions became more personal and inappropriate, such as his query as to whether Harry was a virgin on her wedding day. Although uncomfortable, Harry answered his questions, and the interview concluded.

As she was preparing to leave, Capp asked her if she would give him a kiss good-bye. She attempted to kiss him on the cheek, but he pulled her toward him and kissed her on the lips, forcing his tongue into her mouth. He then exposed himself and, grabbing her neck, forced her head into his lap until his erect penis had penetrated her mouth. He pulled her by the waist into the bedroom and was undressing her when the bedside phone rang. Capp answered it and learned that Patricia Harry's husband, Steve, was waiting for her. Capp ordered her to dress, clean up, comb her hair, and leave.

Steve Harry and the university-appointed assistant were in the hall when Pat left Capp's room. Both noticed that she was upset, and when Steve Harry confronted Capp and asked him what he'd done to her, Capp denied doing anything. Pat explained what had happened only when she and Steve were walking through the hotel's parking lot.

Stephen Caflisch, the news and public affairs director at WBIZ-AM/FM in Eau Claire, saw Capp immediately following the incident at the Holiday Inn. Capp's appearance at the university was a major event for the small town, and Capp had scheduled a press conference prior to his evening performance. According to Caflisch, Capp arrived on time for the press conference, but the normally impeccably dressed cartoonist was "rumpled" in appearance and "sweating profusely" as he met with reporters.

"He looked as if he was really ill," Caflisch remembered. "I have never seen anyone as nervous before a performance as Al Capp was that night." Capp managed to fulfill his engagement, but he was whisked away as soon as it was over, supposedly heading to the Minneapolis/St. Paul area, where he was to appear the following evening.

Over the next three weeks, the Harrys struggled to find a way to prosecute Capp, with no success. Lawrence Durning, Eau Claire's district attorney, felt that Pat hadn't fought aggressively enough during the assault, even when she explained that, while she didn't offer as much resistance as she might have, she'd been sodomized by a relative when she was eight and felt like a young victim in the hands of an older, stronger man. Durning, a conservative, sympathized, but Wisconsin law was clear: "'by force and against her will' means either that her utmost resistance is overcome and prevented by physical violence or her will to resist is overcome by threats of imminent physical violence likely to cause great bodily harm." Since neither strictly applied during her ordeal with Capp, and since she didn't have any bruises to suggest violence, Capp could have argued that he believed that the sexual activity, although rough, was consensual. Then there was the matter of extraditing Capp to Wisconsin for hearings and a trial.

The Harrys, convinced that Durning wasn't motivated to prosecute, continued to push. They called the National Student Government Association and learned about other allegations involving Capp. Pat Harry took and passed a polygraph test. Despite the police and district attorney's efforts to talk her into dropping the case, she persisted.

Stephen Caflisch, who covered the developing story and eventually attended Capp's court hearing, said that Pat Harry's problems went beyond an official reluctance to prosecute. Eau Claire, he remembered, was overrun with outsiders with a strong interest in the case—people determined to prove that Pat Harry was a student agitator trying to ruin Capp's reputation. Harry belonged to campus groups and knew officials in Madison, but, as Caflisch pointed out, she had never been a member of, nor had she consorted with, such groups as the Students for a Democratic Society or the Weathermen. She was well informed about political matters and would attend rallies, but Caflisch insisted that she was "a straight-arrow type of person and absolutely not a radical type." According to Caflisch, the investigators looking into her background made the Harrys' lives "a living hell."

Everything changed with the appearance of Jack Anderson's column on April 22. The Eau Claire paper ran the piece. Durning decided to prosecute. Capp was charged with two felonies and one misdemeanor: with sodomy, for forcibly engaging her in oral sex; for indecent exposure; and, the prosecution having pulled up a rarely enforced law, for adultery.

The charges set off a firestorm of coast-to-coast media coverage. Newspapers that had refused to carry the Jack Anderson column had no choice but to publish accounts of Capp's visit to Wisconsin. AL CAPP IS ACCUSED OF MORALS OFFENSE, the *New York Times* noted in its May 8 edition. AL CAPP IS CHARGED WITH MORALS LAW VIOLATIONS, the *San Francisco Chronicle* declared on that same day.

Capp, issuing a statement from his bed in Boston's Peter Bent Brigham Hospital, where he was supposedly recovering from exhaustion, continued his conspiracy-tinged denials.

"The allegations are entirely untrue," he insisted. "I have been worried for some time now the revolutionary left would try to stop me by any means from speaking out on campuses. My home has been vandalized and I have been physically threatened. This is also part of their campaign to stop me. Those who have faith in me know that I will not be stopped."

He vigorously maintained this position for the rest of his life, insisting that any sex that had taken place was consensual, and that efforts to ensnare him in the legal system and a web of humiliating publicity stemmed from his enemies on the left. In a long, rambling 1974 letter to his old friend Milton Caniff, Capp bitterly repeated his defense.

"If you recall," he wrote Caniff, "I was charged with sodomy (in Wisconsin if a dame goes down on you it's sodomy, if you try to fight it off, an idea that never did occur to me, you are guilty of disorderly conduct)." If not for the intervention of the woman's husband, he further asserted, he would have had sexual intercourse.

Caniff needed no convincing. From the beginning, he believed that Capp had been set up, and immediately following the published reports of the Eau Claire incident, Caniff sent Capp a telegram: "Who do we slug?" Caniff would later characterize his friend, mildly, as a "womanizer," saying that "a womanizer womanizes, he doesn't need to have a reason for it."

While Capp's case worked its way through the legal system, Lawrence Durning learned just how well connected Al Capp was. President Richard Nixon, who would have all sorts of legal problems of his own over the next couple of years, worried about the ramifications of the case, given his public friendship with Capp and a looming reelection campaign. The president conferred with Charles Colson, his special counsel. Colson dispatched an assistant to Eau Claire to try to persuade Durning to dismiss the case "as a favor to Nixon," but the district attorney refused. He reminded his visitor that the White House didn't have the authority to make the request.

There was another far more insidious attempt to save Capp from the embarrassment and expense of a court date. According to Dr. Alvin Kahn, a psychiatrist friend and confidant of Capp's during this period, he was at Capp's Brattle Street home in Cambridge, hanging out and talking as he did on a regular basis, when the telephone rang and Capp became engaged in a loud, animated conversation. Capp, visibly upset, handed the phone to Kahn.

"*You* talk to him," Capp told Kahn.

The call was from Bernie Cornfeld, the controversial international financier, internationally known playboy, and friend of Capp's. Kahn knew Cornfeld only marginally, as a onetime benefactor when Kahn was visiting England and needed a place to stay. Cornfeld had provided his English home.

As Kahn recalled, Cornfeld offered an incredible solution to Capp's problems: he would arrange to have Capp's Eau Claire accuser murdered before the case came before a judge. There would be no possibility of its being traced back to Capp, Cornfeld said, assuring both that he knew capable hit men. Capp would have no part in it, and while Cornfeld sounded serious enough when making the offer, Kahn questioned whether he would have really gone through with it, even had Capp agreed.

Art Buchwald had a better—and totally aboveboard—solution. Buchwald was close friends with Edward Bennett Williams, the high-profile Washington, D.C., attorney and future owner of the Washington Redskins and Baltimore Orioles. Buchwald arranged to have Capp and Williams meet, and Capp wound up retaining Williams's firm to represent him.

He would have his day in court.

There were other victims, too, aspiring actresses duped into auditioning for Capp, unaware that he was operating his own version of the casting couch.

Goldie Hawn dealt with Capp back in her modeling days in New York, before she became a household name on television's *Rowan & Martin's Laugh-In* or earned top billing in the movies. Hawn was still new in the city, on her way to a modeling audition when she ran into a man in his mid-twenties calling himself Bobby. She was carrying a large bag and heading to the subway station at 72nd and Broadway.

Bobby offered to carry her bag, telling her, "You have a very unusual face."

"If he had told me I was beautiful, I would have known he was full of shit," she recollected in a 1985 interview. "But he said the right thing and he gave me a whole line of bull."

Bobby told her he had an aunt named Goldie, that he had a girlfriend who had given him the watch he was wearing. He asked if Goldie had ever heard of a cartoonist named Al Capp, and when she told him that she had, he informed her that a "Li'l Abner" TV movie was about to be made, and they were looking for someone to play the part of Tenderleif Ericsson.

"She's not classically pretty, but she's interesting-looking," Bobby said. "You'd be just perfect for the part." He took her address and phone number and promised to be in touch.

Capp had tried this approach on others.

According to biographer James Spada, Grace Kelly was just starting out as an actress when she learned that a Broadway musical production of "Li'l Abner" was casting for the role of Daisy Mae. Although advised by her manager that she wasn't right for the part, Kelly set up an audition with Capp.

"I took her to Capp's office," her manager, Don Richardson, told Spada, "and waited for her in a little coffee shop nearby. About a half hour later, she came back with her hair messed up, her lipstick smudged, and her dress ripped. Capp had tried to rape her. He physically attacked her. She was in tears and told me how she had tried to flee his office to get away from him. Well, I was ready to kill him, but she pleaded with me not to do anything about it. 'I'm okay,' she said, 'the poor man has only one leg—leave him alone.'"

When Goldie Hawn finally heard from Bobby a couple of weeks after her initial meeting with him, her hopes for landing the role in the "Li'l Abner" television project had faded. Bobby reassured her that Capp was enthusiastic and set up a meeting at the cartoonist's apartment.

Capp arrived late—the butler had let her in—and his first order of business was to slip out of his suit and into a silk bathrobe. Hawn, nervous about meeting the famous cartoonist to begin with, grew more anxious.

Capp, perhaps sensing her apprehension, tried to gain her confidence by having her read from the script and commenting on her performance.

"Goldie, I would now like you to read the part of Daisy Mae," he instructed. "I think you could be very good in that part."

Hawn couldn't believe what she was hearing.

"But she's the lead," she protested. "She's beautiful and sexy and large-breasted! Mr. Capp, I really don't think I look like she does."

"Nonsense!" Capp shouted. "I created her!"

Capp asked her to walk across the room, looking stupid like Daisy Mae might look. Hawn, who had worn an orange-beaded necklace to the audition, dangled the beads from her mouth and pranced around the room, acting, as she later put it, "like a jackass."

Capp's next request was more provocative.

"Go stand in front of the mirror and let me see your legs."

Hawn had mixed feelings about Capp's directive. As a dancer, she worked hard to keep her legs in top condition; she was proud of the way they looked. On the other hand, she wasn't comfortable with Capp's request. Nevertheless, she walked to the full-length mirror and pulled her dress up above her knees.

"Higher," Capp said.

She hiked her dress up another inch or so.

"Higher."

Again she lifted her dress for his approval. She told herself that she would go no further.

"Come over here, Goldie." Capp patted a position on the couch next to *him*.

As Hawn hesitantly approached, she noticed that he had parted his robe and was exposing himself to her.

"Mr. Capp, I will never, ever get a job like this," she told him.

Capp sneered at her. "You'll never get anywhere in this business," he declared. "I've had them all, you know, much better-looking than you. Now go on and get the hell out of here!"

As a parting insult, he tossed a twenty-dollar bill at her.

Hawn rushed from the building, badly shaken and crying, but her integrity intact. Bobby, she realized, had been nothing but a pimp. It was the type of lesson that would prepare her for future encounters in a business that could be very demeaning.

Neither Capp nor his victim in Eau Claire looked forward to an open-court airing of the details of their encounter, with the attendant media coverage.

Lawrence Durning worked out a plea agreement: the indecent exposure and sodomy charges would be dropped if Capp pleaded guilty to the attempted adultery charge. Maximum imprisonment for attempted adultery was eighteen months; the state was recommending probation.

Al Capp, left, *an unidentified man, and Capp's attorney, Al Hochberg,* right, *attending rendition proceedings in Massachusetts' Suffolk County Courthouse in May 1971. Capp pleaded innocent to morals charges originating in Wisconsin, but was ordered by the judge to retain counsel in that state. Nine months later, Capp pleaded guilty.*

Capp appeared in Eau Claire's Circuit Court on February 11, 1972, and to anyone paying attention, it was clear that prosecution and defense alike just wanted the case to go away. The events that brought Al Capp into the courtroom were skimmed over with very little detail; the discussion of resistance was argued in such a manner as to move the case away from an act of aggression toward one of consent. When Judge Merrill Farr asked if it was true that he intended to have sex with the coed if they hadn't been interrupted by the phone call, Capp said, "I am afraid it is."

The judge, conceding that a fine would have little effect on Capp, nevertheless found him guilty by the terms of the plea agreement and fined him $500, plus court costs. No prison time was imposed. If Capp felt any remorse for his actions, he never showed it.

"In Wisconsin, it costs 500 bucks not to score," he later complained.

16 DESCENT

The response to the sex scandals was swift and decisive. The invitations to appear on college campuses evaporated. A planned television show was dropped. A steady stream of newspapers dropped their subscriptions to "Li'l Abner." A career four decades in the making had taken a severe hit from which it would never recover.

Capp remained unrepentant. He told everyone listening, from family members to the press, that he had been set up by enemies hoping to silence him, most likely the Students for a Democratic Society. He couldn't deny that he, once a harsh critic of "the New Morality," had misbehaved in a way that stripped him of that voice; pleading guilty of attempted adultery in Wisconsin had seen to that. He could only hope that, in saying that he had succumbed to temptation by the enemy, he might be understood and eventually forgiven.

Not that the negative publicity forced a change in his behavior. The Jack Anderson column and Eau Claire incidents in 1971 did not appear to dampen Capp's modus operandi, according to one prominent writer. Harlan Ellison was staying with a friend in New York City in 1972 while writing his award-winning short story "The Whimper of Whipped Dogs." His friend, whose name he would not disclose, was a professional photographer who worked for major magazines and provided the still photography for numerous motion pictures.

Ellison said one day the friend went to Al Capp's Park Avenue studio apartment with her equipment on an assignment. Not long afterward, she returned to her own apartment very distraught, telling Ellison that Capp had attacked her. She had not been raped, she said, but Capp had groped her and grappled with her. She fled his apartment, abandoning her camera, tripod, and other equipment.

The notoriously hotheaded Ellison said he immediately stormed over to Capp's place with her and confronted Capp. "How dare you molest her?" He quoted Capp as retorting, "I'm Al Capp. I draw the most beautiful women in the world, and I can molest whomever I want!"

"What an asshole!" Ellison said many years later, when recollecting the incident.. "I punched him out. I hit him with my left fist in the 'V' of his neck, just above the rib cage." Capp lost his balance after the punch and tumbled to the floor. "Then we grabbed her equipment and ran off."

In the wake of all the publicity, and despite the goings-on in his private life, Capp tried to keep a grip on his public image. He had no choice but to maintain the tone of lofty moral superiority that had driven "Li'l Abner," his writings, and his college appearances for years, despite the switch in targets throughout the sixties. A satirist had to clutch a lofty position in order to be effective.

But would the public care? Readers certainly had little use for *The Hardhat's Bedtime Story Book*, a slender volume of musings, scraps from his college lecture tours, reactions to the political foment of the sixties and first year of the seventies, and philosophical meanderings through the minefields of the right. The tone of these brief pieces was cantankerous, but more annoying than convincing; the subject matter offered no surprising insights or memorable salvos. Overall, the miscellany seemed tired and too familiar.

Some of Capp's discontent with America's youth may have stemmed from his ambivalent feelings toward his own adult children. It wasn't merely politics, although Julie, Cathie, and Kim were all liberal in their thinking. Capp had encouraged his children to think freely, and he showed a lot more tolerance toward their views than he ever afforded the students he met on college campuses.

Capp's children depended upon him for different types of support, from housing to cash, and he secretly resented the way they drained his bank account. Even at the height of his success, when money seemed to be gushing in faster than he could count it, Capp never lost his Depression-era fear that it could all come to an abrupt halt and leave him back where he began. He was rightfully proud of the fact that he was a self-made success story, and if he worked himself to the point where he seemed to have run out of time and energy, he did so to meet the needs of all those depending upon him, from his assistants in the studio to his family back home. He could get testy or downright belligerent if he felt he was being taken advantage of, as he had with Nina Luce long ago.

This resentment was also at the core of the pugilistic statements he made on college campuses. His problems with students, he would insist throughout his contentious years of speechifying, did not involve the overwhelming majority of students, who studied hard, worked to help pay their tuition, and treated their learning institutions with respect. It was the tiny minority who felt entitled—to the finest education their parents' (or, worse yet, the state's) money could buy, to the privilege of being able to lash out at their parents, their colleges, their professors, their government. After the deaths at Kent State of four students at the hands of the National Guard mobilized to keep order in the May 4, 1970, demonstrations, Capp declared, in one of the most controversial statements he would ever issue, "The martyrs at Kent State were the kids in National Guard uniforms."

Capp continued to support President Nixon as he began his second term in office. He extended his support to other polarizing conservative figures as well.

"My reaction to Richard Nixon is that he is a towering intellect," Capp wrote in "Let Us Now Praise Famous Men," an essay published in the January 1973 issue of *Penthouse*. "My reaction to Spiro Agnew is that he is a crusader with more courage and usefulness than Ralph Nader." Capp was just getting warmed up. He called Ronald Reagan, then governor of California, "the savior of higher education" in the state. George Wallace, Capp concluded, was "more of a friend to blacks than John Lindsay or LeRoi Jones"—using the birth name of Amiri Baraka in a deliberate insult. Wallace, of course, as governor of Alabama during the civil rights movement, had acted in a way that had been anything but friendly to African Americans.

The essay elicited the predictable angry responses from the left, but a few readers were quite pleased. Reagan sent a complimentary letter to

Penthouse, praising Capp's perception. Nixon, embroiled in the increasing revelations about Watergate, was grateful for Capp's support. He had distanced himself from Capp in the wake of the sex scandals, when he was running for a second term in the White House, but he was touched by Capp's defense of him, in *Penthouse* and elsewhere, while he tried to stave off the disapproval that seemed to be growing with each new Watergate story.

"I very much appreciated the high marks you gave me," he wrote. "You have never been one to mince words or ideas, and you put across your views with no less effectiveness than you have been doing for years as a cartoonist." In another personal letter, written five months later, after Capp had written a piece defending Nixon in the Watergate fiasco, the president expressed gratitude for Capp's taking what was becoming a very unpopular position. "It has always been my experience in my political career that you learn who your friends are—not when the road is smooth, but when it is sometimes rocky," Nixon told Capp.

Yet in this same year, Capp also corresponded personally with his political rivals, the Kennedys. Teddy Kennedy Jr., the twelve-year-old son of his old rival Ted Kennedy, had contracted osteosarcoma and had to have his right leg amputated. On November 19, 1973, two days after Teddy had lost his leg, Capp sent off a letter of encouragement that revealed the rarely seen sweet side of the curmudgeonly cartoonist.

After introducing himself as the creator of "Li'l Abner," Capp wrote of how he'd lost his leg when he was a boy, and how difficult it had been for him to deal with well-meaning people trying to cheer him up. He was frank but gentle.

"It's much better to have two legs," he wrote. "But having one is no tremendous disorder. I've lived an active life and I've accomplished mostly everything I set out to do on one leg."

Capp went on to advise the young Kennedy on how to handle an artificial limb, and how to contend with the psychological trauma that accompanied learning how to walk on the limb and dealing with a permanent limp. People might notice, Capp allowed, but it wouldn't mean anything. In fact, his friends would adjust automatically to his walking pace.

"It's not your missing leg anyone much will notice," he said, "but the rest of you. The rest of you is your character, your intellect, your manliness, and none of that is gone—it's all there to make you and your family happy."

From the tone of the letter, Capp might have been advising his own son, rather than the son of an adversary. The elder Kennedy, taken by Capp's act of kindness, scribbled a note of thanks at the bottom of his son's response to Capp.

Capp kept this strongly personal side of himself private. His work with charitable organizations had been highly touted over the years, but the public knew little about his quietly donating his lecture fees to families of fallen police officers or others just needing help.

Capp guarded his sensitive side as if its revelation would destroy it. His grandson, Will Peirce, would remember watching a television newscast of the Jonestown massacre with his grandfather. Capp sat silently, transfixed as the television reporter related the story of how Jim Jones had ordered his followers to drink poisoned Kool-Aid, and how parents had administered it to their children. When Peirce glanced over at Capp, tears were coursing down the older man's cheeks. Capp wept at the sheer horror and sadness of what he was watching.

Capp's behavior was becoming delusional. He wrote excoriating letters, some to friends and family, some of which he mailed, some of which he crumpled and threw in the trash, almost all lashing out for perceived betrayals, slights, and misdeeds. He fought with his longtime assistants Bob Lubbers, Harvey Curtis, and Larry May, angered when they tried to collect money that he claimed they didn't have coming. He ordered May to destroy much of his art, financial records, correspondence, photographs, and books that were in storage. He became obsessed with his belief that Ted Kennedy had been behind the events in Eau Claire and that his longtime friend, columnist Art Buchwald, had turned him over to Jack Anderson in the University of Alabama scandal.

Some of this behavior might be attributed to the medications he was taking. Although Capp never fully trusted doctors or psychiatrists, he saw plenty of them in the seventies. With more than one doctor writing him prescriptions, it's possible he ingested drugs that, taken together, could

Al Capp, photographed in 1977, the year he retired "Li'l Abner," and two years before his death.

have produced adverse effects leading to his actions. He was taking daily doses of lithium (a medication meant to help control depression and manic behavior), Tofranil (an antidepressant), Haldol (a drug prescribed to help a patient distinguish reality from the imagined), chloral hydrate (a sedative used as a sleep aid), Ritalin (prescribed to help in focusing), and Artane (used to control trembling caused by other drugs).

Neurologist and bestselling author Dr. Oliver Sacks expressed surprise when he heard the list of medications prescribed to Capp. Although they were second cousins, they had not met until 1966, after Sacks had moved from London to New York, and while he was quick to point out that he had never treated Capp, he agreed that the combination of medications constituted "a hell of a cocktail," possibly toxic and certainly capable, depending upon the constitution of the user, of producing unusual, even psychotic, behavior. Sacks, who characterized Capp as "warm-hearted, generous, and someone I enjoyed talking to," also described him as being "contrary," but his anger had always been manifest in his work. His rage as seen in some of the letters was entirely something else.

Although he declined to make a definitive statement about Capp's specific tolerance for a mixture of medications, he did know something of Capp's medical history. His father, Dr. Samuel Sacks, had treated Capp for symptoms of lupus when Capp and his family were visiting England in the early seventies. In all likelihood, the lupus was drug induced: when Samuel Sacks learned that Capp was taking Apresoline, a drug prescribed for hypertension, along with other medications, he ordered Capp to quit taking it, and the symptoms disappeared.

Capp could be a very resistant patient. His regular physician begged him to quit smoking, but he ignored the order—despite his persistent shortness of breath—until 1977. He was placed on an exercise regimen designed to help him strengthen his ailing leg, lose weight, and improve his overall health; he would follow the regimen until he grew bored with it or pains, real or imagined, convinced him that he should stop. He raged when the medical bills rolled in.

"Al became a very nasty and irascible guy in the period just prior to his death," Larry May remembered in 1981. "I knew him on a daily basis for years and easily ascertained his personality quirks, and followed his descent mentally to the acrimonious bed-ridden and guilt-ridden guy he became."

According to May, Capp's depression was so severe and persistent that he contemplated suicide on several occasions. He would type a note, change his mind about committing suicide, toss out the note, and he and May would discuss it later, when Capp's mood had improved enough to allow him to analyze his reasons for wanting to end his life.

One such suicide note, never completed, survives. The letter was unbelievably vitriolic, even by Capp's standards. After citing the problems he'd had with his health—the nonstop pain he'd endured from wearing his wooden leg, the fact that he could barely breathe, the increasing amount of time he was spending in a wheelchair, and his unhappiness with his physical therapy, which he called "a lot of crap"—he turned his anger toward his family: "one of the reasons I want to go." He offered no criticism of Kim but called the women in his life "pitiful and unbearable." He went on to list his complaints about Julie, whom he called "the most promising" of his children, and thus "the most astonishing disappointment." He hated Julie's second and third husbands, both Argentineans—"two of the most detestable frauds I've ever met," "the scrapings of Buenos Aires gutters," who, to hear Capp tell it, were only trying to extract money from him. He ended the note in midsentence, so his feelings about Catherine and Cathie went unwritten.

Not that they were spared in other far less vicious, but still very fierce, letters. In a 1973 business letter to Al Hochberg, he informed his attorney that he intended to move to England and write. He wanted to sell either his Brattle Street home in Cambridge or the New Hampshire farm—Catherine could choose which she wanted to live in—and as far as his money was concerned, he wanted Hochberg to determine a monthly allowance for Catherine, which Capp would provide. As for his children, there would be no more handouts or loans; they were on their own.

"Aside from providing for them, I have no interest in them," he declared. "Their interest in me has been in what they could get out of me, and that has never been so apparent as it has been in the last year. But I'm not doing this out of any bitterness or resentment. I just can't give them any more of myself."

"I am leaving for England," he told Catherine in another letter. "I am sick of all of you, sick of my drudgery to finance Cathie's million-dollar psychiatric binge, Julie's movie ventures, the innumerable trips you all take without a thought as to who pays for the gas or cars . . . Mostly, I am sick of being included only when the money flows, but cursed and abandoned when it stops."

These letters might have been written in moments of extreme rage, when Capp used them as a means of venting his frustration and anger, or they might have been written under the influence of medication that pushed him beyond his normal boundaries of restraint. True, however many suicide notes he wrote, Capp never followed through on his threat, just as he did not mail every vicious letter that he wrote. Still, the letters and notes were specific enough to indicate that Capp had given their content more than a small amount of thought, and that he was very earnest about his complaints. He had indeed given or lent his children large sums of money, and they lived the life of privilege. He'd invested in the movie made by Julie's film-maker husband, only to cringe when he saw the final product. His daughters' medical bills were enormous.

However, as Larry May indicated, Capp's mood swings were extreme. He could be overheated one minute, tender the next. He still had powerful feelings for his family. In a letter to his brother Elliott, Capp spoke of wanting to provide for Catherine, "to keep her warm."

"She has had a painful life with me," he acknowledged.

In another letter, he praised Catherine as "a triumph of strength and sanity. She deserved a better life."

Catherine agreed. She had dealt with her husband's infidelities, his lengthy trips away from a family while she was raising three children, and his recent rages; she'd even heard, through his attorney, that he wanted to leave her. They were two very different people, politically and socially, and they had constructed two very different lives that happened to intersect in a house on Brattle Street. But there was a limit to what anyone could be expected to endure. By 1974, she had concluded, in her diary, that he was the "worst creature I ever could have spent my life with."

Capp might have summed it up best in a 1975 letter to Milton Caniff, when he conceded that the controversies of a few years earlier had whipped him badly and left him feeling "totally helpless."

"I withdrew from damn near everything," he told Caniff. "I think I may be coming out of it. And I'd better hurry if I am. I'm going to be 66 this month."

For all his love of talking about himself, Capp avoided writing his autobiography. He'd written brief memoirs for magazines, but he never attempted a book-length work. There had been a demand for it at one time, but Capp was too tied up by the strip and other projects to block off the period of time needed to write it.

"About 15 years ago, Bennett Cerf gave me an enormous check to write my autobiography," Capp told the *Chicago Tribune*, referring to the publisher and cofounder of Random House, a longtime Capp acquaintance. The offer had been made in the early sixties, and, as Capp recalled, he had to return the advance. "I couldn't write a thing," he admitted. "I was still living it then."

With "Li'l Abner" winding down, his declining health prohibiting travel or any kind of strenuous physical activity, and more time on his hands than he'd had in the past, Capp decided to give the autobiography a try. He had no publisher but, as he told the *Tribune*, all that mattered was the writing itself. He would cover his life beginning with a look back to his ancestors in Lithuania, speak of his parents' meeting and marrying, and move forward in his own life from his birth to the beginning of "Li'l Abner."

This time frame was also covered in a memoir written by his father. Otto Caplin had divorced Tillie, remarried, and moved to Illinois, where he had taken a creative writing class and decided to write a book about his famous son. With the exception of Asa Berger's 1970 *Li'l Abner: A Study in American Satire*, the first book-length critical study of a comic strip artist, there had been no books about Al Capp.

If nothing else, Otto Caplin's manuscript demonstrated where Al Capp's storytelling abilities had originated. Otto had a smooth, engaging style, but his account was overflowing with exaggeration, half-truths, and outright fiction, all mixed together with the truth. Otto cast himself as the all-knowing, always understanding family figurehead, a real-life Ward Cleaver, always ready with instant wisdom or a dollar when needed, a man with a solid work ethic, a successful career, and the patience to guide a strong-willed son like Alfred to the best possible solution to any given problem. When he had completed his manuscript, Otto turned it over to Elliott, hoping that he might find a publisher. Despite strong misgivings about the book, Elliott agreed. Simon & Schuster, to Elliott's relief, rejected it. Elliott found a way to let his father down easily, but the next publisher, Prentice Hall, accepted it. Otto died before the book was issued, and the manuscript was filed away and forgotten.

The Al Capp story, narrated by the person who lived it, wasn't any better than the Otto Caplin version. Capp's version, much less detailed than his father's, conflicted with the elder Caplin's accounts of many of the stories.

It hadn't come easily, either. Capp was always a man with a story, but the discipline of framing the stories eluded him.

"You ask yourself, what is there about my life that makes it worth writing about?" he wondered. "The basic facts of mine seem mighty ordinary: I married a girl I went to school with, same as most everybody; I had three children, which most everybody has; I spent the next forty years supporting them and trying to lay away enough to feed and shelter my widow, and I don't know anybody who hasn't."

Capp, of course, was being modest. Soon enough, he was writing about everything that set him apart from everyone else, and his voice, grumpy at first, when he dragged his audience through his familiar rants about being an outcast conservative, softened as he went, and he became the Al Capp remembered by "Li'l Abner" fans familiar with the strip at its peak. It was as if thirty years had been stripped away and he was young again.

When he finished his second draft, Capp asked Elliott to read it and offer constructive criticism. Elliott, reminded of his troubles with his father's manuscript, reluctantly agreed.

He was stunned by what he read.

"Nowhere in the 70-odd pages did I find the man I knew," Elliott stated in his own memoirs. The book, he told his wife, was "unreal . . . concealing . . . defensive." He approved of many passages, which he found charming and compelling, but the book was largely fiction. He wondered how he could ever discuss it with his brother.

He decided that diplomacy was his only option. He would highly praise the portions of the manuscript that he liked and avoid bringing up his reservations about all the fiction.

The meeting went well—or so Elliott thought until he heard from his sister later in the day. Madeline had spoken to Al, and he'd informed her that Elliott had hated the book.

"My less than stunning performance as a counterfeit critic hadn't fooled him for a minute," Elliott concluded.

Capp never worked on the autobiography again.

In the early days of comics, aspiring commercial artists attended the best art schools in the East, only to learn upon graduation that there were no jobs open to them. Steady freelance work was similarly difficult to find. For

Jewish artists there was the additional matter of prevailing anti-Semitism: top-notch jobs were simply not available to Jews. Needing to earn a living and wanting to use their talents to do so, they would take jobs with comic book publishers, hoping to move on to the more lucrative commercial art and illustrating jobs when times were more favorable.

There had been a pecking order among these artists in terms of their attitudes toward those working in comics. Those in the fine arts deemed all types of comics to be inferior, if they were art at all. Illustrators and commercial artists weren't much kinder in their assessments. Comic strip artists, receiving maximum exposure and, in some cases, huge sums of money for their work, looked down upon comic book artists, whose work was generally produced for young readers on an assembly-line basis and for lowly flat per-page rates. The National Cartoonists Society in its formative years refused to admit those working exclusively in comic books. Comic strip and comic book artists alike resented the lack of respect, but they had little choice except to grind out their work and accept whatever admiration they could garner from their readers and peers.

Al Capp had fought these attitudes from his earliest days in comics. His work was being enjoyed by tens of millions on a daily basis; he was a very high-profile artist, earning more than just a good living. By his own estimation, he was putting a lot more effort into his work than, say, abstract expressionists, who enjoyed international reputations and saw their work hanging in some of the most prestigious galleries and museums in the world. Capp held this kind of art in contempt, grousing that it was "produced by the talentless, sold by the unscrupulous, and bought by the utterly bewildered."

He was further antagonized by the trend of shrinking newspaper comic strips, which had been so reduced in size as to render them almost unreadable. "Li'l Abner" required more panel space than the average strip, yet by the mid-1970s it had shrunk to a size that limited Capp's options as a cartoonist.

As if in retaliation, Capp had opened the seventies with an entirely new artistic endeavor: he'd begun painting on large canvases, acrylics of almost life-sized figures from "Li'l Abner." Each painting was the equivalent of a single panel.

"I hadn't painted since art school," he explained to a reporter from the *New York Post*. "It was fun to work in all that space, instead of small scale."

Catherine had been painting, off and on, over the years, working in a makeshift studio on the New Hampshire farm. She had abandoned her work as an illustrator after the children were born, and her painting, like that of her husband now, had been a creative release. She had been initially upset when Al set aside his painting to work in comics; she'd always envisioned him as a gallery artist. Whatever her feelings about her husband's new series of paintings, she kept them to herself.

Capp might have sold his paintings for a handsome amount of money, but he was too busy with the strip, his writings, and other projects to even consider it. He was gratified, then, when the New York Cultural Center assembled forty of his paintings for an exhibition running from April 15 through May 11, 1975. The showing, receiving wide media coverage, boasted a large overall attendance and featured a gala opening night party; attendees were given the choice of dressing in black tie or Dogpatch style. Capp, who would have preferred being strung up in the town square to being seen in blue jeans or coveralls, donned the black tie.

Speaking to the press, Capp expressed his pleasure in seeing his work being viewed as fine art.

"A work of art is a work of art, regardless of form, size or material," he said in an interview published in the exhibit's catalogue. "People have been brainwashed into thinking that if it appears in a comic strip and in your daily newspaper, and done with pen and ink, it is a contemptible trifle, it isn't art. That is self-swindling snobbishness."

"It occurred to me that my work is being destroyed almost as soon as it is printed," he said in another interview. "One day it is being read; the next day someone's wrapping fish in it. The American comic strip is as unique and as precious an art as jazz. I think it should be preserved."

Capp, of course, was describing the newspaper reproductions of his art. His actual unique comic strip originals were often treated cavalierly, sometimes left on the studio floor to be walked upon, and left abandoned at the syndicate office to be pilfered, while his high-priced gallery paintings and silk screens, being touted as the real thing, were effectively just framed, larger, and more brightly colored versions of the reproductions used for wrapping fish.

On September 13, 1977, Capp was still fighting off a deep depression when he sat down with his family for their customary evening meal. Dinner had always been family time in the Capp household, dating back to the time when his children were growing up and continuing to the present, when Cathie was the only one living in her parents' house. The meals were no longer the loud, rambunctious family gatherings they had once been, when Capp would come home from the studio and regale everyone at the table with his up-to-the-minute plans for "Li'l Abner." Now, the future of the strip was uncertain. Its circulation numbers were still dropping, and Capp, beaten down by emphysema so far that walking had become a chore, was seriously considering retirement. He'd always figured he would give up the strip at sixty-five, but that day had come and gone. Now, less than two weeks from his sixty-eighth birthday, he was rethinking his dedication to the strip.

At one time, he had idealized his retirement years. He had hoped he might still be able to set matters right with Catherine, and that the two of them might finish their lives together in relative ease. This, he now realized, was not going to happen. They didn't quarrel so much as they coexisted, and having their divorced, mentally unstable daughter Cathie living with them added to the strain. Cathie had been troubled for years, as far back as her adolescence, and she had reached a state where she needed people to keep an eye on her. She was still self-sufficient, but marginally so. She could drive, go shopping, and otherwise take care of herself; however, her psychological issues made her unable to hold on to a job. She was heavily medicated and, on some occasions, claimed to hear voices.

After dinner with her parents, her boyfriend, and Julie, Cathie drove her boyfriend home, and Al and Catherine retired for the evening. The next morning when reporting to work, the Capps' maid found Cathie slumped over at the wheel of her car, dead from carbon monoxide poisoning, the Volkswagen's key in the ignition.

The family would question whether she truly intended to commit suicide. This would not have been her first attempt, but in the past, whenever she attempted to end her life, someone had been around to rescue her. When her former husband, Michael Peirce, learned of her death, he wasn't at all surprised. "She finally did it," he said.

Cathie had inherited her mother's looks and her father's rebellious disposition and artistic inclination. Sally Kuhn, who met Cathie in 1952, when both were ninth graders at the Beaver Country Day School, a private all-girls school in the upscale Boston suburb of Brookline, described Cathie as being "talented but not particularly disciplined," interested in boys and getting her driver's license as soon as she was old enough. Cathie's closest friend and an everyday visitor at the Capp home, Sally lived two doors away from the Capps on Brattle Street. She spent a lot of time with Cathie in her room, which was always "messy," with open dresser drawers spilling over with clothing—a sloppiness that irritated her father no end. "There were cashmere sweaters all over the place," Kuhn said. Later, when Cathie began acting out, Sally wondered if this was a sign that she was "more disturbed than any of us knew."

"We considered ourselves Left Bank, bohemian, artistic," she said. "Cathie always dressed with a style—but her own style."

Kuhn remembered an occasion when Capp took the two of them to a taping of his guest appearance on the *Today* show in New York. When host Dave Garroway spotted the three of them walking down the hall, he made a remark about Capp and his girls, drawing an irritated response. "They're not a couple of girls," Capp fired back. "This is my daughter and a friend."

Cathie never attended college, and Capp, who placed the highest value on education, finally ran out of patience with her lack of direction and sloppy demeanor. He wasn't going to stand for her living a lazy existence and sponging off him. He threw her out of the house, and she took an apartment in Cambridge. Unhappy with the arrangement, Cathie asked Sally Kuhn to intercede on her behalf. Capp listened as Sally presented Cathie's case, but he wasn't backing down.

"My daughter's a pig and I won't have her in the house," he growled. He relented when Sally started to cry. "Don't cry," he told her. "I can't stand it when women cry. I'll take her back."

Cathie met and married Michael Peirce, the son of painter Waldo

Peirce. Michael was a fashion photographer, and Cathie worried that she wasn't as bone-thin as the models he shot. She dieted and, after failing to slim down to her satisfaction, began taking diet pills, which contributed to erratic behavior. Capp sank a substantial amount of money into finding her psychiatric treatment, and she was hospitalized for psychological observation, but nothing worked. Peirce eventually left her and they divorced, with Michael taking primary responsibility for their children, William and Gabrielle.

Capp worried about how best to handle her, his thoughts influenced by his own struggles with depression. At first, before the problems became too great for her to handle, Capp paid for an apartment and offered her an allowance. He resented the sheer amount of money her day-to-day living expenses and medical bills were costing him and talked to Al Hochberg, his attorney, about cutting her payments and allowance, but he ultimately returned to his lifelong belief that he had a responsibility to see that her needs were met. He and Catherine, recognizing the severity of her "nervous difficulties," as Capp described her condition, invited her to move in with them. "She is a silent, ghostly presence, heavily loaded with lithium, and pleasant," Capp wrote about her.

Neither Capp nor Catherine, paralyzed by shock in the immediate aftermath of their daughter's death, could handle the disposal of Cathie's remains, so their maid, Dicey, called a funeral parlor and had her body taken away. The graveyard funeral service was for family only.

Tragedy struck again, before Capp had time to recover from the loss of his daughter, when he took an early-morning call informing him that Tammy Manning, his favorite grandchild, had been killed in an automobile accident. Tammy, Julie's daughter, had been a rising star. After graduating from the University of California at Berkeley, she had taken a job with a newspaper in Newark, New Jersey, and established herself as a top-flight reporter. She and another reporter were out on an assignment when the Toyota driven by Tammy's co-worker was slammed into by a drunk driver running a red light. She was killed instantly. The accident occurred on November 24, just over two months after Cathie's death.

Capp would never recover from the loss.

*   *   *

Capp found a reason to fight with almost everyone during the years of discontent near the end of his life. He could detect a slight in the most innocuous comment, a case of thievery in any discussion about money. He could not understand why an assistant couldn't see that a pay reduction was a simple business decision and nothing personal, or that an employee had every right to inquire about why Capp was so slow in paying a debt owed. The slightest provocation sent Capp to the typewriter, where he'd pound out an angry letter to whoever he felt had offended him.

Harvey Curtis, an employee for forty years, caught the full brunt of Capp's anger—"you are a vicious, indecent, dishonorable ingrate, who, in the end, stabbed the best friend he ever had in the back"—but Bob Lubbers, Larry May, and Bill Gordon, a well-known inventor and psychologist who was Capp's friend and neighbor and did occasional scripting work for him, also caught flak. Al Hochberg found himself mediating payment disputes.

In a letter to Hochberg, Gordon summed up how difficult it was to work with a man weakened by such heavy medication that he had a hard time thinking straight. In the past, Gordon explained, he and Capp worked quickly; now it was taking nearly six hours to prepare him for an hour's work.

"It is extremely difficult to plan around his condition," Gordon told Hochberg. "As often as not, by 11 his eyes begin to close and we have to come to a halt. Or he calls a few minutes before 10 to set a new time. Or he calls a few minutes before I leave to say that he just must go up and sleep for a while."

Hochberg was caught in the middle. He had encouraged Gordon to work for Capp, and now he was hearing from a disgruntled employee making perfect sense in his complaints.

"Frankly, I am a little hurt by what I consider unfair treatment," Gordon continued. "I am flabbergasted by his refusing to pay me for the last month but it may tell me something about the way Al is thinking."

Studio employees weren't the only ones that Capp found too expensive for his bank account. The household help, including Dicey, a fixture in the house since Capp's children were young, were suddenly under Capp's scrutiny. They were too expensive, he felt; they weren't pulling their weight. On several occasions, he considered cutting them loose, only to relent after considering it further.

It was a familiar complaint, dating back to the formation of Capp Enterprises and his initial disputes with his brother Bence. Capp felt, with some justification, that others were being too loose with his money. He was the creative force behind the different enterprises, from the strip to the marketing, earning a small fortune, the man who worked and traveled and worried about all the projects connected to his name, yet others ripped through his money as if there were no end to it. His earnings had dropped off substantially in recent years, and Capp was concerned that he might not have enough left to remain comfortable in his advancing years and, after he died, take care of Catherine.

He wasn't about to watch it frittered away without raising some hell.

The deaths of his daughter and granddaughter, coupled with his failing health and bouts of depression, wounded Capp beyond recovery. It was bad enough that he was spending almost all his time off his feet, often in a wheelchair; the decades of heavy smoking had destroyed his lungs to the extent that he could no longer take more than a few steps before being overcome by shortness of breath. He was having trouble with his wooden leg and was still racked by phantom pains in his missing limb. His medications left him dull and drained of energy, and almost unable to stay awake beyond midmorning.

Capp's mood swings intensified. He bounced back and forth between rage and depression. After spending a lifetime as a teetotaler, he began to drink, never in large amounts, but enough and often enough, when combined with his medications, to numb him even further.

"Li'l Abner" had reached the end. The strip hadn't been anywhere near approaching the standard Capp set in its early years; only occasional flashes of humor remained. The art, at one time as strong as any in comics, had slipped noticeably. Capp had fooled himself into believing that he could recover enough of his previous inspiration and energy to make the strip relevant again, but it didn't happen. The number of subscribing newspapers, in the neighborhood of a thousand during the strip's salad days, had dwindled to just a few hundred. Even the *Boston Globe*, Capp's flagship newspaper, stopped carrying the strip.

Rather than face further decline in the strip's quality and more cancellations from subscribing papers, Capp announced that he was retiring the daily "Li'l Abner" strip effective November 5, 1977, with the final Sunday entry to run on November 13. No one would be taking over the feature, as often occurred when an artist retired, and there would be no fanfare at the end. He would simply conclude the current continuity and the proverbial stage would go dark after a forty-three-year run.

Capp insisted that there was no direct correlation between the recent tragedies in his life and the ending of the strip. He'd reached his decision, he told *People* magazine, weeks before Cathie's death.

"I talked with my syndicate, my brother, my lawyer," he explained. "I knew sooner or later I'd have to stop. I knew it was time. In a way, it's a relief."

"Li'l Abner," he admitted in interviews leading to the strip's last day, had been fading for years—maybe as far back as 1973. He'd quit traveling during that period, and travel had always goosed his inspiration and ideas. He'd never been afraid of work, but "Li'l Abner" had become sheer labor, more job than joy.

"I grew more and more tired of drawing the strip," he said, "and the strip began to show it. So finally I said, 'What the hell' and quit."

Capp wondered if he shouldn't have taken a hint from the strip's declining circulation, but he hesitated to walk away from forty-three years of working on something so totally connected to his own identity. He'd been too proud and stubborn to acknowledge that he had no comebacks in him.

"If you have any sense of humor about your strip, and I had a sense of humor about mine, you knew that for three or four years Abner was wrong," he said. "Oh hell, it's like a fighter retiring. I stayed on longer than I should have."

Capp's announcement drew international attention. Newspapers and magazines printed articles tracing his long, successful career; television newscasts gave it respectful treatment. Fellow cartoonists weighed in on Capp's importance.

"He's like a Dickens," said Dik Browne, creator of "Hagar the Horrible," drawing a comparison that undoubtedly pleased Capp. "He was ahead of his time. He forecast the age of irreverence, and he was a technically fabulous cartoonist."

In its waning years, the quality of "Li'l Abner" spiraled downward. In this strip from 1976, Capp attempted to revive his once enormously popular shmoo as a winged creature. The art, probably ghosted by Bob Lubbers, little resembles Capp's classic style and lettering. Even his trademark signature is unrecognizable.

Charles Addams, whose *New Yorker* cartoons earned him a position among the greats, placed Capp's importance in a historical perspective.

"He's created some characters that will go down in the history of our times," he told the *New York Times*. "The names and general connotations have become a part of the language."

Capp was leaving characters who, over the years, had become as real to him as living people. For more than four decades, he'd let his mind wander through Dogpatch, Skonk Hollow, Lower Slobbovia, and all places in between; it was a good bet that he'd be wandering long after his final strip had been sent to the engraver.

"I keep thinking of all kinds of things to do with Li'l Abner even now," he stated after his announcement. "But he's had the most fantastic run for 43 years. I think this is a decent way to end it all."

The demise of "Li'l Abner" left Capp in an unfamiliar position. He'd not only been working since he was in his early twenties; he'd been famous for the better part of a half century, a dominant presence in American popular culture. Less than a decade ago, he'd sparred with students on college campuses; now he was mostly imprisoned in a wheelchair, silent a good portion of the day, and lacking the audience that had boosted his sense of self-importance. His health had declined so sharply that he knew he didn't have long to live.

Capp had always resisted sentimentality, and he made a conscious effort to avoid it in his final decline. When asked by a reporter if he had any regrets, he responded with typical Capp bluster: "Regrets? I'm sure I've regretted every other act—doesn't everyone? Maybe I should've taken better care of my health. But what the hell, I think I've managed it so that these days I don't have an awful lot to regret."

He did, however, make some attempt to tie up loose ends. Art Buchwald had written him about his accusation that Buchwald had set him up for negative publicity by turning over information to Jack Anderson. In his letter, the columnist denied doing any such thing and said he was "quite bewildered" by Capp's charges. "Although we haven't seen much of each other during the years, I don't think I would have done anything to hurt you,"

Buchwald wrote. "I know you have had a lot of tragedies in the last few years and I have been meaning to write to you and tell you how saddened I have been by it all."

Capp responded by thanking Buchwald for his letter and bringing him up to date on his health issues. "For the last few years, I have left my home fewer and fewer times," he told Buchwald. "In the last couple of years, not at all."

In a letter to Elliott, Capp praised his youngest brother for managing affairs in the family and becoming a sort of "father of us all."

"Our family has, suddenly, begun to fall apart," he noted, writing about the deaths of Cathie and Tammy, saying that he would be the next. "I had a pretty good life," he continued. "It has been the last few years that were dull. After Harvey and Andy left the strip, I made a half-hearted attempt to go on, but there seemed to be no compelling reason to, and I have never regretted giving it up. I thought I would, and I find it odd not to."

He never fully reconciled with his other brother. Bence had attempted to offer an olive branch six years earlier, in 1973, and although Capp responded with a letter saying that he just wasn't up to seeing or speaking to him—"I can't take any upsetting scenes"—he had thawed considerably from the angry, aggressive tone he'd taken with him in the past. "My dearest wishes to you [and] my thanks for your efforts to try to do something for me," he wrote in his closing to the letter.

The decline of his health was rapid now. He was diagnosed with throat cancer. That, along with the emphysema, placed an enormous burden on his heart, leaving him bedridden, with Catherine and Julie attending to him as it became clear that the end was near. He was taken to Mt. Auburn Hospital in Cambridge, where he died on the evening of Monday, November 5, 1979.

The obituaries were respectful in their accounts of the cartoonist whose work had given so many people pleasure, whose shift in politics had infuriated so many others, and whose missteps had proven to be his undoing. Along the way, he had become "an American institution," "the Mark Twain of cartoonists." He had left behind a legacy reflected in the satire in comic strips everywhere, most prominently in Garry Trudeau's Pulitzer Prize–winning strip, "Doonesbury." Some of the words and expressions he'd invented for "Li'l Abner"—"as any fool can plainly see," "double whammy," "writ by hand," "oh, happy day," "going bananas"—had become part of the American idiom.

"The things Capp said would be said with more refinement and circumspection by others," noted the *Saturday Review*. "But nobody said them better, because he spoke the truth with the special confidence of the comedian, who knows that the truth will be recognized even when it comes without formal credentials, and that a good joke will always triumph over a respectable thesis."

John Updike, at one time a frustrated would-be cartoonist, might have summed up Capp's contributions most succinctly when he observed, "Li'l Abner was a comic strip with fire in its belly and a brain in its head."

There was no formal funeral service. The family gathered for a graveside service, and Alfred G. Capp was laid to rest. Chiseled into his headstone were two lines from Thomas Gray's "Elegy Written in a Country Church-yard":

> *The ploughman homeward plods his weary way,*
> *And leaves the world to darkness and to me.*

In California, the former Nina Luce read Capp's obituary and remembered a time, almost exactly forty years earlier, when a brash young artist had watched her perform and introduced himself with an autographed drink coaster.

Her life had taken a direction much different than she had planned in the days when she and Al Capp were romantically involved. After splitting with Capp, she'd held several jobs, eventually working in Oak Ridge, Tennessee, in the high-security site of the Manhattan Project developing the atomic bomb. She'd met Murray Bevis, an engineer and scientist nine years younger; they'd married and had two children, a son and a daughter.

Although she had once been signed to a recording contract, Nina never recorded an album. Her nightclub days ended, but she never quit singing. At the sight of a piano and pianist, she would break into song, and she could always pull it off, even when she grew older.

The last two times she had seen Al Capp face-to-face had reflected the nature of their relationship—a dramatic high and low. Capp had visited her in Oak Ridge, when she was already committed to Bevis, and the meeting had been ugly. When he had left, she hoped she would never see him again.

But there would be another time—a chance encounter that became a humorous story that she would tell her daughter, Rita, when she was old enough to appreciate it.

In the fall of 1945, Nina and her husband went to Ohio to visit Murray's parents, Howard and Alma Bevis. Howard Bevis served as president of Ohio State University from 1940 to 1956, and they lived in the president's mansion. On the weekend Nina and Murray visited, Al Capp was in town for a fund-raiser, and a reception was held at the mansion.

When Nina and Murray came down to dinner, Alma introduced Capp as the guest of honor, the creator of "Li'l Abner."

"In telling the story, my mother would just laugh and tell how Al Capp kept kicking her under the table and grinned during the laughter and small talk. I'm sure my father was steaming because he knew that my mother and Al Capp had had a pretty intense relationship at one time. My father never let on, though, during the entire dinner. He generally just ignored him. As far as my grandparents were concerned, this must have been a special treat for the daughter-in-law from Texas, to meet such a notable guest."

After dinner, Nina and Capp found a way to talk in private. Capp had two questions for Nina.

"Are you happy?" he asked.

When she replied that she was, Capp asked: "Is your husband happy? If he's not, he cannot be made happy."

Nina read the clipping about Capp's death with mixed feelings. She knew that she and Capp would never have lasted as a couple even if circumstances had been different and they had reunited as planned in Texas. They were both too strong-minded to be compatible.

When she finished reading the obituary, Nina placed it in her Bible, where it would remain for the rest of her life.

NOTES

1 Flashpoint

1   "Al Capp may have been . . ." Dave Schreiner, "The Storyteller," *Li'l Abner: Dailies*, vol. 1, 1934 (Princeton, WI: Kitchen Sink Press, 1988), p. 7.

1   "Capp was one . . ." ibid.

2   Fifty-cent piece: In a strange yet unlikely addendum to the story, retold on a number of occasions in years to come, Capp would claim that, when he regained consciousness in the hospital, he still had the fifty-cent piece clutched tightly in the palm of his hand. His mother would take the coin from him, place it in a drawer at home and, from time to time, take it out and look at it, sobbing a little at the memory. She'd hang on to the sacred relic until, a dozen years later, during the Depression, she'd stare at the coin one last time and spend it on groceries.

2   "you could get . . ." Capp, AUTO 1, p. 2. Al Capp would attempt to write his autobiography on two occasions, but as of this writing, neither has been published. The two autobiographies, typed on legal paper, covered essentially the same material—his life up to the creation of "Li'l Abner" and subsequent Fisher disputes—but they differed slightly. In these notes, they will be referred to as AUTO 1 and AUTO 2, accompanied by a manuscript page number. Capp also left unfinished fragments that he intended to work into the autobiography.

2   "I hopped on . . ." ibid., p. 3.

2   "There was just nothing . . ." William Furlong, "Recap on Al Capp," *Saturday Evening Post*, Winter 1971.

4   "Her expression . . ." Elliott Caplin, *Al Capp Remembered* (Bowling Green, OH: Bowling Green State University Popular Press, 1994), p. 128.

4   "How are you doing?" O. P. Caplin, *Dogpatch Road*, unpublished manuscript. Otto Caplin wrote a lengthy autobiography focusing on his eldest son, covering approximately the same time frame of Al Capp's unpublished autobiographies. The typed manuscript and accompanying book proposal run more than five hundred pages. Elliott Caplin submitted the manuscript to Simon & Schuster on his father's behalf, but it was rejected. The manuscript was eventually accepted by Prentice Hall, but Otto died before the book was published and it was withdrawn. Otto Caplin's account of his son's losing his leg, while differing from Capp's in some of its details, is harrowing, and it is the only other known "eyewitness" account of the accident and its aftermath.

4   "There is no more . . ." Capp, AUTO 1, p. 2.

4   "They took my leg . . ." O. P. Caplin, *Dogpatch Road*.

5   "With two legs . . ." Capp, "My Well-Balanced Life on a Wooden Leg," *Life*, May 23, 1960, reprinted in *My Well-Balanced Life on a Wooden Leg* (Santa Barbara, CA: John Daniel, 1991).

5   "Alfred fidgeted . . ." O. P. Caplin, *Dogpatch Road*.

6   "Shut up, Momma": Elliott Caplin, *Al Capp Remembered*, p. 5.

6   "My brother never mastered . . ." ibid., p. 5–6.

7 "To this day . . ." Capp, "Autobiography of a Freshman," published in *My Well-Balanced Life*, p. 16. This memoir was also published in Elliott Caplin's *Al Capp Remembered*.

8 "My rooster toughness . . ." Capp, "My Well-Balanced Life."

9 "It would have been . . ." ibid.

11 "Dear Chip . . ." Letter, Capp to Mel "Chip" Dinker, May 28, 1964.

11 "Very good, sir . . ." Capp, "My Well-Balanced Life."

2 Young Dreams and Schemes

12 Yanishok: To this point, it has always been written that Al Capp's ancestors were from Latvia. (A few sources even had them originating in Russia.) However, there is no record of a Yonishak—or Yanishek, as Al Capp spelled it in his unpublished autobiography—in Latvia. Research revealed a town by the name of Joniskis—Yanishok, in Yiddish—in Lithuania, a very short distance from the Latvian border.

12 "If you walked . . ." Capp, AUTO 2, p. 1.

13 "Any Jewish father . . ." ibid., p. 3.

13 Name change from Cowper to Caplan/Caplin: According to Don Caplin, his father, Elliott Caplin, told him that his grandfather Sam Cowper changed his name on the boat taking him to the United States. "You won't get business in America if you don't have a Jewish name," he was told—an irony, given the popular practice of Anglicizing Jewish names to avoid anti-Semitism.

14 "my favorite creature": Capp, AUTO 2, p. 6.

16 "Her hair turned white . . ." William Furlong, "Recap on Al Capp," *Saturday Evening Post*, Winter 1971.

17 "anxious and scolding . . ." Capp, AUTO 1, p. 4. Al Capp's description of his mother matched those of others in the family. Otto Caplin, along with Al's two brothers, Bence and Elliott, shared similar feelings about a woman who seemed so unhappy with her life. As they learned later, she had a warm, generous side that she rarely displayed. After he had become wealthy and internationally known, Al, along with his siblings, sent money to Tillie to give her some comfort as she grew older. In "Mother and Her Secret," a brief memoir published in the March 1964 issue of *Reader's Digest*, Capp wrote about how Tillie never improved the quality of her life after her children started sending her monthly checks. She lived in the same apartment, wore the same clothes, didn't hire someone to help her with the housework, and never took vacations. The siblings reasoned that she was putting the money away and would have had a substantial amount saved when she died. They were mistaken. When they went through her papers, they were stunned to discover that she had cashed every one of the checks and used the money to arrange, through a refugee foundation, to have four European war orphans brought to the United States. She sponsored them in every way: "She'd set them up in a home near hers, and for 20 years she'd educated them, seen them through sickness and teen-age problems, and, in two cases, into marriage." She never mentioned any of it to her children, probably, Al reasoned, because she didn't want their disapproval of "her going through the whole mess all over again."

17 "He always triumphed . . ." Furlong, "Recap on Al Capp."

18 "constantly marrying 'Follies' girls": Capp, AUTO 2, p. 9.

18 "block-gang-warfare jungle": Capp, "Memories of Miss Mandelbaum," *Atlantic Monthly*, May 1951, reprinted in *My Well-Balanced Life on a Wooden Leg*, p. 18.

19 "The experiment went on . . ." E. J. Kahn Jr., "OOFF!! (SOB!) EEP!! (GULP!) ZOWIE!!!—II," *New Yorker*, December 6, 1947.

19 "I was just a kid . . ." Ibid.

21 "Momma hastily packed . . ." Elliott Caplin, *Al Capp Remembered* (Bowling Green, OH: Bowling Green University Popular Press, 1994), p. 31.

21 "a gifted artist . . ." Furlong, "Recap on Al Capp."

21 "He was a dreamer . . ." Caplin, *Al Capp Remembered*, p. 34.

22   "solid": Capp, AUTO 1, p. 21.

23   "But how do I . . ." ibid., p 24.

3 The Hills

25   "she was quite old . . ." Capp, AUTO 1, p. 27.

26   "I don't know . . ." Capp, AUTO 2, p. 16.

27   "If it [was] simple . . ." Capp, AUTO 1, p. 27. In an interview with the authors, Todd Capp, Al Capp's nephew, recalled Gus Levy being a topic of conversation long after his trip with Alfred Caplin. As Todd Capp remembered, Gus was a friend of both Al and Bence Caplin, and might have even concocted a scheme in partnership with Otto Caplin: "A charming scoundrel, Gus was famous within the family for his schemes and scams. One, which Otto [Caplin] may have helped with, involved taking orders for fur coats from Yale students. Gus would describe, perhaps show pictures of, high-quality overcoats and even have the students meticulously measured to ensure proper fit. He took their deposits, gave them receipts, and of course the coats never materialized. The oft-repeated tale was a source of great mirth at family gatherings, especially those in New Haven." In interviews over many years in which his trip through Appalachia was discussed, Al Capp maintained that it was his other lifelong friend, Don Munson, who accompanied him, undoubtedly because he wanted to distance himself from Levy, a lifetime scammer, and because he didn't tell some of the stories about Levy that he would finally relate in his unpublished autobiography.

28   "What the hell": Capp, AUTO 2, p. 18.

29   "This must be worth . . ." ibid., p. 19.

31   "These people had . . ." Al Capp, "Unforgettable Li'l Abner," *Reader's Digest*, June 1978.

31   "It was a hot day . . ." n.a., "The Men Who Make You Laugh," undated promotional article issued by the United Feature Syndicate.

31   "Whatcha doing?" Virginia Irwin, "Al Capp and His Fertile Imagination," *St. Louis Post-Dispatch*, February 14, 1949.

32   "Hello, Mom": Capp, AUTO 2, p. 21.

32   "It was just as well . . ." ibid.

32   "No one was able . . ." O. P. Caplin, *Dogpatch Road*, p. 126. For all his skepticism, Otto Caplin enjoyed hearing Alfred's stories, if for no other reason than their sheer entertainment value. "He had a flair for injecting a measure of excitement in his stories," he said. "He enjoyed his own narratives and laughed boisterously."

33   "Cartooning is something . . ." Gail Matthews, "Interview with Al Capp," *Yankee*, April 1965.

34   "So it's your ambition . . ." O. P. Caplin, *Dogpatch Road*, p. 144.

4 Uncle Bob's Generosity

38   "I want to dance . . ." O. P. Caplin, *Dogpatch Road*.

38   "The Academy . . ." Capp, AUTO 2, pp. 26–27.

41   "the most awful . . ." Capp, AUTO 1, p. 42.

43   "She was so beautiful . . ." ibid., p. 43. In all likelihood, Capp exaggerated his account of meeting Catherine Cameron, although Catherine supported much of his story in her written account of the meeting. Oddly enough, while Capp said that he was attracted by her open act of kindness in the episode of lending him her smock when he tore his pants, he did not mention another incident that apparently occurred before that. "One day, a fire broke out somewhere in the building that housed the school," Catherine recalled. "Everyone had to leave the classroom, down a fire escape. Since Al had a wooden leg, he was a bit slower than the others, so I stayed with him while we escaped." As for the hole in his pants, Catherine recalled a slightly different story than the one Capp presented about his ripping his trousers on the street. "We met in art school [and] had our first date over a cup of coffee during recess," she remembered. "At the time

I was much impressed with the beautiful raccoon coat he was wearing, only to find out later that it was borrowed from his roommate to hide a terrific rip in the seat of his only pair of pants."

43 "I resolved . . ." ibid.

44 "My mother . . ." ibid.

5 Breaking into the Business

47 "a long way . . ." Wilson Hicks, "Discoverer Remembers a Promising Pair," *Life*, December 7, 1959.

47 "sort of ruptured . . ." Richard Marschall, "Al Capp: The Last Interview with Comics' Master Satirist," *Comics Journal* 54 (March 1980).

47 "You said . . ." Capp, AUTO 1, pp. 45–46.

51 "Don't . . ." ibid., p. 47–48. All citations in this passage are from this source. As improbable as Capp's account of his and Caniff's "hotel watching" might be—especially the idea that he would have stepped out onto a ledge—Wilson Hicks, in his 1959 memoir about his hiring of Capp and Caniff, confirmed that the artists seated near the windows got a case of "bulging right eyes" from staring out the corner of their eye at the window at the hotel.

53 "[Caniff] knew many . . ." Al Capp, "I Don't Like Shmoos," *Cosmopolitan*, June 1949.

53 "Al used to write . . ." Milton Caniff and Jules Feiffer, "Strip-time: The Comics Observed," *The Festival of Cartoon Art*, catalogue (Columbus, OH: Ohio State University Libraries, 1986), p. 22.

54 Capp's leaving AP: There is some inconsistency and disagreement, even in Capp's own accounts, about how he left the Associated Press. Typically, Capp told or modified his story to suit his audience. In his autobiography, Capp wrote that he left voluntarily, after submitting a letter of resignation. However, in the September 19, 1949, issue of *Newsweek*, Capp identified Russ Councilman (then photo editor of the magazine, but AP's art director in 1932) as the man who "fired" him. Capp even drew a humorous panel depicting Councilman literally kicking him out. Milton Caniff, in 1983, said that Capp "just walked out." Wilson Hicks, Capp's boss, wrote that Capp quit.

54 "a fairy tale week": Capp, AUTO 2, p. 39.

55 "Never have I worked . . ." Hicks, "Discoverer Remembers a Promising Pair."

56 "The Camerons . . ." Capp, AUTO 2, p. 43.

56 "You damned idiot!" Capp, AUTO 1, pp. 50–51.

6 Hatfield and McCoy

59 "seemed to [have been] drawn . . ." Capp, AUTO 2, p. 41.

62 "We thought . . ." Catherine Capp Halberstadt, introduction to *Li'l Abner: Dailies*, vol. 1, *1934–1935* (Princeton, WI: Kitchen Sink Press, 1988), p. 6.

63 "culture in the United States . . ." M. Thomas Inge, Introduction to *Li'l Abner: Dailies*, vol. 26, *1960* (Northampton, MA: Kitchen Sink Press, 1997), p. 6.

64 "One of the characters . . ." Capp, AUTO 1, p. 53.

68 "The story . . ." Capp, AUTO 2, p. 58.

68 "If you can get . . ." ibid.

70 "Great strip . . ." Richard Marschall, "Al Capp: The Last Interview with Comics' Master Satirist," *Comics Journal* 54 (March 1980).

70 "it was my . . ." ibid.

71 "I don't think . . ." Capp, AUTO 2, p. 52. More than forty-five years after he worked for Fisher, Al Capp's emotions still ran high when he discussed the details of his employment and Fisher's character. He was becoming so enraged when typing the manuscript that he would punch holes in the paper when he was typing lower-case *o*'s. Entire pages dealing with Fisher are perforated, whereas all of the other pages are clean.

72 "Mr. Fisher . . ." ibid., p. 53.

72 "He stole money . . ." ibid., p. 54.

7 Li'l Abner

75 "all hell broke loose": Capp, AUTO 1, p. 56

76 "Suspense was what . . ." Capp, "'It's Hideously True': The Creator of Li'l Abner Tells Why His Hero Is (Sob!) Wed," *Life*, March 31, 1952.

76 "I simply couldn't . . ." ibid.

81 "No artist who can write . . ." Catalina Kitty Meyer, "Interview with Al Capp," *Al Capp: Paintings*, catalogue from exhibit at New York Cultural Center, April–May 1975, p. 11.

81 "I don't think . . ." Alvin Toffler, "The *Playboy* Interview: Al Capp," *Playboy*, December 1965.

81 "At times . . ." Edward D. Brown, "'Li'l Abner' Artist Learned How at Boston Art Museum School," *Boston Globe*, March 3, 1935.

82 "We work . . ." Toffler, "*Playboy* Interview."

85 "He emphasized . . ." n.a., "Raeburn Van Buren," *Cartoonist Profiles*, December 1980.

86 "When the idea . . ." Letter, Capp to Raeburn Van Buren, undated, ca. late 1936.

86 "We took them . . ." n.a., "Raeburn Van Buren."

87 "strange mountain custom . . ." Capp, "Li'l Abner" (comic strip), November 13, 1937.

87 "I would always . . ." Capp, *The Best of Li'l Abner* (New York: Holt, Rinehart, and Winston, 1978), p. 7.

89 "We would always . . ." ibid.

90 "I was so ashamed . . ." Mary Cremmen, "Take a Lesson from Al Capp," *Pageant*, March 1950.

90 "Let's keep the strip . . ." Letter, William Lamb to Capp, December 14, 1938.

90 "Make it burlesque . . ." Letter, William Lamb to Capp, April 12, 1939.

91 "They said I implied . . ." n.a., "Fifteen Minutes with Al Capp," *Pageant*, September 1951.

91 "Who ever would . . ." E. J. Kahn Jr., "OOFF!! (SOB!) EEP!! (GULP!) ZOWIE!!!—II, *New Yorker*, December 6, 1947.

8 Nina

92 "While, if it ever . . ." Letter, George A. Carlin to Capp, August 9, 1939.

93 Nina Luce: Rita Castillo, Nina's daughter, supplied much of the background information about her mother. "First of all, her name was not Nina Gaye Luce," she told the authors. "When she was born it just said 'Baby Girl' on her birth certificate. Her mother named her Nina, pronounced 'Nine-ah.' When my mom got older, she became fluent in Spanish as a teenager in Texas and decided to change the pronunciation to 'Neenya' and added the tilde over the second *n*. She corrected anyone who said 'Nine-ah,' including her mother. She added a middle name 'Rae' to her signature sometime in the 'thirties . . . Al Capp is the only person that I know that ever called her Gaye. Often she would use a stage name, 'Leila Foster.' Her ancestor was Stephen Foster, so maybe that was in reference to him." Capp's pet name for her, "Gaye," was a derivative of Gay Carrol, her stage name when she was singing for Freddie Packard's band in San Diego.

95 "There are lots . . ." Letter, Capp to Nina Luce, undated, postmarked July 27, 1940. Capp rarely dated his letters. There is a large volume of letters written by Capp to Luce, and to assemble a chronology, the authors had to match postmarks on envelopes with separated letters and set up an order with some educated guesswork based on the letters' content, matching stationery, typewriter clues, and handwriting.

97 "a swell . . ." Letter, Capp to Nina Luce, undated, ca. mid-July 1940.

97 "my sister . . ." Letter, Capp to Nina Luce, undated, ca. mid-July 1940.

97 "talked and talked . . ." Letter, Capp to Nina Luce, undated, ca. mid-July 1940.

97 "brutish and selfish . . ." ibid.

98 "NO BACKSLIDING!! . . ." Letter, Capp to Nina Luce, undated, ca. mid-July 1940.

98 "I feel like . . ." Letter, Capp to Nina Luce, undated, ca. late July 1940.

99 "It was a sweet . . ." Letter, Capp to Nina Luce, undated, postmarked July 24, 1940.

99 "I've never wanted . . ." Letter, Capp to Nina Luce, July 28, 1940.

99 "My heart has not . . ." Letter, Nina Luce to Capp, undated, probably July 23, 1940.

99 "Why did you . . ." Letter, Capp to Nina Luce, undated, postmarked July 26, 1940.

100 "presarved turnips": Capp, "Li'l Abner" (comic), December 25, 1939.

101 "a grim city": Letter, Capp to Nina Luce, undated, postmarked August 5, 1940.

101 "You'll be chucking . . ." ibid.

102 "It was all about . . ." Letter, Capp to Nina Luce, undated, postmarked December 10, 1940.

102 "I came to you . . ." Letter, Nina Luce to Capp, undated, ca. late December 1940.

9 Merry-Go-Round

103 "merrygoround": Letter, Capp to Nina Luce, undated, ca. mid-January 1941.

105 "I am trapped . . ." Letter, Capp to Nina Luce, undated, postmarked February 28, 1941.

105 "I'm desperately unhappy . . ." Letter, Capp to Nina Luce, undated, ca. early March 1941.

105 "My kids . . ." ibid.

106 "Inside of me . . ." Letter, Capp to Nina Luce, undated, postmarked March 14, 1941.

106 "The more I feed . . ." Letter, Capp to Nina Luce, undated, postmarked October 24, 1941.

106 "Your silence . . ." Letter, Capp to Nina Luce, undated, postmarked May 13, 1941.

107 "I've been working . . ." Letter, Capp to Catherine Capp, undated, postmarked July 24, 1941.

107 "You should have . . ." Letter, Capp to Catherine Capp, undated, ca. August 1941.

108 "I won't intrude . . ." Letter, Capp to Nina Luce, undated, postmarked December 30, 1941.

108 Capp and World War II: As a Jew, Capp had especially strong feelings about Hitler's rise in Europe and about the importance of the Allies' winning the war at all costs. For all his patriotism, he feared a possible German victory in Europe and the effect it would have on Jews worldwide. In an October 7, 1942, letter to Nina Luce, he described a dream that detailed his fears for the worst and its effects on him personally: "When England has been beaten to its knees and when the United States is forced to turn out its Roosevelts, its Hulls, and knuckle under to our Lindberghs and Wheelers, when our way of life is gone, and the Fascist way of life is forced upon us, and when hatred and intolerance run amok, I, as a Jew, may be a millstone to my kids. It may be that my kids can be happier without me, safer without me."

109 "Dear Friends . . ." Capp, "Li'l Abner" (comic), July 4, 1942.

110 "a blow to . . ." Letter, Capp to Nina Luce, undated, ca. mid-March 1941.

110 Fearless Fosdick: Al Capp may have had more than Chester Gould's Dick Tracy in mind when he created bumbling detective Fearless Fosdick. Artists and comics historians Peter Poplaski and Frank Stack believe Capp's previously uncredited influence was *Holt of the Secret Service,* a fifteen-chapter serial film released by Columbia Pictures in 1941. Fearless Fosdick first appeared in "Li'l Abner" in November 1941. Secret Service agent Jack Holt plays it straight in the serial, but with his similar hat, mustache and square jaw he looks very much like a human version of Capp's detective.

110 "His relations with . . ." Capp, preface to *Fearless Fosdick: His Life and Deaths* (New York: Simon & Schuster, 1956), unpaginated.

112 "stoopid iggorant hill-billies": Capp, "Li'l Abner" (comic), August 30, 1942.

112 "whar nothin' kin . . ." Capp, "Li'l Abner" (comic), September 20, 1942.

112 "without doubt . . ." Capp, "The Terrifying Adventures of Fearless Fosdick," *Pageant*, May 1952.

112 "Fosdick's duty . . ." Capp, preface to *Fearless Fosdick*.

113 "I'm getting . . ." n.a., "Strip Tease," *Newsweek*, July 17, 1944.

113 "Because I am kidding . . ." n.a., "Superwoman's Dive," *Newsweek*, July 12, 1943.

113 "Gone wif the Wind": n.a., "Apology for Margaret," *Time*, January 11, 1943. In interviews about

the parody, Capp took a lighthearted approach to the controversy, but in private he was terrified about the prospects of litigation, so much so that he altered a November 25, 1942, daily strip that introduced a washed-up movie star named Lorna Doon. A careful examination of the strip reveals awkward spacing in the lettering in the fourth panel—lettering inconsistent with the usual impeccably balanced lettering. The reason for this is simple: "Lorna Doon" was a replacement name. The original name for the unpleasant actress had been "Scarlett O'Horror," but after the flap over "Gone wif the Wind," Capp thought better of using the name and pasted a new, shorter name over "Scarlett O'Horror" in the dialogue bubble, creating the awkward spacing.

116 "Sometime in late May . . ." Dave Schreiner, "Stage Settings: The Beginnings of a Roll . . . ," *The Spirit* 20 (June 1986). All quotations in this passage are from this source.

10 Greetings from Lower Slobbovia

120 "I couldn't very well . . ." E. J. Kahn Jr., "OOFF!!! (SOB!) EEP!! (GULP!) ZOWIE!!!—II," *New Yorker*, December 6, 1947.

121 "I'm Al Capp . . ." Norman Katkov, "Li'l Abner's Pappy," *Saga*, November 1955.

121 "Everybody is worried . . ." ibid.

122 "rigorous course . . ." Elliott Caplin, *Remembering Al Capp* (Bowling Green, OH: Bowling Green State University Popular Press, 1994), p. 6.

122 "resumed his starboard . . ." ibid.

123 "He would narrate . . ." Interview with Julie Cairol.

124 "the most egomaniacal . . ." Rick Marschall, "Al Capp and Li'l Abner in 1946: Schoolbook Lessons in Producing a Comic Strip," *Li'l Abner: Dailies*, vol. 12, 1946 (Princeton, WI: Kitchen Sink Press, 1991), p. 6.

125 "possibly the strip's . . ." Dave Schreiner, "1946: Hallo, Switty-pie!" *Li'l Abner: Dailies*, ibid., p. 16.

11 The Shmoo, the Kigmy, and All One Cartoonist Could Ever Want

128 "Every month . . ." E. J. Kahn Jr., "OOF!! (SOB!) EEP!! (GULP!) ZOWIE!!!—I" *New Yorker*, November 29, 1947.

128 "Capp regards himself . . ." ibid.

130 "There was an unwritten . . ." Rick Marschall, "Saying Something About the Status Quo: Al Capp, Master Satirist of the Comics," *Nemo*, April 1986.

131 "consonant with . . ." n.a., "Little Abner Creator Sues for 14 Million," *New York Times*, July 12, 1947.

132 "The time has come . . ." Judith Crist, "Horror in the Nursery," *Collier's*, March 27, 1948.

133 "I deplore them . . ." Transcript of ABC radio program, "What's Wrong with the Comics?" published in *Town Meeting: Bulletin of America's Town Meeting of the Air* 13, no. 45 (March 1948). All other citations in this passage, unless otherwise indicated, are from this source.

133 *True Comics*: Amy Kiste Nyberg, *Seal of Approval: The History of the Comics Code* (Jackson: University Press of Mississippi, 1998), pp. 6–7.

135 "As drawing . . ." William Laas, "A Half-Century of Comic Art," *Saturday Review of Literature*, March 20, 1948.

136 "bad fo' chillen . . ." Capp, "Li'l Abner" (Sunday comic), August 8, 1948. Reprinted under the title "Li'l Abner Fights for His Rights," *Li'l Abner* (comic book), vol. 2, no. 9 [#69] (Harvey Publications, February 1949).

136 "those psy-cho-logists . . ." ibid.

136 The shmoo: Newspapers and magazines usually referred to the shmoo's shape as being that of a bowling pin or ham. Critics, most notably Capp's nemesis, Ham Fisher, complained that the shmoo was phallic in design, and that Capp used that design as a way to slip dirty jokes into "Li'l Abner." Even the creature's name was brought into question. As Asa Berger wrote in his book-length critical study of "Li'l Abner": "The word 'shmoo' is quite probably a modification of the Jewish term Schmo or Schmuck. Which means either 'fool' ('booby,' 'nitwit') or 'penis.'" *Lil'Abner: A Study in American Satire* (New York: Twayne, 1970), p. 115. Two panels in the November 23, 1948, strip offer credence to shmoo detractors' claims. In these panels, Li'l Abner is hiding in a hollowed-out tree, trying to elude his Sadie Hawkins Day pursuers. He has a shmoo in the tree with him, and the shmoo, standing in front of Abner, looks like an erect penis poking out of Abner's pants. When the shmoo sings to attract Daisy Mae's attention, Li'l Abner refers to it as a "Benedick Arnold." There is no possibility that all this was unintended, and Fisher would use this strip and others as part of his "evidence" that Capp was a pornographer.

136 "strange moosic": Capp, "Li'l Abner" (comic), August 20, 1948.

136 "th' greatest menace . . ." Capp, "Li'l Abner" (comic), August 30, 1948.

136 "Why did I call . . ." Capp, "I Don't Like Shmoos," *Cosmopolitan*, June 1949.

138 "Wif these around . . ." Capp, "Li'l Abner" (comic), September 2, 1948.

138 "everything including . . ." n.a., "Taming of the Shmoo," *Newsweek*, September 5, 1949.

138 "Capp-italist Revolution": n.a., "Capp-italist Revolution," *Life*, December 20, 1948.

139 "My first sensation . . ." n.a., "The Miracle of Dogpatch," *Time*, December 27, 1948.

140 Nancy O: The solution to the Nancy O mystery involved another Al Capp contest. Nancy O, as Capp depicted her in his strip, had the figure of a typical Capp knockout, but she possessed a face identical to Mammy Yokum's. Li'l Abner, of course, fell madly in love with her, but she wanted a change—a makeover that a plastic surgeon said he could provide. He would change her into a woman with the sweetest face in the world, a sort of Lena the Hyena in reverse. In the March 24, 1951, "Li'l Abner" strip, Capp announced a contest. Readers were encouraged to submit photographs of their sweetest girl. The contest would end on April 21, and the winner would be announced on May 14. Capp would apply the sweetest girl's face to Nancy O, and the contest winner would appear on Milton Berle's popular television show. Entries flooded in. The winner, Kitty Pankey, a University of Florida student, was pictured in the May 14 strip and, after receiving a plug in the next day's "Li'l Abner," she appeared on Berle's show the following evening. For Capp, what began as an inside joke between him and his assistants wound up gaining the strip countless dollars in free publicity. For Li'l Abner, the transformation was devastating: as soon as he saw the new Nancy O, he dropped his pursuit of her. He'd fallen in love with her because she was a ringer for his mother, and the new look put her in the same category as—gasp!—Daisy Mae.

140 "mah Sure-Fire . . ." Capp, "Li'l Abner" (comic strip), October 1, 1949.

140 "And there yo' has . . ." ibid.

140 "a handy-sized . . ." Capp, "Li'l Abner" (comic strip), October 3, 1949.

141 "Since the Kigmy . . ." Capp, in typed notes on "Li'l Abner" stationery. The notes were published in Dave Schreiner's "The Evolution of the Kigmy," introductory essay in *Li'l Abner: Dailies*, vol. 15, 1949 (Princeton, WI: Kitchen Sink Press, 1992), p. 10. All other citations in this passage are from this source.

142 Affair with Carol Saroyan: See John Leggett, *A Daring Young Man: A Biography of William Saroyan* (New York: Alfred A. Knopf, 2002), pp. 231–43.

144 "an open and notorious . . ." Letter, William Saroyan to Carol Saroyan, January 28, 1950.

144 "With the immeasurable . . ." ibid.

144 "to help her . . ." Letter, William Saroyan to Capp, January 28, 1950.

145 Toby Press: Named after one of Elliott Caplin's daughters, Toby Press was, according to Don Caplin, an enterprise involving the entire family. The press paid newsstands an allowance for prominent display of Toby Press titles, and Otto Caplin was hired to go from newsstand to newsstand and make certain that the titles were given the correct attention.

145 "nothing but a menace . . ." Jane McMaster, "'Li'l Abner' Sideline Is Shmoopendous," *Editor & Publisher*, July 16, 1949.

146 "a flurry of letters . . ." n.a., "Many Protest to Syndicate on Shmoo Tieup," *Editor & Publisher*, September 3, 1949.

146 "We think this is . . ." n.a., "Capp Answers Criticism of Exploitation," *Editor & Publisher*, August 27, 1949.

146 "If through the use . . ." ibid.

148 Capp and the *Daily Mirror*: By all indications, Capp had a legitimate complaint about the fees the *New York Daily Mirror* was paying for "Li'l Abner" and the placement the strip was receiving in its Sunday paper. In an undated letter to his editor at the *Daily Mirror*, Capp accused the paper of giving him the "run-around": "I think that there is little doubt that for the last couple of years, 'Abner' has been your top comic, that it has long since rated the front page of the Mirror, and I want to know why this hasn't happened," he wrote. As for the fee the paper was paying, it was practice for the smaller papers to pay less, but in the case of a large-circulation paper like the *Mirror*, the price was ludicrously low. "['Li'l Abner'] has rated the highest prices ever paid for any comics," Capp reminded his editor. "The Mirror pays less than one-fourth than is paid in Philadelphia, less than one-third than is paid in Boston, etc. The Mirror gets 'Abner' cheaper than any large city in America."

148 "These matters . . ." Letter, Capp to Jerome "Bence" Capp, undated, ca. summer 1949. "Li'l Abner" replaced "Joe Palooka" on the front page of the *Sunday* Daily *Mirror* comics in August 1949.

149 "This is not . . ." Letter, Capp to Jerome "Bence" Capp, undated, ca. early 1949.

150 "In the Sunday . . ." Letter, Capp to Jerome "Bence" Capp, undated, ca. spring 1949.

12 Demise of the Monster

152 "grave charges": Capp, AUTO 2, p. 60.

152 "I knew . . ." ibid.

153 "He grew richer . . ." Capp, "I Remember Monster," *Atlantic Monthly*, April 1950.

155 "Do you believe . . ." Amy Kiste Nybert, *Seal of Approval: The History of the Comics Code* (Jackson: University Press of Mississippi, 1998), p. 54.

156 "Practitioners of . . ." David Hajdu, *The Ten-Cent Plague: The Great Comic-Book Scare and How It Changed America* (New York: Farrar, Straus and Giroux, 2008), p. 173.

156 "The doctor . . ." Alvin Toffler, "The *Playboy* Interview: Al Capp," *Playboy*, December 1965.

156 "The fact that . . ." Capp, "'It's Hideously True': Creator of Li'l Abner Tells Why His Hero Is (Sob!) Wed," *Life*, March 31, 1952. All other citations in this passage are from this source.

160 "Li'l Abner" and television: Television producers had tried to find a way to produce a live-action series based on the comic strip, but it had never happened. One of the great "what-if's" occurred in 1949, when a "Li'l Abner" television program was being developed. Actor Warde Donovan was favored for the Li'l Abner part, and, in what might have changed her career, Marilyn Monroe was picked for the role of Daisy Mae. Monroe dropped out when her agent couldn't come to terms with the producers. The program never escaped the development stage.

160 "a novelty . . ." Tom Andrae, "Fearless Fosdick: A 'Lost' Television Classic," *Li'l Abner: Dailies*, vol. 19, *1953* (Northampton, MA: Kitchen Sink Press, 1994), unpaginated.

162 "it was going . . ." John Steinbeck, introduction to *The World of Li'l Abner* (New York: Ballantine Books, 1952). All other citations in this passage, unless otherwise indicated, are from this source.

163 "No one on earth . . ." Letter, Capp to Jerome "Bence" Capp, undated, ca. late November 1952.

164 "There must be . . ." Letter, Capp to Madeline Gardner and Elliott Caplin, undated, ca. early February 1953.

164 "Every prediction . . ." Letter, Capp to Elliott Caplin, undated, ca. early February 1953.

164 "You are and have been . . .": Letter, Jerome "Bence" Capp to Capp, February 26, 1953.

165 "charity": Letter, Capp to Jerome "Bence" Capp, undated, ca. early March 1953.

165 "The last six years . . ." ibid.

165 "suffer the mortification . . ." Letter, Jerome "Bence" Capp to Capp, March 5, 1953.

165 "Are you so swept . . ." ibid.

166 "It is tragic . . ." Letter, Capp to Jerome "Bence" Capp, undated, ca. May 1953.

166 "I certainly wish . . ." Letter, Al Foster to Jerome "Bence" Capp, May 11, 1953.

169 "The pay was wonderful . . ." Frank Frazetta, *Icon: A Retrospective by the Grand Master of Fantastic Art* (Grass Valley, CA: Underwood Books, 1998).

169 "This claim . . ." Richard Marschall, "Al Capp: The Last Interview with Comics' Master Satirist," *Comics Journal* 54 (March 1980).

170 "Instead of getting . . ." Denis Kitchen, "Fame and Anonymity," introductory essay published in *Al Capp's Li'l Abner: The Frazetta Years*: vol. 1, *1954–1955* (Milwaukie, OR: Dark Horse, 2003), p. 13.

172 "a leading critic . . ." Capp, "Li'l Abner" (comic), November 11, 1955.

173 "I became an expert . . ." E. J. Kahn Jr. "OOFF!! (SOB!) EEP!! (GULP!) ZOWIE!!!—II," *New Yorker*, December 6, 1947.

173 "These are forgeries . . ." n.a., "Capp v. Fisher," *Time*, February 14, 1955.

176 "To be quite blunt . . ." Letter, Walt Kelly to Capp, December 16, 1954.

176 "We cannot entertain . . ." ibid.

176 "Be careful . . ." Letter, Morris L. Ernst to Capp, December 15, 1954.

177 "father confessor": Interview with Morris Weiss.

177 "He was very unhappy . . ." ibid.

177 "I think . . ." Affidavit: William H. Mauldin, December 9, 1954.

177 "the questioned notations . . ." Deposition: Charles A. Appel Jr., December 20, 1954.

178 "He came to our . . ." Interview with Blanche Weiss.

178 "I did sincerely . . ." Interview with Morris Weiss.

178 "I don't want . . ." ibid.

179 "My sight has gone . . ." n.a., "Cartoonist Ham Fisher Found Dead," *New York Daily News*, December 28, 1955.

179 "I stood . . ." Interview with Morris Weiss.

179 ""He has ennobled . . ." Jay Maeder, "Spitting on Pictures: Funny Papers, 1955," *New York Daily News*, September 18, 1998.

179 "With the FCC business . . ." Letter, Capp to Milton Caniff, undated, ca. September 1956.

13 Bright Lights

181 "They asked me . . ." Mark Evanier, "Li'l Abner on Broadway," *Li'l Abner: Dailies*, vol. 22, *1956* (Northampton, MA: Kitchen Sink Press, 1995), p. 6. This article provided much of the background for this section.

183 "Not only did he . . ." Edie Adams and Robert Windeler, *Sing a Pretty Song: The "Offbeat" Life of Edie Adams* (New York: William Morrow, 1990), pp. 191–92.

185 "One day in November . . ." Alberto Becattini, "The Good Girl Art of Bob Lubbers," *Comic Book Marketplace*, April 2002.

185 People to People meeting: Dwight D. Eisenhower to Capp, June 1, 1956.

186 "We cartoonists . . ." James Vance, "The Feuds That Were and Never Were," in *Li'l Abner: Dailies*, vol. 23, *1957* (Northampton, MA: Kitchen Sink Press, 1996), p. 12.

186 "Make him suffer . . ." Capp, "Li'l Abner" (comic strip), September 1, 1957.

188 "Mary Worth is . . ." Phyllis Lauritz, "Friends A-Feudin' in So-Called Funnies; More Takeoffs Lurking in Fertile Minds," *Oregonian*, August 29, 1957.

188 "unpardonable slander . . ." n.a., "Rap for Capp," *Time*, September 9, 1957.

188 "Al Capp is surrounded . . ." Lauritz, "Friends A-Feudin'."

188 "thinly disguised attack . . ." n.a., "Rap for Capp."

188 "the most dangerous . . ." Al Capp, "Li'l Abner" (comic strip), September 22, 1957.

189 "insisted that his name . . ." Mark Evanier, "Li'l Abner in Hollywood," in *Li'l Abner: Dailies*, vol. 25, 1959 (Northampton, MA: Kitchen Sink Press, 1997), p. 10. Much of the background for this section was obtained from this source.

192 "Fearless Fosdick" animated television program: Apparently producer/director Ralph Bakshi worked on that never-produced animation development early in his career, and he came away with deep respect for Al Capp. In April 2008, at the ASIFA Animation Archive in Hollywood, Bakshi had this to say about the influence of the "Li'l Abner" creator and his influence on comics: "Capp is one of the great unsung heroes of comics. I've never heard anyone mention this, but Capp is 100% responsible for inspiring Harvey Kurtzman to create *Mad* magazine. Just look at '*Fearless Fosdick*'—a brilliant parody of 'Dick Tracy' with all those bullet holes and stuff. Then look at *Mad*'s 'Teddy and the Pirates,' 'Superduperman!' or even 'Little Annie Fanny.' Forget about it—slam dunk! Not taking anything away from Kurtzman, who was brilliant himself, but Capp was the source for that whole sense of satire in comics. Kurtzman carried that forward and passed it down to a whole new crop of cartoonists, myself included. Capp was a genius. You wanna argue about it? I'll fight ya, and I'll win!"

193 "Maybe you're . . ." Letter, Capp to Jerome "Bence" Capp, undated.

195 "would call the apartment . . ." Interview with Todd Capp.

195 "When the editors . . ." n.a., "What Changes Will the Sixties Bring?" *Esquire*, January 1960.

198 "life, death . . ." Bob Abel, "The Philosopher from Dogpatch," *Pageant*, May 1964.

200 "Under today's corruption . . ." Alvin Toffler, "The *Playboy* Interview: Al Capp," *Playboy*, December 1965. All other citations in this passage are from this source.

14 In the Halls of the Enemy

201 "something to fill . . ." Al Capp, "Li'l Abner" (comic strip), January 3, 1967.

201 "You'll take her . . ." ibid.

202 "The whole thing . . ." n.a., "'Joanie' Draws a Protest," *St. Petersburg Times*, January 11, 1967.

202 "I've never seen . . ." n.a., "Strip Tease," *Newsweek*, January 23, 1967.

202 "She should remember . . ." n.a., "Which One Is the Phoanie?" *Time*, January 20, 1967.

203 "told me he wouldn't . . ." Interview with Colin "Kim" Capp.

203 "Joan Baez refuses . . ." Bob Abel, "Al Capp vs. Just About Everybody!" *Cavalier*, July 1967.

203 "the greatest war-time . . ." Andy Sugar, "On the Campus Firing Line with Al Capp," *Saga*, December 1969.

203 "in the same Olympic league . . ." n.a., "Al Capp Talks to Larry Rivers," *Interview*, June 1975.

203 "Nobody is going . . ." Abel, "Al Capp vs. Just About Everybody!"

204 "It suddenly occurred . . ." Frank Leeming Jr., "Dogpatch in Arkansas," *St. Louis Post-Dispatch*, April 1, 1968.

205 "Of all the by-products . . ." Leroy Donald, "With Turn of Shovel, Dogpatch Is More than Paper and Ink," *Arkansas Gazette*, October 4, 1967.

206 "You have forty-eight hours . . ." Interview with Colin "Kim" Capp.

206 "It is every kid's . . ." n.a., "'Terribly Excited' Al Capp on Hand as Dogpatch Becomes a Real Place," *Arkansas Gazette*, May 19, 1968.

206 "I find 'Peanuts' . . ." Alvin Toffler, "The *Playboy* Interview: Al Capp," *Playboy*, December 1965.

207 "I told him . . ." n.a., "Al Capp Yields to 'Mr. Peanuts,'" *Milwaukee Journal*, October 18, 1968.

207 "I wouldn't do . . ." ibid.

207 "It is the duty . . ." n.a., "Is Nothing Sacred?" *Big Ten*, October 1967. In an interview with the authors, Tony Gardner, son of Capp's sister, Madeline, offered the following story to illustrate the complexity of his uncle's political stance in the 1960s: "I was in high school when the 'Mao' jacket came into style. My parents took me clothes shopping—at Saks, I think—and there was a rack of Mao jackets. I wanted one desperately but my parents refused, pointing out that it was not appropriate for school and, besides, it was just a fad and after a month I'd stick it in the closet and never wear it again. I was crushed. The next day, when I got home from school, there was a letter waiting for me from Al. It read, roughly, 'Tony, I was appalled by your mother's story of her refusal to buy you a Mao jacket. When I was your age, I, too, wanted to dress like an enemy of my people. As I recall, I wanted an Adolph Eichmann jacket.' A check was enclosed. I bought the jacket, loved it for a month, and stuck it in my closet, never to be worn again."

208 "I took his cue . . ." Interview with Millie Maffei Selvitella.

209 "as long as . . ." Laura Wertheimer, "Capp Denounces Student Left," Penn State University *Daily Collegian*, May 27, 1969.

209 "was not in the spirit . . ." n.a., "Capp Barbs Irk Students," *Boston Globe*, May 26, 1969.

209 "He did not come here . . ." Denise Bowman, "Embarrassment over Capp", Penn State University *Daily Collegian*, May 27, 1969.

210 "hired a performer . . ." Laura Wertheimer, "Shall Holds Back Presentation of Lion Trophy to Capp," Penn State University *Daily Collegian*, May 27, 1969.

210 "Any concerted booing . . ." Andy Sugar, "On the Campus Firing Line with Al Capp," *Saga*, December 1969.

210 "I think Mr. Capp . . ." William F. Buckley Jr., "The Campus Destroyers," *Firing Line Newsletter*, undated (April 1969).

210 "Now we must . . ." Wills quoted in William F. Buckley Jr., "Al Capp at Bay," *New York Post*, October 1, 1970.

211 "I'm that dreadful . . ." John and Yoko encounter, as seen in the film *Imagine: John Lennon*, directed by Andrew Solt, 1988. All citations in this passage are from this source.

215 "That surreptitious attack . . ." August 2, 1960, letter in Al Capp's FBI file. The identity of the author of the letter, as per FBI custom, has been obscured by white-out. All other citations in this section, unless otherwise noted, are from Capp's FBI file.

216 Bence and the Communist Party: United States Senate: Report of Proceedings, Hearing Held Before Subcommitee to Investigate the Administration of the Internal Security Act and Other Internal Security Laws of the Committee on the Judiciary: Mass Communications, December 17, 1958; interview with Todd Capp.

218 "into the pigpen . . ." Capp, "Al Capp Reprimands Harvard," *Boston Globe*, June 25, 1969.

218 "Harvard . . ." ibid.

218 Capp and Galbraith: Capp's politics gravely affected his friendships with fellow Cambridge residents John Kenneth Galbraith and Arthur Schlesinger, to the point where they were not only no longer friendly, they would have nothing to do with each other. "I remember meeting Galbraith at the Registrar of Motor Vehicles, where I was getting a license renewal," Capp's daughter Julie Cairol told the authors, "and he said, 'Oh, hello Julie, it's so nice to see you. And how is your dear mother?' Almost the same thing happened one time [after] a big snowstorm and I met Arthur Schlesinger in the subway in New York. (That was the only way you could get anyplace.) He said almost exactly the same thing! Neither mentioned a word about my father."

219 "Instead of being . . ." Capp, "Letter to the Globe from Al Capp," *Boston Globe*, June 25, 1969.

220 "hordes of people": Carol Liston, "Capp in Wrong Party to Oppose Kennedy," *Boston Globe*, June 25, 1970.

220 "dollar for dollar . . ." n.a., "Al Capp May Race Kennedy," *Milwaukee Journal*, May 27, 1970.

221 "I think it's fine . . ." Liston, "Capp in Wrong Party."

222 "I will remain . . ." Capp, "Statement," July 2, 1970.

222 "one of the most . . ." n.a., "The Metamorphosis of Al Capp," *Worcester Telegram*, July 22, 1970.

222 "I was always . . ." Capp, "Al Capp Here: A No Man," column, n.d., included in his Al Capp television show press kit. In his autobiography, *In Joy Still Felt*, prolific science fact and fiction writer Isaac Asimov wrote of the remarkable change he observed in Al Capp between the time he met him over lunch in 1953 and when he ran into him at a party fifteen years later. The two had crossed paths when both were campaigning for Lyndon B. Johnson in 1954 and still held similar views, but by 1968 Capp was an entirely different person. "It was not that he had become disillusioned in his liberalism; he had joined the enemy camp with enthusiasm," Asimov wrote. They argued "vehemently" about civil rights and Black Power, with Capp taking what Asimov considered to be "a distressingly anti-black stand." The two locked horns later, when Asimov wrote the *Boston Globe* and criticized a "Li'l Abner" sequence that he perceived to be "anti-black propaganda." Capp responded immediately, threatening Asimov with a lawsuit unless he recanted his accusation. Asimov refused. Nothing ever came of it, but as Asimov wrote, "for twenty-four hours I had been a very frightened person." Taking on Al Capp was not for the fainthearted.

222 "Believe me . . ." Tim Metz, "Leftists (for Once) Feel Satire's Sting," *Wall Street Journal*, March 31, 1970.

223 "The TV show . . ." n.a., untitled Thayer/Bruce Together press release, October 27, 1970.

223 "Whoever thought . . ." Sally Quinn, "Appreciating Agnew," *Washington Post*, November 13, 1970. Capp's assistant Larry May told a story about this event that sheds light on Capp's complexity. Despite his conservatism and the setting, Capp took May's gay roommate, David, to the event. (Catherine, still liberal and barely tolerant of Spiro Agnew's politics, refused to go.) David, May noted, had long hair and was a pacifist, but it didn't stop Capp from taking him. "He was very much aware of gays' problems in society, and felt they had the same rights every American citizen had," May said. "I heard him on more than one occasion stop someone from telling a gay 'joke,' or an anti-black joke."

15 Scandals

225 made "suggestive comments": Jack Anderson, "Capp on Campus," *New York Post*, April 22, 1971. All other citations in this passage are from this source.

The Jack Anderson column was the first public mention of allegations focusing on Capp's involvement in inappropriate or even criminal sexual behavior. Other incidents, detailed later in this chapter, were kept quiet. These incidents dated as far back as 1948 or 1949, when a woman at Simmons College, an all-women's school, supposedly received indecent telephone calls from Capp. Nothing came of this until at least late 1955 or early 1956, when the Boston Police Department became involved in the woman's complaints. Capp reacted swiftly when the complaints were brought to his attention, and by the time the investigation had reached its conclusion, Capp had enlisted the help of his attorneys, a private detective, and at least one member of the Boston Police Department—all at a substantial financial investment on Capp's part. The private investigator was able to secure a statement from Jane Louise Mesick, the retired dean of Simmons College, who, during her twenty-six years as dean, had heard many complaints of inappropriate phone calls. In her statement to the private detective, Mesick said she knew nothing of Al Capp, other than from "Li'l Abner," and that she would have known if someone of his stature had been involved in such behavior. A member of the Boston Police Department, familiar with the investigation but fearing reprisals if he became involved, declined to make a formal statement on the case, although he clearly knew of the allegations against Capp. The private investigator advised the police officer that Simmons College "would raise the roof off the Boston Police Department if such a false story were circulated." Harriet F. Pilpel, Capp's attorney at Greenbaum, Wolff & Ernst, a New York law firm, saw the reports filed by Bob Swanson, the private detective, and in a letter dated May 16, 1956, advised Capp that while Swanson's efforts "did not come out to a final termination of the matter as we hoped . . . we do feel that his recommendation to leave the matter lie for the moment is a good one." Nothing further came of the case, and Capp was never publicly implicated, but he took a significant financial hit from it—as he would later, in cases in which he was named and, in one case, charged for inappropriate sexual behavior.

226 "We found out . . ." Brit Hume, interview with Brian Lamb, C-SPAN, July 9, 2008.

228 "What had been described . . ." Brit Hume, *Inside Story* (Garden City, NY: Doubleday, 1974), p. 67. All other citations from this passage are from this source.

   Without trying to diminish in any way what Hume uncovered about Capp, it might be important to mention the possible significance of Hume's religious convictions at this point. Hume cites Anderson's Mormon beliefs as context for his boss's aversion to Capp's "you know how these young babes are" rationalization, but he doesn't reference his own religious beliefs as a possible motive for going after Capp. Hume left Anderson in 1973 to work for ABC News, and then, in 1987, he joined Fox News, the conservative network owned by Rupert Murdoch. Hume was Fox's news anchor for a decade, retiring in 2008 "to pursue the three G's: God, granddaughters and gold," but continued as a senior political analyst and as a regular panelist on *Fox News Sunday*. In his latter capacity Hume publicly revealed a judgmental moral position almost unheard of among prominent newscasters and commentators when Tiger Woods, golf's biggest name, became engulfed in his own sex scandal in late 2009 and early 2010. "The extent to which [Woods] can recover," Hume said on air, "depends on his faith. He is said to be a Buddhist. I don't think that faith offers the kind of forgiveness and redemption that is offered by the Christian faith. My message to Tiger would be, 'Tiger, turn to the Christian faith and you can make a total recovery and be a great example to the world.'"

229 Capp meeting with Anderson and Hume: Al Capp's account of his meeting with Jack Anderson and Brit Hume in Washington, D.C., found in an unpublished autobiographical fragment, could not have been more different from Hume's published version. Rather than offer the two journalists' names, Capp referred to them as "the columnist" and "the assistant": "The columnist was big, forty-five-ish, and overweight. His assistant was thirtyish, blonde, and in every way a Greek god. I had never seen either before, but somehow they seemed familiar to me, like old photographs of Oscar Wilde and young Lord Douglas. The columnist said my assistant has been working on this stuff, I've just had time to glance at it, but it looks crazy to me. I said I wasn't surprised that it did, and I preferred not to make any comment, but, if after investigating, any part of it needed explaining, I would come down and tell them the truth. The columnist said, fine, we will let you know. He walked me out to the elevator. He chuckled that a good-looking boy like that gets wound up in something like this which, of course, he wouldn't touch, for he was a great admirer of mine . . . I called my friend, the lawyer, told him it was over, and went back to Boston."

231 "wholly and ludicrously . . ." Hume, *Inside Story*, p. 79.

231 Capp/Eau Claire: n.a., "Al Capp Denies Coed's Sex Claim," *Milwaukee Journal*, May 8, 1971; n.a., "Al Capp Is Accused of Morals Offense," *New York Times*, May 8, 1971; n.a., "Al Capp Is Charged with Morals Law Violations," *San Francisco Chronicle*, May 8, 1971; n.a., "Al Capp Put in Hospital for Rest," *Milwaukee Journal*, May 2, 1971; n.a., "Capp to Answer Morals Charge," *New York Post*, July 21, 1971; n.a., "Capp Freed on Bond in Morals Case," *Milwaukee Journal*, October 13, 1971. Transcript of *State of Wisconsin vs. Al Capp*, February 1, 1972. Interviews with Patricia Harry, Stephen Caflisch, and Dr. Alvin Kahn. The FBI kept a close watch on the developments in Eau Claire, and Capp's FBI file contains many news clippings on the case.

232 "rumpled" and "sweating profusely": Interview with Stephen Caflisch.

232 "I have never seen . . ." ibid.

233 "by force . . ." Wisconsin Statute, Section 944.16.

233 "a straight-arrow . . ." ibid.

234 "AL CAPP IS ACCUSED . . ." Headline: *New York Times*, May 8, 1971.

234 "AL CAPP IS CHARGED . . ." Headline: *San Francisco Chronicle*, May 8, 1971.

234 "The allegations . . ." n.a., "Al Capp Denies Coed's Sex Claim," *New York Times*, May 8, 1971.

234 "If you recall . . ." Letter, Capp to Milton Caniff, March 7, 1974.

234 "Who do we slug?" Milton Caniff and Jules Feiffer, "Strip-time: The Comics Observed," *The Festival of Cartoon Art*, catalogue, Ohio State University Libraries, Columbus, OH, 1986.

234 "a womanizer . . ." ibid., p. 260.

235 "as a favor . . ." n.a., "Nixon Meddled in Case of Al Capp," *Milwaukee Journal*, December 8, 1992.

235 "You talk to him . . ." Interview with Al Kahn.

236 "You have a very . . ." Lawrence Grobel, "The *Playboy* Interview: Goldie Hawn," *Playboy*, January 1985. Sally Kuhn, a close friend of Capp's daughter Cathie, offered a story almost identical to Hawn's, this one involving a friend who had been approached by a stranger on the street. The stranger identified himself as someone working for Al Capp, and he told Kuhn's friend that she looked like she would make a good Daisy Mae in an upcoming theatrical production of "Li'l Abner." He set up a meeting between the young woman and Al Capp. The two met, and things went well until the young woman, undoubtedly trying to gain an advantage by dropping a name that Capp recognized, mentioned that she was a good friend of Sally Kuhn's. Capp was suddenly very uninterested and the meeting ended quickly.

236 "If he had told me . . ." ibid.

236 "She's is not classically pretty . . ." Goldie Hawn with Wendy Holden, *Goldie: A Lotus Grows in the Mud* (New York: G. P. Putnam's Sons, 2005), p. 92.

236 "I took her . . ." James Spada, *Grace: The Secret Life of a Princess* (New York: Doubleday, 1987), p. 37. The theatrical production of "Li'l Abner" that Kelly "auditioned" for was not the one that eventually appeared on Broadway. It was an earlier, unsuccessful attempt to bring the strip to the stage.

237 "Goldie, I would now . . ." Hawn, *Goldie*, p. 97. All other citations, unless otherwise noted, are from this source,

237 "like a jackass": Grobel, "*Playboy* Interview."

239 "I am afraid . . ." Transcript of *State of Wisconsin vs. Al Capp*, February 1, 1972.

239 "In Wisconsin . . ." Letter, Capp to Milton Caniff, March 7, 1974,

16 Descent

241 "How dare you . . ." Interview with Harlan Ellison.

242 "The martyrs at . . ." M. J. Wilson, "Millionaire Capp Tackles College Militants," *San Francisco Sunday Examiner & Chronicle*, August 23, 1970.

242 "My reaction to . . ." Capp, "Let Us Now Praise Famous Men," *Penthouse*, January 1973.

243 "I very much . . ." Letter, Richard Nixon to Capp, February 5, 1973.

243 "It has always . . ." Letter, Richard Nixon to Capp, July 12, 1973.

243 "It's much better . . ." Letter, Capp to Teddy Kennedy Jr., November 19, 1973.

245 "a hell of a cocktail": Interview with Oliver Sacks. All other quotes attributed to Sacks are from this source.

246 "Al became . . ." Letter, Laurence T. May to Alvin S. Hochberg, March 20, 1981.

246 "a lot of crap": Capp, discarded suicide note, retrieved by Larry May. The other citations in this passage are from this source.

247 "Aside from providing . . ." Letter, Capp to Al Hochberg, undated. In the letter, Capp mentioned that he was sixty-three, and from the content one might conclude that it was written in 1973, before his sixty-fourth birthday.

247 "I am leaving . . ." Letter, Capp to Catherine Capp, undated, ca. 1973. From the content of the letter, it is clear that it was written at the same time as the letter to Al Hochberg. It's possible that this letter was discarded before it was sent or delivered.

248 "to keep her warm . . ." Letter, Capp to Elliott Caplin, undated.

248 "a triumph . . ." Letter, Capp to "Ole Boy" (almost certainly intended for either Don Munson or Gus Levy), undated, but 1975 or 1976 based on references in the letter.

248 "worst creature . . ." Catherine Capp, diary entry, courtesy of Caitlin Manning.

248 "totally helpless": Letter, Capp to Milton Caniff, September 2, 1975.

248 "About 15 years ago . . ." Carol Oppenheim, "Al Capp's Denizens of Dogpatch run out of Time," *Chicago Tribune*, November 13, 1977.

250 "You ask yourself . . ." Capp, autobiographical fragment, unpublished.

250 "Nowhere in the . . ." Elliott Caplin, *Al Capp Remembered* (Bowling Green, OH: Bowling Green University Popular Press, 1994), p. 124.

250 "My less than . . ." ibid., p. 126.

252 "I hadn't painted . . ." Eugenia Sheppard, "The Morning After," *New York Post*, April 18, 1975.

252 "A work of art . . ." Catalina Kitty Meyer, "Interview with Al Capp," catalogue of *Al Capp: Paintings*, catalogue from exhibit at New York Cultural Center, April–May 1975, p. 8. Capp's belief in comics as art dated back three decades. In a November 24, 1947, cover profile in *Newsweek*, he stated: "The most significant art of the '40s will not be some tired landscapes, not some aborted attempts of abstractionists and surrealists, but the comic strip. It is the most beloved way of telling a story and the most fanatically followed, and the realization of this is beginning to take shape now."

252 "It occurred . . ." n.a., "For the Art Crowd, a Choice of Picasso or Dogpatch," *People*, May 5, 1975.

254 "She finally . . ." Interview with Sally Kuhn. All quotations attributed to Kuhn in this passage are from this source.

255 "nervous difficulties": Letter, Capp to "Ole Boy," (almost certainly intended for either Don Munson or Gus Levy), undated, but 1975 or 1976 based on references in the letter.

255 "She is a silent . . ." ibid.

256 Capp and his employees: Capp could be both generous and stingy with his employees. He did not provide health insurance and retirement benefits, for instance, but until he hired Frank Frazetta in 1953, he gave each of his two key assistants a generous 10 percent of the "Li'l Abner" take—which, in effect, doubled their salaries. His loyalty to Andy Amato and Walter Johnston was admirable; even if Capp's bonus system was a pragmatic defensive position inspired by his own unpleasant experience as Ham Fisher's assistant, he seems to have developed a genuine bond with them. In an interview for this book, Nancy LeBlanc, Johnston's daughter, spoke of how her father began having severe headaches in early 1962 and suffered a stroke on Groundhog Day that same year. During Johnston's lengthy rehabilitation process, Capp sent him unused penciled strips to practice his inking on, but Johnston never recovered enough to work again. His eye-to-hand coordination was gone. Nevertheless, even though he had no legal obligation to offer assistance to Johnston, Capp, LeBlanc said, "put my father on half-pay for the rest of his life." Johnston died in 1969.

256 "you are a vicious . . ." Letter, Capp to Harvey Curtis, undated, ca. 1977.

256 "It is extremely . . ." Letter, Bill Gordon to Al Hochberg, August 8, 1977.

256 "Frankly, I am a little . . ." ibid.

258 "I talked with . . ." Gail Jennes, "Falling Popularity, Bad Health and a Family Tragedy Persuade Al Capp to Erase 'Li'l Abner,'" *People*, October 24, 1977.

258 "I grew more . . ." Daniel Q. Haney, "Li'l Abner Retires, Takes All Dogpatch with Him," *Milwaukee Journal*, November 13, 1977.

258 "If you have . . ." n. a., "Mr. Dogpatch," *Time*, November 19, 1979.

258 "He's like a Dickens . . ." Israel Shenker, "Al Capp, Harbinger of the Age of Irreverence, Gives Up Cartoon but Not Irascibility," *New York Times*, November 11, 1977.

260 "He's created . . ." ibid.

260 "I keep thinking . . ." n.a., "Dogpatch Is Ready for Freddie," *Time*, October 17, 1977.

260 "Regrets? . . ." John Halbrooks, "Al Capp: Curmudgeon Emeritus," *Ambassador*, June 1978.

260 "quite bewildered": Letter, Art Buchwald to Capp, September 21, 1978.

261 "For the last . . ." Letter, Capp to Art Buchwald, undated, ca. early 1978.

261 "father of us all": Letter, Capp to Elliott Caplin, undated, ca. 1979.

261 "I can't take . . ." Letter, Capp to Jerome "Bence" Capp, undated, ca. 1973.

261 "an American institution": n.a., "Sad Day in Dogpatch: Al Capp Dies," *Boston Globe*, November 6, 1979.

261 "the Mark Twain . . ." n.a., "Mr. Dogpatch," *Time*, November 19, 1979.

262 "The things . . ." n.a., "Al Capp, R.I.P.," *Saturday Review*, November 23, 1979.

262 "Li'l Abner . . ." John Updike, foreword to Al Capp's posthumously published collection of memoirs, *My Well-Balanced Life on a Wooden Leg* (Santa Barbara, CA: John Daniel, 1991), p. 9.

263 "In telling the story . . ." Interview with Rita Castillo. All other citations in this passage are from this source.

BIBLIOGRAPHY

Books

Adams, Edie, and Robert Windeler. *Sing a Pretty Song: The "Offbeat" Life of Edie Adams*. New York: William Morrow, 1990.

Beaty, Bart. *Fredric Wertham and the Critique of Mass Culture*. Jackson: University Press of Mississippi, 2005.

Berger, Arthur Asa. *Li'l Abner: A Study in American Satire*. New York: Twayne, 1970.

Caplin, Elliott. *Al Capp Remembered*. Bowling Green, OH: Bowling Green State University Popular Press, 1994.

Capp, Al. *Al Capp's Bald Iggle: The Life It Ruins May Be Your Own*. New York: Simon & Schuster, 1956.

———. *Al Capp's Li'l Abner: The Frazetta Years*. 4 vols., with introductions and annotations by Denis Kitchen. Milwaukie, OR: Dark Horse Books, 2003.

———. *Al Capp's Shmoo: The Complete Comic Books*. Introduction and annotations by Denis Kitchen. Milwaukie, OR: Dark Horse Books, 2008.

———. *Al Capp's Shmoo: The Complete Newspaper Strips*. Introduction and annotations by Denis Kitchen. Milwaukie, OR: Dark Horse Books, 2011.

———. *The Best of Li'l Abner*. New York: Holt, Rinehart, and Winston, 1978.

———. *Fearless Fosdick*. Princeton, WI: Kitchen Sink Press, 1990.

———. *Fearless Fosdick: His Life and Deaths*. New York: Simon & Schuster, 1956.

———. *Fearless Fosdick: The Hole Story*. Princeton, WI: Kitchen Sink Press, 1992.

———. *The Hardhat's Bedtime Story Book*. New York: Harper & Row, 1971.

———. *The Life and Times of the Shmoo*. New York: Simon & Schuster, 1948.

———. *Li'l Abner*. San Diego, CA: IDW [Idea and Design Works] Publishing, American Library of Comics. Ongoing series publishing every "Li'l Abner" strip, daily and Sunday, each volume containing two years of strips.

———. *Li'l Abner: Dailies*. Princeton, WI, and Northampton, MA: Kitchen Sink Press. 27 vols., each covering a year of daily strips.

———. *My Well-Balanced Life on a Wooden Leg: Memoirs*. Foreword by John Updike. Santa Barbara, CA: John Daniel, 1991.

———. *The World of Li'l Abner*. Introduction by John Steinbeck. Foreword by Charles Chaplin. New York: Farrar, Straus and Young, 1953.

Eisner, Will. *Will Eisner's Shop Talk*. Milwaukie, OR: Dark Horse Comics, 2001.

Gray, Harold. *Arf! The Life and Hard Times of Little Orphan Annie, 1935–1945*. Introduction by Al Capp. New Rochelle, NY: Arlington House, 1970.

Hajdu, David. *The Ten-Cent Plague: The Great Comic-Book Scare and How It Changed America*. New York: Farrar, Straus and Giroux, 2008.

Harvey, Robert C. *Meanwhile. . . .* Seattle, WA: Fantagraphics Books, 2007.

———, ed., *Milton Caniff Conversations*. Jackson: University Press of Mississippi, 2002.

Hawn, Goldie, with Wendy Holden. *Goldie: A Lotus Grows in the Mud*. New York: G. P. Putnam's Sons, 2005.

Hume, Brit. *Inside Story*. Garden City, NY: Doubleday, 1974.

Inge, M. Thomas. *Comics as Culture*. Jackson: University Press of Mississippi, 1990.

Kilbourne, Jean. *Deadly Persuasion*. New York: Free Press, 1999.

Leggett, John. *A Daring Young Man: A Biography of William Saroyan*. New York: Alfred A. Knopf, 2002.

McLuhan, Herbert Marshall. *The Mechanical Bride*. New York: Vanguard, 1951.

Michaelis, David. *Schulz and Peanuts*. New York: HarperCollins, 2007.

Nyberg, Amy Kiste. *Seal of Approval: The History of the Comics Code*. Jackson: University Press of Mississippi, 1998.

O'Sullivan, Judith. *The Great American Comic Strip*. Boston: Bulfinch Press, 1990.

Sheridan, Martin. *Classic Comics and Their Creators*. Boston: Cushman and Flint, 1942; rpt. Arcadia, CA: Post-Era Books, 1973.

Spada, James. *Grace: The Secret Lives of a Princess*. Garden City, NY: Dolphin Doubleday Books, 1987.

Theroux, Alexander. *The Enigma of Al Capp*. Seattle, WA: Fantagraphics Books, 1999.

Waugh, Coulton. *The Comics*. New York: Macmillan, 1947.

Wertham, Fredric. *Seduction of the Innocent*. New York: Rinehart, 1954.

White, David Manning. *From Dogpatch to Slobbovia: The Gasp!! World of L'il Abner, as Seen by David Manning White, with Certain Illuminating Remarks by Al Capp*. Boston: Beacon Press, 1964.

Magazine and Newspaper Articles

n.a. "Al Capp a Hit as WEA Lecturer," *Milwaukee Journal*, November 8, 1969.

———. "Al Capp, Critic," *Newsweek*, April 1, 1963.

———."Al Capp Denies Coed's Sex Claim," *New York Times*, May 8, 1971.

———. "Al Capp Is Accused of Morals Offense," *New York Times*, May 8, 1971.

———. "Al Capp Is Charged with Morals Law Violations," *San Francisco Chronicle*, May 8, 1971.

———. "Al Capp May Race Kennedy," *Milwaukee Journal*, May 27, 1970.

———. "Al Capp Meets Some Dogpatchers," *American Youth*, January/February 1960.

———. "Al Capp Put in Hospital for Rest," *Milwaukee Journal*, May 2, 1971.

———. "Al Capp Reprimands Harvard," *Boston Globe*, June 25, 1969.

———. "Al Capp, R.I.P.," *Saturday Review*, November 23, 1979.

———. "Al Capp Says Comics Are Today's Fine Art," *Cleveland Plain Dealer*, March 17, 1969.

———. "Al Capp's Wondrous Li'l Abner," *Satellite*, August 1957.

———. "Al Capp Yields to 'Mr. Peanuts,'" *Milwaukee Journal*, October 18, 1968.

———. "Amateur Boxer to Play Li'l Abner in the Movies," *Boston Globe*, September 9, 1940.

———. "Apology for Margaret," *Time*, January 11, 1943.

———. "Are You a Citizen of Dogpatch?" *Argosy*, November 1948.

———. "Bane of the Bassinet," *Time*, March 15, 1948.

———. "Btfsplk Does It," *Time*, October 18, 1948.

———. "Capp Answers Criticism of Exploitation," *Editor & Publisher*, August 27, 1949.

———. "Capp Attacks Madison Window Smashers," *Milwaukee Journal*, February 14, 1970.

———. "Capp Freed on Bond in Morals Case," *Milwaukee Journal*, October 13, 1971.

———. "Capp-italist Revolution," *Life*, December 20, 1948.

———. "Capp Says 'McCommunism' Now Holding Sway in Senate," *Durham Sun*, May 8, 1954.

———. "Capp's Cuts," *Time*, April 11, 1969.

———. "Capp's Funny Spelling Lands in Textbooks," *Editor & Publisher*, July 13, 1963.

———. "Cappsulizing a Cartoonist's Views," *San Francisco Examiner*, May 14, 1969.

———. "Capp Tells Police They Get Hard Time on Hard Pay," *Cleveland Press*, October 5, 1966.

————. "Capp to Answer Morals Charge," *New York Post*, July 21, 1971.

————. "Capp to Put a Cap on 'Li'l Abner' Strip," *Milwaukee Journal*, October 4, 1977.

————. "Capp v. Fisher," *Time*, February 14, 1955.

————. "Cartoonist Ham Fisher Found Dead," *New York Daily News*, December 28, 1955.

————. "Cartoonist Is Liable in Amount of $75,000,000," *Amesbury Daily*, January 11, 1943.

————. "City Club to Hear Li'l Abner Creator," *Cleveland Press*, November 24, 1955.

————. "Defending Fosdick," *Arkansas Gazette*, December 11, 1965.

————. "Did Sex Ruin the Darling of Dogpatch?" *Picture Digest*, June 1955.

————. "Die Monstersinger," *Time*, November 6, 1950.

————. "Dogpatch Is Ready for Freddie," *Time*, October 17, 1977.

————. "Fifteen Minutes with Al Capp," *Pageant*, September 1951.

————. "For the Art Crowd, a Choice of Picasso or Dogpatch," *People*, May 5, 1975.

————. "For Your Information," *Newsweek*, September 19, 1949.

————. "Fosdick Bad for the Law, Chief Claims," *Arkansas Gazette*, December 10, 1965.

————. "Harvest Shmoon," *Time*, September 13, 1948.

————. "Inhuman Man," *Time*, February 6, 1950.

————. "Is Long Sam America's Ideal Woman?" *People Today*, February 22, 1956.

————. "Is Nothing Sacred?" *Big Ten*, October 1967.

————. "Joan Baez Protests Comic Strip 'Joanie,'" *Milwaukee Journal*, January 11, 1967.

————. "'Joanie' Draws a Protest," *St. Petersburg Times*, January 11, 1967.

————. "Joe Palooka vs. Li'l Abner," *Tops*, May 1954.

————. "Kigmy Sweet," *Newsweek*, October 3, 1949.

————. "Lazonga to Shmoo," *Newsweek*, July 12, 1948.

————. "Leviticus vs. Yokums," *Newsweek*, November 29, 1948.

————. "Li'l Abner," *Variety*, December 31, 1959.

————. "Li'l Abner—Broadway," *Life*, January 14, 1957.

————. "Li'l Abner Creator Sues for 14 Million," *New York Times*, July 12, 1947.

————. "Li'l Abner Goes to Town," *Saturday Review*, February 29, 1964.

————. "Li'l Abner's Mad Capp," *Newsweek*, November 24, 1947.

————. "Li'l Abner to Have Southland Adventure; Cartoonist Capp Here to Plan for Trip," *Los Angeles Times*, June 17, 1940.

————. "Many Protest to Syndicate on Shmoo Tieup," *Editor & Publisher*, September 3, 1949.

————. "Mellowed Kickapoo," *Newsweek*, February 22, 1965.

————. "The Metamorphosis of Al Capp," *Worcester Telegram*, July 22, 1970.

————. "The Miracle of Dogpatch," *Time*, December 27, 1948.

————. "Missionary to the Campus," *Newsweek*, June 22, 1970.

————. "Mr. Capp Finds SDS Full of Yokum," *Washington Daily News*, June 17, 1969.

————. "Mr. Dogpatch," *Time*, November 19, 1979.

————. "New Picture," *Time*, December 21, 1959.

————. "Nixon Meddled in Case of Al Capp," *Milwaukee Journal*, December 8, 1992.

————. "Pappy Yokum Caught Reading," *Editor & Publisher*, August 10, 1963.

————. "Parashmoopers Take Off to Be Dropped on Berlin," *Cleveland Press*, October 13, 1948.

————. "Rap for Capp," *Time*, September 9, 1957.

————. "The Roaring Presses," *Time*, May 10, 1948.

————. "Sacking of the Shmoo," *Time*, May 23, 1949.

————. "Sad Day in Dogpatch: Al Capp Dies," *Boston Globe*, November 6, 1979.

————. "Sen. McCarthy Called 'Bum' by Al Capp," *Haverhill Gazette*, April 17, 1953.

————. "Shmoos Make Noos," *Newsweek*, October 11, 1948.

————. "The Shmoo's Return," *New Yorker*, October 26, 1963.

————. "The (Sob!) Ugliest," *Time*, October 28, 1946.

———. "Speaking of Pictures . . . Al Capp Puts the Likenesses of Famous People in His 'Li'l Abner,'" *Life*, June 12, 1944.

———. "Speaking of Pictures . . . 500,000 People Draw Lena the Hyena," *Life*, October 22, 1946.

———. "Strip Tease," *Newsweek*, July 17, 1944.

———. "Stuff of Dreams," *Time*, December 1, 1947.

———. "Superwoman's Dive," *Newsweek*, July 12, 1943.

———. "Taming of the Shmoo," *Newsweek*, September 5, 1949.

———. "'Terribly Excited' Al Capp on Hand as Dogpatch Becomes a Real Place," *Arkansas Gazette*, May 19, 1968.

———. "Trials of Li'l Abner: He's So Real That Food Gifts Pour in for Gaunt Yokums," *Newsweek*, February 26, 1940.

———. "U. N. Take Note," *Quick*, October 10, 1949.

———. "The Unthinkable," *Time*, March 31, 1952.

———. "The U.S. Becomes Shmoo-Struck," *Life*, September 20, 1948.

———. "What Changes Will the Sixties Bring?" *Esquire*, January 1960.

———. "Which One Is the Phoanie?" *Time*, January 20, 1967.

———. "Yokum Hokum," *People Today*, February 1957.

Abel, Bob. "Al Capp vs. Just About Everybody!" *Cavalier*, July 1967.

———. "The Philosopher from Dogpatch," *Pageant*, May 1964.

Alden, John. "Li'l Abner, World's Leading Comic; Drawn By 28-Year-Old Cartoonist in Cambridge," *Boston Globe*, August 30, 1938.

Armstrong, Walter. "What Really Made Ham Fisher Decide to Die?" *Uncensored*, May 1956.

Atwood, Margaret. "The Comics Generation," *Playboy*, December 2008.

Becattini, Alberto. "The Good Girl Art of Bob Lubbers," *Comic Book Marketplace*, April 2002.

Brady, Frank. "How Li'l Abner Got His Start," *Quill*, October 1937.

Brown, Edward D. "'Li'l Abner' Artist Learned How at Boston Art Museum School," *Boston Globe*, March 3, 1935.

Buchwald, Art. "Capp's Spoiled Girls Become Model Wives," *Boston Globe*, February 26, 1960.

———. "Don't Be a Pal to Your Son," *American Mercury*, August 1959.

Buckley, William F., Jr. "Al Capp at Bay," *New York Post*, October 1, 1970.

———. "The Campus Destroyers," *Firing Line Newsletter*, April 1, 1969.

Caniff, Milton. "No Free Trips to DAMA," *Milton Caniff's Steve Canyon Magazine*, September 1984.

Capp, Al. "A Blasting Capp," *Ergo*, May 28, 1969.

———. "Advice to Princeton Alumni," *National Review*, September 22, 1970.

———. "Al Capp by Li'l Abner," *Life*, June 24, 1946.

———. "Al Capp Here: Anarchy, Anyone?" *New York Daily News*, September 27. 1970.

———."Al Capp Here: The Concerned Coed," *New York Daily News*, September 20, 1970.

———. "Al Capp Here: Share the Wealth!" *New York Daily News*, May 10, 1970.

———. "Ál Capp Here: Willy's World," *New York Daily News*, April 26, 1970.

———. "Al Capp's America," *Pageant*, March 1953.

———. "Back to the Democrats' Drawing Board," *Penthouse*, March 1973.

———. "Can TV Be Saved?" *Esquire*, December 1963.

———. "The Care and Feeding of Sacred Cows," *Saturday Evening Post*, September/October 1973.

———. "The Comedy of Charlie Chaplin," *Atlantic Monthly*, February 1950.

———. "The Day Dream," *Show*, December 1962.

———. "Dear Mammy," *Argosy*, January 1960.

———. "Gulp!" *New York Review of Books*, March 19, 1964.

———. "I Don't Like Shmoos," *Cosmopolitan*, June 1949.

———. "I Remember Monster," *Atlantic Monthly*, April 1950.

———. "I Remember Rube, the Chaplin of the Funny Pages," *Smithsonian*, November 1970.

———. "'It's Hideously True': The Creator of Li'l Abner Tells Why His Hero Is (Sob!) Wed," *Life*, March 31, 1952.

———. "Letter to the Globe from Al Capp," *Boston Globe*, June 25, 1969.

———. "Let Us Now Praise Famous Men," *Penthouse*, January 1973.

———. "Li'l Abner's Gals," *Playboy*, May 1957.

———. "The Man Who Came Back," *New York Herald Tribune*, July 30, 1951.

———. "Memories of Miss Mandelbaum," *Atlantic Monthly*, May 1951.

———. "Mother and Her Secret," *Reader's Digest*, May 1964.

———. "My Life as an Immortal Myth," *Life*, April 30, 1965.

———. "My Well-Balanced Life on a Wooden Leg," *Life*, May 23, 1960.

———. "The Other Capp," *Saturday Evening Post*, March/April 1973.

———. "O, Whither Hast Thou Led Me, Egypt? The Roman Spring of Al Capp," *Show*, June 1962.

———. "The Person Who Changed My Life," *Seventeen*, April 1965.

———. "The Real Powers in America," *Real*, December 1952.

———. "The Terrifying Adventures of Fearless Fosdick," *Pageant*, May 1952.

———. "There Is a Real Shmoo," *New Republic*, March 21, 1949.

———. "The Thinking Capp," *This Week*, February 23, 1969.

———. "They Don't Make Millionaires Anymore the Way They Did in Betty Grable's Time," *Saturday Evening Post*, December 1974.

———. "Unforgettable Li'l Abner," *Reader's Digest*, June 1978.

———. "Why I Am Not Rich," *Saturday Evening Post*, March 1974.

———. "Why Watergate?" *Spectator*, April 21, 1974.

Capp, Cathy [sic]. "Cathy Capp Says Dad Is Okay Guy," *Boston Globe*, January 2, 1953.

Casey, Phil. "Capp-turing Laughter and Applause," *Washington Post*, June 17, 1969.

Cooper, Morton. "Profile of a Character," *Modern Man*, October 1958.

Cornell, John. "Yokel Boy Makes Good," *Los Angeles Times*, July 21, 1940.

Cremmen, Mary. "Take a Lesson from Al Capp," *Pageant*, March 1950.

Crist, Judith. "Horror in the Nursery," *Collier's*, March 27, 1948.

Crowther, Bosley. "The Screen: Li'l Abner," *New York Times*, December 12, 1959.

Dobson, Gwen. "Al Capp—No One Is Neutral," *Oakland Tribune*, July 5, 1970.

Doherty, John Stephen. "The Ribald Humor of Al Capp," *Climax*, July 1959.

Domeier, Douglas. "Al Capp, Art Linkletter Speak Out for America," *Dallas Morning News*, February 16, 1970.

Donald, Leroy. "With Turn of Shovel, Dogpatch Is More Than Paper and Ink," *Arkansas Gazette*, October 4, 1967.

Du Brow, Rick. "Al Capp Will Be Featured in Hour-Long NBC Special," *Memphis Press-Scimitar*, February 4, 1970.

Edgar, James. "Joe Palooka: Richest Pug in the World," *Maclean's*, August 1, 1950.

Fiddick, Peter. "Perennial Wiseguy," *Guardian*, January 2, 1971.

Flanagan, James B. "Daly in Lions' Den with Capp, Condon," *Cleveland Plain Dealer*, June 14, 1965.

Flowers, Paul. "Cartoonist Al Capp a Dinosaur," *Memphis Commercial Appeal*, August 22, 1971.

Freeman, Donald. "Al Capp on GOP Switch, 'Hillbillies' and Lawsuits," *San Diego Union*, June 25, 1970.

Furlong, William. "Recap on Al Capp," *Saturday Evening Post*, Winter 1971.

Galton, Lawrence N. "Al Capp: His Hillbilly Characters Are American Institutions," *Pageant*, December 1945.

Gerrard, Michael. "Fascism's Foe from Dogpatch," *Columbia Daily Spectator*, December 4, 1969.

Goldberg, Hyman. "2 Daisy Maes Fight for Their Creator's Favor," *New York Mirror*, June 8, 1947.

Goldstein, Kalman. "Al Capp and Walt Kelly: Pioneers of Political and Social Satire in the Comics," *Journal of Popular Culture*, Spring 1992.

Grobel, Lawrence. "The Playboy Interview: Goldie Hawn," *Playboy*, January 1985.

Halbrooks, John. "Al Capp: Curmudgeon Emeritus," *Ambassador*, June 1978.

Haney, Daniel Q. "Li'l Abner Retires, Takes All Dogpatch with Him," *Kansas City Star*, November 13, 1977.

Harris, Harry. "Al Capp and Ustinov Square Off on Merv Griffin 'Love-In' Show," *Philadelphia Inquirer*, May 1970.

Hazen, David W. "Meet Li'l Abner's Real-Life Pappy," *Oregonian*, January 16, 1938.

Heckman, Richard. "An Interview with Al Capp," *Boston*, February 1964.

Hicks, Wilson. "Discoverer Remembers a Promising Pair," *Life*, December 7, 1959.

Howard, Edwin. "Blam! That's Capp: Students Go Zap!" *Memphis Press-Scimitar*, November 12, 1969.

Inge, M. Thomas. "Li'l Abner, Pogo, and Friends: The South in the American Comic Strip," *Southern Quarterly*, Winter 2011.

Irwin, Virginia. "Al Capp and His Fertile Imagination," *St. Louis Post-Dispatch*, February 14, 1949.

Jennes, Gail. "Falling Popularity, Bad Health and a Family Tragedy Persuade Al Capp to Erase 'Li'l Abner,'" *People*, October 24, 1977.

Jiler, George H. "Li'l Abner, Born Here 5 Years Ago, Heads for Movies," *Bridgeport Post*, August 13, 1939.

Jones, Pat. "Happy Job for Marryin' Sam," *Arkansas Gazette*, October 29, 1968.

Kahn, E. J., Jr. "OOFF!! (SOB!) EEP!! (GULP!) ZOWIE!!!—I," *New Yorker*, November 29, 1947.

———. "OOFF!! (SOB!) EEP!! (GULP!) ZOWIE!!!—II," *New Yorker*, December 6, 1947.

Katkov, Norman. "Li'l Abner's Pappy," *Saga*, November 1955.

Kraus, Dick. "The Story of Al Capp," *Calling All Boys*, December–January 1947.

Kutner, Nanette. "Li'l Abner's Mistuh Capp," *Esquire*, April 1957.

Laas, William. "A Half-Century of Comic Art," *Saturday Review of Literature*, March 20, 1948.

Lauritz, Phyllis. "Friends A-Feudin' in So-Called Funnies; More Takeoffs Lurking in Fertile Minds," *Oregonian*, August 29, 1957.

Leeming, Frank. Jr., "Dogpatch in Arkansas," *St. Louis Post-Dispatch*, April 1, 1968.

Liston, Carol. "Capp in Wrong Party to Oppose Kennedy," *Boston Globe*, June 25, 1970.

Long, Barbara. "A Day at the Buckleys: Big Blight at Great Elm," *Village Voice*, September 17, 1970.

Maeder, Jay. "Spitting on Pictures: Funny Papers, 1955," *New York Daily News*, September 18, 1998.

Maitland, Leslie. "Dogpatch, U.S.A., Joins World of Fine Arts," *New York Times*, April 16, 1975.

Mann, D. L. "Al Capp," *Open Road*, December 1952.

Mannes, Marya. "Junior Has a Craving," *New Republic*, February 17, 1947.

Manning, Annabel. "My Grandfather Draws Li'l Abner," *Jack and Jill*, April 1973.

Marschall, Richard. "Al Capp: The Last Interview with Comics' Master Satirist," *Comics Journal* 54 (March 1980).

Marschall, Rick. "Saying Something About the Status Quo: Al Capp, Master Satirist of the Comics," *Nemo*, April 1986.

Matthews, Gail. "Interview with Al Capp," *Yankee*, April 1965.

Mattingly, Ignatius G. "Some Cultural Aspects of Serial Cartoons," *Harper's*, December 1955.

McCabe, Charles. "Old at 30?" *San Francisco Chronicle*, June 4, 1970.

McMaster, Jane. "Capp's Position on Strip Opinion Draws Dissent," *Editor & Publisher*, June 24, 1950.

———. "Editor, Capp Disagree on Opinions in Strips," *Editor & Publisher*, June 10, 1950.

———. "'Li'l Abner' Sideline Is Shmoopendous," *Editor & Publisher*, July 16, 1949.

Metz, Tim. "Leftists (for Once) Feel Satire's Sting," *Wall Street Journal*, March 31, 1970.

Nuhn, Roy. "Farewell to Li'l Abner and Daisy Mae," *Antique Trader Weekly*, August 30, 1978.

Oppenheim, Carol. "Al Capp's Denizens of Dogpatch Run Out of Time," *Chicago Tribune*, November 13, 1977.

Ownes, Wayne. "'Expert on Nothing' Has Many Opinions," *Lake Charles American Press*, April 16, 1970.

Peak, Mayme Ober. "Movie Mammy Yokum Has Plenty of Sock," *Boston Globe*, August 11, 1940.

Perkin, Robert L. "Al Capp Has Turned into Inc. Enterprise," *Rocky Mountain News*, May 30, 1954.

Quinn, Sally. "Appreciating Agnew," *Washington Post*, November 13, 1970.

Rivers, Larry. "Al Capp Talks to Larry Rivers," *Interview*, June 1975.

Rodell, Fred. "Everybody Reads the Comics," *Esquire*, March 1945.

Seidenbaum, Art. "Liberals Fret: Is Li'l Abner Turning Against Them, Too?" *Milwaukee Journal*, April 4, 1967.

Shenker, Israel. "Al Capp, Harbinger of the Age of Irreverence, Gives Up Cartoon but Not Irascibility," *New York Times*, November 11, 1977.

Sheppard, Eugenia. "The Morning After," *New York Post*, April 18, 1975.

Storin, Matthew V. "Al Capp May Run Against Kennedy," *Boston Globe*, June 19, 1970.

Sugar, Andy. "On the Campus Firing Line with Al Capp," *Saga*, December 1969.

Toffler, Alvin. "The *Playboy* Interview: Al Capp," *Playboy*, December 1965.

Wechsler, James A. "Non-Comic Strip," *New York Post*, May 23, 1969.

———. "Secrets of 'Success,'" *New York Post*, February 15, 1973.

Whiting, Thelma. "'Acid Al' Capp Talks Politics," *Daily Hampshire Gazette*, August 13, 1970.

Whitman, Howard. "Li'l Abner Makes a Killing," *Coronet*, November 1941.

Wilson, M. J. "Millionaire Capp Tackles College Militants," *San Francisco Sunday Examiner & Chronicle*, August 23, 1970.

Woodley, Richard. "Cappital Punishment," *Esquire*, November 1970.

Manuscripts

Capp, Al. Autobiographical fragments. Loose pages, including three false starts to the longer autobiographies listed below.

———. "Gus and Alvin." Five typed, unpublished autobiographical fragments, presented as short stories.

———. Untitled autobiography—1. 79-page typescript on yellow legal paper.

———. Untitled autobiography—2. 80-page typescript on yellow legal paper.

Caplin, O. P. *Dogpatch Road*. A memoir written by Capp's father. 498-page typescript.

Documents

Federal Bureau of Investigation Files on Al Capp, Cartoonist, Cambridge, Massachusetts. n.d.

State of Wisconsin Circuit Court, Eau Claire County: *State of Wisconsin, Plaintiff, vs. Al Capp, Defendant*, February 11, 1972.

United States Senate: Report of Proceedings: Subcommittee to Investigate the Administration of the Internal Security Act and Other Internal Security Laws of the Committee on the Judiciary: Mass Communications, December 17, 1958.

Plays

Caplin, Elliott. *A Nickel for Picasso*. A two-act, loosely biographical play, focusing on Al Capp's childhood accident and its aftermath, offered as a fictional account. Capp and his parents are given especially strong portrayals. n.d.

Film/DVD

Imagine: John Lennon. Directed by Andrew Solt. Written by Sam Egan and Andrew Solt. Released by Warner Bros. on October 7, 1988.

Untitled. Unreleased black-and-white footage of John Lennon and Yoko Ono's confrontation with Al Capp in Montreal, provided by Will Peirce. n.d.

Recordings

Al Capp on Campus. Folkways Records No. FC 7353, 1959.

ACKNOWLEDGMENTS

Every biography promises challenges to the biographer, and we knew, going into our research, that a biography of Al Capp would require special vigilance. As of this writing, he had been dead for more than three decades, so we had to rely on his interviews, statements, and writings to delve into his feelings about his life and times. Even so, as we mention elsewhere in this book, he had issues with the unvarnished truth, often because he favored a flavorful story in lieu of the vanilla one, which might be fine for the purposes of entertainment, but could be problematic for someone trying to re-tell the story of his life. In addition, Capp's memory was faulty, particularly when it came to dates. (In his unpublished autobiography, he even got the year wrong when he wrote about losing his leg, and the date of his marriage.) Then there was the usual issue of revisionist history: people prefer to remember events in a specific way, even if the facts say otherwise. Capp had many professional acquaintances and friends, but very few close friends; most have died.

We spent countless hours constructing timelines, checking and cor-roborating the facts, reading through thousands of pages of news clippings, letters, and official documents; we watched old recordings of his television appearances. We interviewed, in person, over the phone, and via e-mail, any-one who could supply us with needed information and details. We continued to interview, even after we had submitted the manuscript of this book, and we were able to obtain vital information that we added to the edited version.

As always, the biography became a group effort, and we want to thank the many people who helped us along the way.

First and foremost, we wish to thank Julie Cairol, Al Capp's daughter, for talking about her father and permitting us to examine documents, let-ters, clippings, and other materials long relegated to storage.

Colin "Kim" Capp, Al Capp's son, spoke at length about what it was like growing up in the Capp household; of his experiences at Dogpatch USA; and of the burdens of holding on to one's identity while bearing the name of someone as famous as his father.

Todd Capp, son of Al Capp's brother Bence, provided the authors with a copy of the unpublished manuscript of Otto Caplin's memoirs, the transcript of his father's appearance before the Senate Subcommittee investigating communism in the United States, and the often contentious correspondence between his father and uncle. Todd's notes and comments supplied us with invaluable information for this book.

William Peirce, son of Capp's daughter Cathie, offered valuable insight into Al Capp's life as a father and grandfather, and was very helpful in assisting us in securing needed documents for this book. He offered clarification of some of the events in his grandfather's life, even though some were painful to remember and discuss.

Don Caplin, Elliott's son, supplied us with a copy of his father's play, *A Nickel for Picasso*—a two-act dramatization of Al Capp's childhood and accident, fictionalized for the stage.

Thanks to other family members for their insights and help: Julian Cairol (Julie's husband), Louis Gardner (husband of Capp's sister, Madeline), Tony Gardner (Louis and Madeline's son), Alexa Gardner Lesser (Louis and Madeline's daughter), and Caitlin Manning (Julie's daughter).

Rita Castillo was extremely generous with her time and help with this book. Her mother Nina Luce's affair with Capp, aside from his marriage, was the most enduring love affair of Al Capp's life, and Rita offered the authors access to scores of his letters, as well as to photos and other vital information. Her interviews helped shed light on a side of Capp rarely seen by the public. Thanks also to Louie Castillo, Rita's husband, for his interview and assistance on archival matters.

Deepest gratitude to Patricia Harry for her courage in recalling the events in Eau Claire, Wisconsin. These events are still very difficult for her to discuss, more than four decades after their taking place, and it's clear that it was painful for her to offer details about something that quite literally changed her life. Thanks also to Stephen Caflisch, a radio news director and reporter who followed and covered the story from the beginning, whose memories speak volumes of the exceedingly difficult time Patricia Harry and her late husband, Steve, endured in the months following Capp's visit to Eau Claire.

Sally Kuhn, close friend of Capp's daughter Cathie, offered a clear, concise picture of Cathie's troubled life, as well as a definitive insider's look at day-to-day goings-on in the Capp household. Kuhn's frank memories of Capp's darker side helped corroborate accounts given by Goldie Hawn, Patricia Harry, and other women who encountered Capp on his worst behavior.

Thanks to Dr. Alvin Kahn, a psychiatrist, neighbor, and friend of Capp's, who spent many hours visiting Capp at his home (though never in an official capacity) in the 1970s. Kahn accompanied Capp to his court hearing in Eau Claire and was party to his telephone conversation with Bernie Cornfeld, when Cornfeld offered to help arrange a "hit" on Patricia Harry.

Dr. Oliver Sacks, neurologist, psychologist, and bestselling author (and Capp's second cousin), graciously agreed to talk to us about Capp, and while he never formally treated him, he was able to provide us invaluable details about the effects of some of the prescribed medications Capp was taking in the last decade of his life.

Mort Walker, creator of "Beetle Bailey" and "Hi and Lois," and long-time professional acquaintance of Capp's, spoke eloquently about the Al Capp/Ham Fisher feud, the issues that led to the National Cartoonists Society's eventually expelling Fisher from its membership, and Capp's ups and downs during the time they knew each other.

Millie (née Maffei) Selvitella talked about the time she spent as Capp's secretary and personal assistant, and Laurence May offered unflinching details about the near-decade he worked as Capp's assistant. Morris Weiss, who discovered Ham Fisher's body after the "Joe Palooka" cartoonist committed suicide, provided details of Fisher's last day, as well as information about his feud with Capp.

There were many others who agreed to interviews, helped us with arranging interviews, and otherwise gave their time to, or offered assistance in, this effort: E. B. Boatner, Andrew Cooke, Randy Dahlk, Kate Edgar, Ann Eisner, Harlan Ellison, Danny Fingeroth, Mike Fontanelli, Kelts Gordon, Michael Gordon, George Hagenauer, Judy Hansen, R. C. Harvey, Tom Heintjes, Karen Henell, Ann Hochberg, Esq., Jeff Hutchins, Esq., Bill Janocha, Nancy

LeBlanc, John Lind, Lesleigh Luttrell, Margaret Maloney, Bill Morgan, Peter Poplaski, Dan Rea, Trina Robbins, Rodney Schroeter, Anthony F. Smith, Joe Suggs, Anthony Tollin, Blanche Weiss, and Pablo Yglesias.

Agent David Black offered guidance and assistance at critical points, and it was greatly appreciated. Thanks also to Allison Hemphill and Antonella Iannarino at the David Black Literary Agency for their help and good cheer.

Finally, special thanks to Stacey Kitchen, empress of the scanning machine, who put up with it all.

Michael Schumacher
Denis Kitchen
April 2012

INDEX

A NOTE ON THE AUTHORS

Michael Schumacher has written biographies of Allen Ginsberg, Eric Clapton, Phil Ochs, Francis Ford Coppola, George Mikan, and, most recently, comics pioneer Will Eisner. His other recent books include *Wreck of the* Carl D.: *A True Story of Loss, Survival, and Rescue at Sea,* and *Mighty Fitz: The Sinking of the* Edmund Fitzgerald. He lives in Wisconsin.

Denis Kitchen was a pioneering underground cartoonist and publisher, whose Kitchen Sink Press published R. Crumb, Will Eisner, Harvey Kurtzman, Art Spiegelman, Al Capp, and many others during its thirty-year existence. He also founded the Comic Book Legal Defense Fund, curates art exhibits, and represents talent. *The Oddly Compelling Art of Denis Kitchen*, a monograph of his art career, was published in 2009. He lives in western Massachusetts.